Successful Sewing

Mary G. Westfall, C.F.C.S.
Author of Home Economics
Instructional Materials
Kelso, Washington

Publisher
The Goodheart-Willcox Company, Inc.
Tinley Park, Illinois

The idea, the opportunity,
and the ability to do this work
came from Another —

and with deep appreciation
to my husband for his help.

Library of Congress Catalog Card Number 90-2913
International Standard Book Number 1-56637-010-8

  2 3 4 5 6 7 8 9 10   94   98 97 96

Library of Congress Cataloging-in-Publication Data

Westfall, Mary G. (Mary Glenda)
  Successful sewing / Mary G. Westfall.

    p. cm.
    ISBN 1-56637-010-8
    1. Sewing.   I. Title.
  TT705.W47   1990
  646.2--dc20   90-2913
                                                  CIP

Introduction

If you have just made the decision to learn to sew, you will need help in gaining an understanding of basic sewing skills. This textbook will provide all of the information and activities you will need to achieve your goal. If you are an experienced sewer, this book will help you brush up on your present skills. It will also challenge you to try new techniques.

The following is a brief summary of the units included in this textbook. It will give you an idea of what to expect as you work through the materials.

Unit 1: An Introductory Activity

The textbook begins with an introductory lesson that will acquaint you with what is ahead. You will find out what is to be learned and discover just how much you may already know.

Unit 2: Evaluating Your Knowledge and Planning Your Learning

In this section you will need to take a pretest. Don't worry! You aren't expected to know all the answers. The test is to help you plan your learning. Other activities are also included to help you develop your own plan for learning to sew.

Unit 3: Learning the Basics

Unit 3 contains lessons providing all the basic information needed to learn to sew. If you have sewn before, you may not need to complete all of the lessons. Your pretest, your teacher, and your personal goals will help you decide which lessons you need to complete.

The information in the basic lessons is presented in a way that may be completed through self study. It may also be completed by working with other members of your class. Sometimes your teacher may ask you to work by yourself. At other times, he or she may ask you to work with your classmates. This arrangement will help you meet your personal learning needs quickly and easily.

The lessons have been designed around three types of learning processes: gathering information, practicing, and evaluating learning. You will find learning easier if you do all the activities in the order they are given. This method of study will also help you retain information longer.

Unit 4: Assessing Your Learning

This unit includes a posttest similar to the pretest you took in Unit 2. Taking the test will help you see how much you have learned. It will also help you identify any skills that you are still weak in. Analyzing the results of the posttest will allow you to review needed skills before beginning work on your project.

Unit 5: Project Selection and Planning

In this unit, you will find activities designed to assist you in selecting and planning your sewing project. You will also find a list of steps to help you begin your project.

Unit 6: Constructing the Project

This section includes additional lessons that will give you helpful suggestions for constructing each detail of your sewing project. For instance, suggestions for constructing a pocket or a sleeve can be found here. The purpose of these lessons is to help you avoid common problems and mistakes. You will work through only those lessons needed to complete your sewing project. When working with these lessons, you will still use the instruction sheet that comes with your pattern.

Also included in Unit 6 are evaluation forms to be completed as you finish each detail of your sewing project. These evaluations will help you complete your project successfully.

Unit 7: Learning to Sew with Sergers

This unit will open up exciting new avenues of sewing possibilities. You will discover how to operate sergers. You will learn how to construct garments using techniques very different from those used with conventional sewing machines.

To complete this unit, your teacher may help you work through the materials. If you have a serger at home, you may want to study the information and complete the activities on your own.

Unit 8: Evaluating the Project

In this unit, you will find several forms. They will help you evaluate your completed conventional and serged sewing projects. They will also help you take stock of the total learning you have achieved in this class.

Unit 9: Additional Experiences

In the last unit of this textbook, you will find ideas for expanding your sewing knowledge and skill. Your teacher may assign an in-class project that includes some techniques suggested in this section. You may also be encouraged to explore some of these ideas on your own. You may be allowed to complete some projects incorporating techniques from this unit for extra credit. Other projects, you may choose to do just for fun.

Contents

Contents

Unit 1 An Introductory Activity

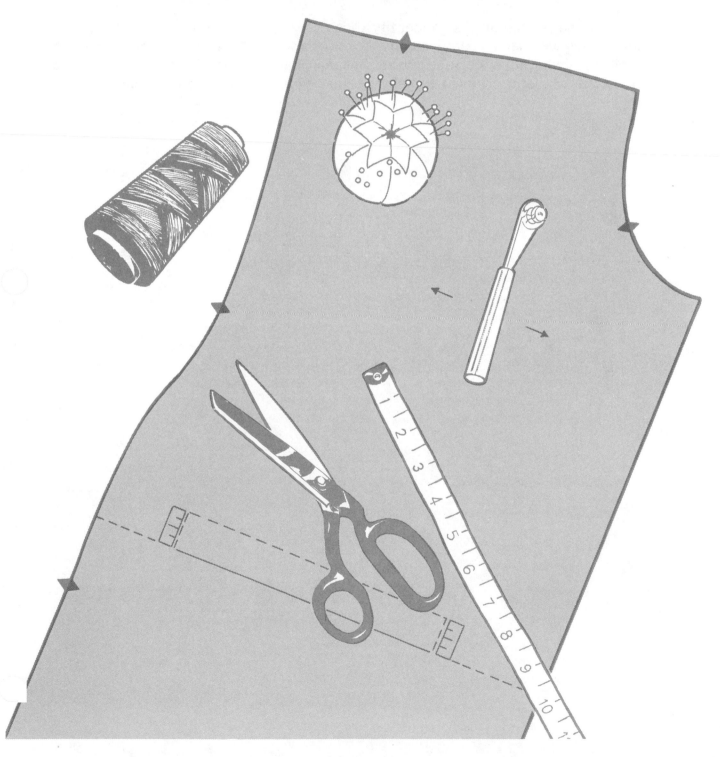

Unit 1
An Introductory Activity

The purpose of this unit is to identify those sewing skills with which you are acquainted. This will then help you identify those skills with which you are not acquainted. You will be given a chance to organize these skills into a logical learning order. The resulting list will later be used to help you plan your own program of learning.

Name _____

Date _____   Period _____

AN INTRODUCTORY ACTIVITY

Step 1: Listing What You Know

In the space provided below, write a list of all the sewing skills and concepts with which you are familiar. One way of doing this would be to think about a garment. Think about the steps you might take to make that garment. What information do you need to know? Write down the points that come to mind.

Cutting out pattern pieces   _____

Learning fabric care requirements   _____

_____   _____

_____   _____

_____   _____

_____   _____

_____   _____

_____   _____

_____   _____

_____   _____

_____   _____

Step 2: Compiling Information

Work in small groups to compile your list with those of your classmates. After forming a single list, look over it and see if anything is missing. Thumb through this textbook to find more ideas. Add any new ideas to the list.

Group all similar ideas together. For instance, cutting out a sleeve is similar to cutting out a collar. Measuring a hem is similar to pinning a hem.

Place items in an order that you think would be helpful when completing a sewing project. What might you need to know first, second, and so on. When the list has been completed, write it down in the space below. This list will help you later to plan your own program of learning.

1. _____   6. _____

2. _____   7. _____

3. _____   8. _____

4. _____   9. _____

5. _____   10. _____

(Continued)

Name _____

11. _____ 28. _____

12. _____ 29. _____

13. _____ 30. _____

14. _____ 31. _____

15. _____ 32. _____

16. _____ 33. _____

17. _____ 34. _____

18. _____ 35. _____

19. _____ 36. _____

20. _____ 37. _____

21. _____ 38. _____

22. _____ 39. _____

23. _____ 40. _____

24. _____ 41. _____

25. _____ 42. _____

26. _____ 43. _____

27. _____ 44. _____

Step 3: Forming a Conclusion

Answer the following question in the space below: What problems might occur in constructing your sewing project if you do not have all the skills on your list?

_____

_____

_____

_____

_____

_____

_____

_____

Unit 2 Evaluating Your Knowledge and Planning Your Learning

Unit 2
Evaluating Your Knowledge and Planning Your Learning

This unit is designed to help you discover how much sewing knowledge you already have. You will then use this information to plan your classroom learning. This unit consists of three parts.

Basic Sewing Skills Pretest

Unit 3 in this textbook deals with basic sewing skills. Learnings such as marking pattern symbols, fabric preparation, and pattern layout are organized into individual lessons. If you already have the skills needed for a specific lesson, you may not need to complete it. This pretest will help you determine which of the lessons you will need to complete.

Student Program Plan Sheet

This part of the unit consists of a form to be completed after your pretest has been corrected. The form will indicate sewing skills with which you are already familiar. It will also indicate skills that you need to study. The information summarized on this form will be used to help you plan your program of learning.

Weekly Plan Sheet

This form is a schedule for your classroom learning. Your teacher can help you plan when different topics are to be covered. This will allow you to prepare for lessons and make you aware of when assignments are due.

This form is also a record of your progress. It can help you keep track of when you complete various activities. And it can show you how to catch up when you return from an absence.

Pretest Score _____

Name _____

Date _____ Period _____

BASIC SEWING SKILLS PRETEST

This pretest will help you identify the areas of clothing construction in which you have adequate knowledge and skill. It will also help you identify those areas in which you need more work. You will be planning your direction of study based on the results of this pretest.

Read each question carefully. Select the best answer and write the letter in the blank. When you have finished, your teacher will give you directions regarding how the test is to be corrected.

Remember, this is a pretest. You are not expected to know all the answers. Do the best you can.

_____ 1. When taking a back waist length measurement, the tape measure should be placed:
   a. From the top of the shoulder to the waist.
   b. From the waist to the desired finished garment length.
   c. From the prominent bone at the back of the neck to the waist.

_____ 2. When taking a man's sleeve length measurement, the measuring tape is placed from the:
   a. Elbow to the wrist.
   b. Top of the spine to the wrist.
   c. Shoulder bone to the wrist.

_____ 3. You are making a shirt for a friend with the following measurements: bust 32, waist 26 1/2, hips 36. Which pattern size would you select? (Refer to the chart below.)
   a. Size 10.
   b. Size 12.
   c. Size 14.

Size	10	12	14	16
Bust	32 1/2	34	36	38
Waist	25	26 1/2	28	30
Hips	34 1/2	36	38	40

(Continued)

Name _____

____ 4. How much fabric would be required for View A in a size 12, if the fabric were 44/45″ wide? (Refer to the chart below.)
   a. 3 3/8 yards.
   b. 3 1/8 yards.
   c. 3 1/4 yards.

VIEW A	8	10	12	14
35″ fabric	3 1/4	3 3/8	3 3/8	4 3/8
44/45″ fabric	3	3 1/8	3 1/8	3 1/4
60″ fabric	1 1/2	1 7/8	1 7/8	2
VIEW B				
35″ fabric	3 1/2	3 1/2	4 3/8	4 3/8
44/45″ fabric	3 1/4	3 1/4	3 1/4	3 1/2
60″ fabric	2	2	2	2 1/8

____ 5. The yardage requirement table for various views, sizes, and widths of fabric is found on the:
   a. Back of the pattern envelope.
   b. Front of the pattern envelope.
   c. Guide sheet.

____ 6. Which of the following types of information would not be found on the pattern envelope?
   a. A description of the garment.
   b. Suggested fabric from which to construct the garment.
   c. A list of pattern pieces needed for the garment view being constructed.

____ 7. The lengthwise grain of the fabric:
   a. Runs from cut edge to cut edge.
   b. Runs from selvage to selvage.
   c. Forms a 45 degree angle with the selvage edge.

____ 8. The ends of woven fabric should be straightened by cutting along a pulled crosswise thread when the fabric has been:
   a. Cut from the bolt.
   b. Torn from the bolt.
   c. Either cut or torn from the bolt.

____ 9. To determine whether or not a piece of fabric is on grain, the fabric should first be folded:
   a. Crosswise.
   b. On the bias.
   c. Lengthwise.

____ 10. How can you determine whether or not the ends of the fabric are straight with the grain?
   a. Fold the fabric lengthwise to see if the raw, cut edges match.
   b. See if one crosswise thread ravels from selvage to selvage without being stopped by other crosswise threads.
   c. Pull on the true bias every few inches.

(Continued)

Name _____

In questions 11 through 16, match the pattern symbols with the letter that represents the symbol on the diagram. Use diagram A for questions 11 through 13. Use diagram B for questions 14 through 16.

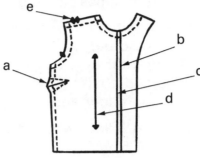

_____ 11. Grain line.

_____ 12. Center front line.

_____ 13. Notch.

DIAGRAM A

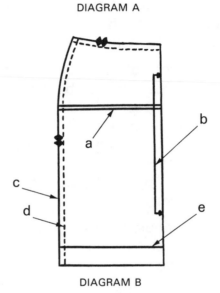

_____ 14. Seamline.

_____ 15. Place on the fold line.

_____ 16. Length adjustment line.

DIAGRAM B

_____ 17. To see if a pattern piece is placed on the fabric straight with the grain, measure the distance from:
    a. Both ends of the grainline arrow to the center front line.
    b. Both ends of the pattern piece to the selvage edge.
    c. Both ends of the grainline arrow to the selvage edge.

_____ 18. When pinning the pattern to the fabric, pattern pieces should:
    a. All be placed on the fabric before pinning any of them in place.
    b. Be placed on the fabric and pinned one at a time.
    c. Be pinned and cut out one at a time.

_____ 19. When cutting out a pattern piece, notches should be cut:
    a. In, toward the seam allowance.
    b. Straight across the notch.
    c. Out, away from the seam allowance.

_____ 20. Which of the following is not a method for removing marks left by special fabric marking pens?
    a. Apply a cleaning compound made especially to remove the marks.
    b. Rub marks gently with a dampened cloth.
    c. Allow the marks to fade without doing anything.

(Continued)

Name _____

_____ 21. Marks made with a tracing paper and wheel:
   a. Should always be on the right side of the fabric.
   b. Should always be on the wrong side of the fabric.
   c. Are sometimes placed on the wrong side and sometimes on the right side.

_____ 22. The best method to use when transferring pattern symbols to a thick, fuzzy fabric would be:
   a. Tailor's tacks.
   b. Pins and chalk.
   c. Tracing paper and wheel.

_____ 23. The rule to follow when threading the sewing machine needle is to thread the needle from:
   a. The side of the last thread guide.
   b. Right to left.
   c. Left to right.

_____ 24. When the bobbin thread lies along the lower surface of the fabric, which statement below would be correct?
   a. The upper tension is too loose, so the tension regulator is turned to a smaller number.
   b. The upper tension is too tight, so the tension regulator is turned to a smaller number.
   c. The upper tension is too loose, so the tension regulator is turned to a larger number.

_____ 25. How should a sewing machine needle be placed in a machine?
   a. The short groove on the needle should be on the side of the last thread guide.
   b. The needle can be put in either way.
   c. The long groove on the needle should be on the side of the last thread guide.

_____ 26. The purpose of the sewing machine feed dog is to:
   a. Hold the thread in place.
   b. Move the fabric along.
   c. Control tightness of the thread and move the thread through the machine.

_____ 27. The correct direction for pressing horizontal darts is:
   a. Up, toward the armhole.
   b. Down, toward the hem.
   c. In either direction.

_____ 28. The general rule for pressing is to press:
   a. Each piece immediately after stitching.
   b. When the garment is finished.
   c. After several steps have been completed.

_____ 29. Which of the following garment areas should be pressed on the curved surface of a pressing ham?
   a. The darts.
   b. The hems.
   c. The cuff seams.

(Continued)

Name _____

____ 30. Plain seams are usually pressed:
   a. To one side.
   b. On a curved surface.
   c. Open, using the point of the iron.

____ 31. In general, vertical darts should be pressed to the:
   a. Right.
   b. Center of the garment.
   c. Left.

____ 32. The purpose of staystitching is to prevent:
   a. Raveling while the garment is being made.
   b. Facings from showing on the right side of the garment.
   c. Stretching while the garment is being made.

____ 33. When should staystitching be done?
   a. As the first stitching process on a garment piece.
   b. Just before the final pressing.
   c. At any point during the construction process.

____ 34. The direction for staystitching should be:
   a. From the narrow to the wide part of the garment piece.
   b. Away from the center of the garment piece.
   c. With the grain of the fabric.

____ 35. Where should staystitching be done?
   a. 1/4 inch from the cut edge of a garment piece.
   b. 1/2 inch from the cut edge of a garment piece.
   c. On the seam line of a garment piece.

____ 36. A plain seam is stitched with:
   a. Right sides of the garment pieces together.
   b. Wrong sides of the garment pieces together.
   c. The right side of one garment piece against the wrong side of the other garment piece.

____ 37. How far from the cut edge are most plain seams stitched?
   a. 3/8 inch.
   b. 1/2 inch.
   c. 5/8 inch.

____ 38. If a very sturdy seam is desired, which of the following would be the best choice?
   a. Flat-felled seam.
   b. Plain seam.
   c. Double-stitched seam.

____ 39. To conceal the seam allowance on a sheer fabric, which of the following would be the best seam choice?
   a. Plain seam.
   b. French seam.
   c. Flat-felled seam.

(Continued)

Name _____

_____ 40. Which of the seam allowances in a shirt is not trimmed?
    a. The facing seam allowance.
    b. The side seam allowance.
    c. The neckline seam allowance.

_____ 41. The purpose of trimming seam allowances is to:
    a. Relieve the strain on the seam allowance.
    b. Eliminate bulk.
    c. Allow the seam to spread and make a smooth curve.

_____ 42. Seam allowances that need trimming should be trimmed to:
    a. 1/4 inch.
    b. 1/16 inch.
    c. 1/2 inch.

_____ 43. The term grading means to:
    a. Clip through the various layers of the seam allowance.
    b. Trim the seam allowance.
    c. Trim each layer of the seam allowance to a different width.

_____ 44. If the guide sheet tells you to clip a seam allowance, what should you do?
    a. Cut into the seam allowance several times at right angles to the seamline.
    b. Cut off part of the seam allowance parallel to the seamline.
    c. Cut into the seam allowance at center front.

_____ 45. When using heavy fabric that ravels, which of the following seam finishes would work best?
    a. Turned and stitched.
    b. Stitched and pinked.
    c. Zigzagged.

_____ 46. Which of the following is not a reason for finishing seam edges?
    a. To prevent the seam from raveling during laundering and wearing.
    b. To give the interior of the garment a finished look.
    c. To prevent the seam allowances from stretching.

_____ 47. When using very lightweight fabric that ravels, which of the following seam finishes would work best?
    a. Stitched and pinked.
    b. Turned and stitched.
    c. Zigzagged.

_____ 48. The selection of a seam finishing method to be used on a garment depends most on:
    a. The fabric weight.
    b. The garment design.
    c. The care requirements of the finished garment.

_____ 49. To clean finish the raw edge of a garment piece, you would turn the edge under:
    a. 1/8 inch.
    b. 1/2 inch.
    c. 1/4 inch.

(Continued)

Name _____

_____ 50. The purpose of clean finishing the raw edge of a garment piece is to:
   a. Maintain the grainline.
   b. Prevent raveling.
   c. Prevent stretching.

_____ 51. Which of the following garment pieces should be clean finished?
   a. Sleeve placket.
   b. Neckline seam.
   c. Facing.

_____ 52. The purpose of understitching is to:
   a. Keep the facing turned to the underside.
   b. Form a line on which to turn under the hem.
   c. Keep the outside edge of the facing from raveling.

_____ 53. To understitch you would:
   a. Stitch through the facing, seam allowance, and the outer layer of the garment.
   b. Stitch 1/4 inch along the facing edge, turn under, press, and stitch again close to the facing edge.
   c. Stitch the facing to the seam allowance close to the seamline.

_____ 54. Which of the following garment areas might be understitched?
   a. Collar.
   b. Waistline seam.
   c. Placket opening.

_____ 55. Gathering requires the use of:
   a. One row of stitching.
   b. Two rows of stitching.
   c. Three rows of stitching.

_____ 56. When the instruction sheet tells you to ease the shoulder seam, this means to:
   a. Sew two lines of long stitches on the shoulder seam allowance.
   b. Match notches and work in the extra fabric.
   c. Match the garment pieces at the neckline and trim off the extra at the shoulder.

_____ 57. The size of stitches used for gathering as compared to those used for seams should be:
   a. Longer.
   b. Shorter.
   c. The same size.

_____ 58. In which of the following areas of a garment is there no ease?
   a. Waist seam.
   b. Underarm portion of armhole seam.
   c. Placket opening.

USING THE STUDENT PROGRAM PLAN SHEET

The questions in the pretest related only to the lessons listed in section A of the chart on the next page. To determine which lessons in this section you will need to complete, refer to your corrected pretest. Circle the numbers in the first column of the chart that correspond with the test questions you answered correctly. The numbers in the second column tell how many questions must be answered correctly to exempt you from completing each lesson. If you have missed more than the allowed number of questions for any lesson, place a check in the third column. This will indicate that you need to complete the lesson.

Your pretest may indicate that you do not need to complete a specific lesson. But your teacher may ask that certain lessons be completed by all students. For instance, your teacher may ask everyone to complete the lesson on Operating the Sewing Machine. He or she may feel that everyone in the class needs to learn to operate the sewing machines in your classroom.

You were not asked questions related to the lessons in section B of the chart for several reasons. First, some of these lessons include information that even experienced students may need to review. Second, some of these skills are more advanced and may not be included in every basic sewing class. The lessons on sergers fall into this group. Finally, some of these lessons involve skills that are best tested through demonstration rather than with written questions. Your teacher will tell you which lessons in section B you are to complete.

After your teacher has explained your class requirements, complete your plan sheet. Your teacher will then tell you how to use it to schedule activities on your weekly plan sheet.

Name _____

Date _____ Period _____

STUDENT PROGRAM PLAN SHEET

SECTION A			
Questions Answered Correctly (Circle)	**Correct Number Needed**	**Lessons To Be Completed (✓)**	**Lessons**
1 2 3	3		1—Taking Measurements & Selecting Size
4 5 6	3		2—The Pattern Envelope
7 8 9 10	3		4—Fabric Preparation
11 12 13 14 15 16	5		6—Pattern Symbols
17 18 19	3		8—Pattern Layout, Pinning, & Cutting
20 21 22	3		9—Transferring Pattern Symbols
23 24 25 26	4		11—Operating the Sewing Machine
27 28 29 30 31	4		12—Pressing as You Sew
32 33 34 35	3		13—Staystitching
36 37 38 39	4		14—Seams
40 41 42 43 44	4		15—Clipping, Notching, Trimming, & Grading
45 46 47 48	4		16—Seam Finishes
49 50 51	3		17—Clean Finishing
52 53 54	3		18—Understitching
55 56 57 58	3		19—Easing & Gathering
SECTION B			
Number of lessons from section A to be completed. _____			3—Making Fabric Choices
			5—Reading the Instruction Sheet
Number of lessons from section B to be completed. _____			7—Pattern Adjustments
			10—Small Equipment & Notions
Total _____			20—Interfacing
			21—Topstitching
			22—Hand Stitching
			23—Hemming Methods
			44—Operating the Serger Machine
			45—Serger Construction Techniques
			46—Constructing a Serged Project
			47—Additional Experiences

Name _____

Date _____ Period _____

WEEKLY PLAN SHEET

This sheet is divided into blocks for planning your weekly learning. In the first column, list the dates of each of your classes.

In the second column, fill in what topics or activities are to be covered each day. These topics should include each of the lessons checked on your Program Plan Sheet. Be sure to note when demonstrations will be given and when assignments will be due. Also note when each of the steps of your sewing project should be completed. Your teacher will provide you with this information and tell you how many weeks in advance to plan.

At the end of each class period, record in the third column what you actually accomplished. This will help you see whether or not you are on schedule. It will also show you what topics you missed during an absence. You and your teacher can use this record to evaluate your progress.

DATE	TOPIC OR ACTIVITY	ACCOMPLISHMENTS

(Continued)

DATE	TOPIC OR ACTIVITY	ACCOMPLISHMENTS

(Continued)

DATE	TOPIC OR ACTIVITY	ACCOMPLISHMENTS

(Continued)

DATE	TOPIC OR ACTIVITY	ACCOMPLISHMENTS

notes

Unit **3**   **Learning the Basics**

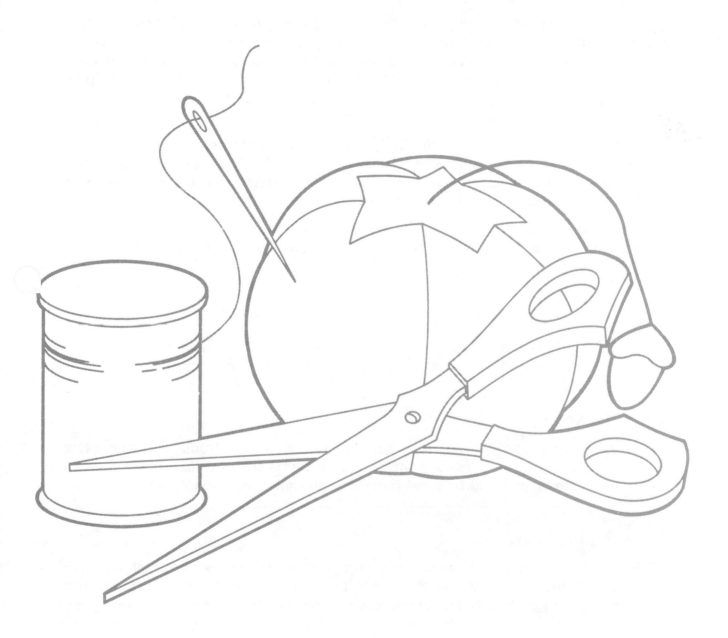

Unit 3
Learning the Basics

This unit consists of lessons about basic sewing information. Studying these lessons will help you become familiar with common sewing terms and techniques. If you are a beginner, you will need to study all of the lessons. If you have sewing experience, you may not need to study every lesson. The pretest you took in Unit 2 will help pinpoint skills with which you are not familiar. You and your teacher can use this information to decide which lessons you need to complete.

Your teacher will tell you how the lessons in this unit are to be completed. You may complete some of the lessons on your own. Your teacher may give demonstrations and lead class discussions for some lessons. And other lessons may be completed working with your classmates in small groups.

As you study each lesson, read the information carefully. Complete the activities and turn them in for evaluation according to your teacher's instructions. The lessons include five sections.

Objectives

This part of the lesson will tell you what you are to learn. It will list skills you should be able to demonstrate after you have finished studying the lesson.

Words to Know

This part of the lesson will list basic sewing terms that are introduced in the lesson. (This part is not included in lessons where no new terms are introduced.) As you read, watch for these words and become familiar with their meanings.

Gathering Information

This part of the lesson will provide information about a basic sewing skill. It is divided into sections to help you remember specific points. Illustrations are often used to help increase your understanding of the lesson. You will be learning other sewing skills based on this information. Therefore, read this part of the lesson carefully and refer back to it as needed.

Practicing Activities

This part of the lesson will provide you with skill building activities. You may be asked to interpret or restate the information you have just read. You may also be asked to demonstrate a technique or practice making actual samples.

Some of the activities may be turned in to your teacher. Others you may keep for your own reference. But in both cases, you should be prepared to discuss your work as you complete the activities.

Evaluating Learning

This part of the lesson will help you see what you have learned. It may also point out skills or information that you need to study further.

Some evaluation activities include forms for evaluating samples completed as practice activities. Both you and your teacher can use these forms. You may be asked to complete these forms so you can assess your own learning. Or your teacher may wish to complete them so he or she can keep track of your progress. In either case, they can be used to identify areas of weakness and success in your learning of sewing skills.

notes

Lesson 1 Taking Body Measurements and Selecting Your Pattern Size

Objectives

This lesson will help you to:
1. Identify how body measurements are taken for both men and women.
2. Take your own body measurements with the assistance of another individual.
3. Use a measurement chart to find your body type and pattern size.

Gathering Information

One of the first sewing decisions you will have to make is choosing a pattern to fit your body. Selecting the correct size depends on taking accurate body measurements. It also requires knowing which pattern body type is most suitable for you. This lesson will help you to make these decisions.

The following information gives instructions for taking measurements and determining pattern size for both men and women. Read all the information giving special attention to the portion that pertains to your body.

HOW TO TAKE WOMEN'S MEASUREMENTS

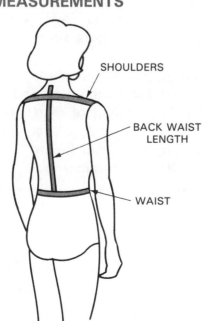

SHOULDERS

BACK WAIST LENGTH

WAIST

Note: For greatest accuracy, women should have their measurements taken while wearing undergarments or leotards.

Height. Without wearing shoes, stand with your back against the wall. Find your height on the wall by placing a level object, such as a ruler, on your head. Mark where the object touches the wall. Measure from the floor to the mark.

Waist. Tie a string around your waist area. It will roll to your natural waistline. Use the string as a guide for placing the tape measure around your waist. Hold the tape snug but not tight.

Back waist length. Measure down from the most prominent bone at the back of the neck to the string tied at your waist.

Shoulders. Measure across the back from shoulder bone to shoulder bone.

(Continued)

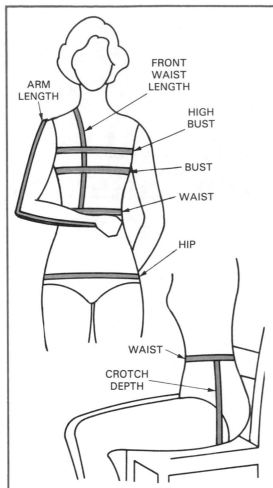

Full bust. Holding the tape snug but not tight, measure over the fullest part of the bust. The tape should ride over the shoulder blades in the back.

High bust. Measure around the widest part of the back, under the arms, and above the full bustline.

Hips. Measure around the fullest part of the hips. This should be 7 to 9 inches below the waist. Make a note of how far below the waist you took your hip measurement.

Arm length. With your arm bent in front of you, measure around the elbow from the shoulder bone to the wrist bone.

Front waist length. Measure from below the ear on the shoulder, over the bust to the string at your waist.

Crotch depth. While sitting on a flat surface, measure from the waist to the flat surface.

HOW TO SELECT FIGURE TYPE FOR WOMEN

Pattern companies have developed seven basic figure types for women. These figure types vary in a number of ways. You will find differences in height and length of arms and legs. Height and shape of the bust and slope of the shoulders will also differ. Age is not necessarily an indication of figure type.

To determine your figure type, look at a chart located in a pattern catalog or one provided by your teacher. Read the description of each figure type and select the best one for you. Base your decision on the description, your height, and your back waist length measurements.

HOW TO TAKE MEN'S MEASUREMENTS

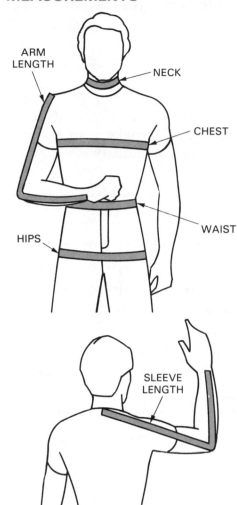

Note: For greatest accuracy, men should have their measurements taken while wearing an undershirt and lightweight pants.

Height. Same as women.

Neck band. Measure around the base of the neck. Add 1/2 inch to your measurement for comfort.

Waist. Start at the navel and measure around the body.

Hips (seat). Measure around the widest part of the hip area.

Chest. Place the tape under the arms and measure around the fullest part of the chest.

Crotch depth. Same as women.

Inseam. Measure from the crotch along the inside of the leg to the desired hem length.

Arm length. The arm should be bent at a right angle. Measure from the shoulder bone under the elbow to the wrist bone.

Sleeve length. Bend arm at a right angle. Measure from the top of the spine around the elbow to the wrist bone.

HOW TO FIND PATTERN SIZE FOR MEN AND WOMEN

Compare your measurements to those listed under your body type on a figure chart. Find the size nearest to your measurements. Use the following guidelines for further assistance in identifying your pattern size:

1. If you fall between two sizes, select the smaller of the two for a tight fit. Select the larger size if you prefer a looser fit.
2. For coats, jackets, shirts, and dresses, select pattern size by the bust or chest measurement. This area of the garment is the most difficult to alter.
3. For slacks, skirts, and shorts, women should select their pattern sizes by the hip measurement. Men should select their pattern sizes by the waist measurement.

Name _____

Date _____ Period _____

Activity 1-1: Practicing Taking Women's Measurements

Supplies needed:
  tape measure
  ruler
  string

Complete the chart below. Begin by asking someone to help you take your measurements. Then find your body type and pattern size. To make your selection, use a chart found in a pattern catalog or one provided by your teacher.

MEASUREMENTS—WOMEN

To find body type
Height   _____
Back waist length   _____

To find pattern size
Full bust   _____
Waist   _____
Hips   _____

Additional measurements
High bust   _____
Crotch depth   _____
Arm length   _____
Shoulders   _____
Front waist length _____

Body type _____

Dress/Blouse pattern size
(select by bust measurement)

_____

Pant pattern size
(select by hip measurement)

_____

Name _____

Date _____ Period _____

Activity 1-2: Practicing Taking Men's Measurements

Supplies needed:
   tape measure
   ruler

Complete the chart below. Begin by asking someone to help you take your measurements. Then find your pattern size using a chart found in a pattern catalog or one provided by your teacher.

MEASUREMENTS—MEN

To find pattern size
Height _____

Neckband (add 1/2'' to
   your measurement) _____

Chest _____

Waist _____

Hips (seat) _____

Sleeve length _____

Shirt/Jacket pattern size
(select by chest measurement)

_____

Pant pattern size
(select by waist measurement)

_____

Additional measurements
Crotch depth _____

Inseam _____

Arm length _____

Name _____

Date _____ Period _____

Activity 1-3: Evaluating Learning

Check your understanding of taking measurements, selecting body type, and selecting pattern size by taking the quiz below.

1. If you were going to make a shirt or jacket, you would pick a pattern that fits your _____ measurement.

2. If a woman were going to make slacks, she would purchase a pattern that fits her _____ measurement.

3. Crotch depth is measured from the _____ to a flat surface while sitting.

4. When taking a man's sleeve length, it is measured from the _____ to the _____ with the arm bent.

5. When taking a woman's arm length, it is measured from the _____ to the _____ with the arm bent.

6. Explain how to measure your height.

    _____

    _____

7. The inseam is measured from the _____ to _____.

8. If your measurements fall between two sizes on the chart, would you select the larger or smaller size? _____ Justify your answer._____

    _____

9. Would two women who have the same bust, waist, and hip measurements necessarily be the same body type? _____ Explain your answer.

    _____

    _____

10. Briefly, explain how you should go about finding your pattern size.

    _____

    _____

Lesson 2 The Pattern Envelope

Objectives

This lesson will help you to:
1. Identify the various types of information that may be found on a pattern envelope.
2. Use the information on a pattern envelope.

Words to Know

multisized pattern
napped fabric
notions
stretch knits

Gathering Information

The pattern envelope is an important source of sewing information. It offers guidelines for selecting and purchasing all the materials you will need to construct your project. Making use of this information will get your sewing project off to a good start. As you read the following information, refer to the diagram on page 41.

PATTERN CLASSIFICATIONS	Pattern companies have attempted to make sewing easier for beginners by labeling patterns to indicate the level of difficulty. The level of difficulty may be based partly on the number of pattern pieces included in the envelope. The estimated amount of time needed to complete the pattern may be another factor that determines difficulty.
	Patterns for beginners require few detailed sewing skills such as applying zippers and constructing collars. Most beginner patterns call for easy to handle fabrics. Some include how-to lessons on fashion, fabric, and sewing techniques.

PHOTOGRAPHS AND FASHION SKETCHES	The front of the pattern envelope shows photographs or fashion sketches of finished garments. This allows you to see what each garment will look like. Some patterns allow you to vary design details such as sleeve length or collar treatment. In this case, different views of the garment will appear to show each variation.

FIGURE TYPE AND SIZE	The figure type and size of a pattern will appear on the front of a pattern envelope. Generally, only one size is included in an envelope. However, some patterns are multisized. Multisized patterns include cutting lines for several sizes. For instance, sizes 8, 10, and 12 may all appear on the same pattern tissue. Multisized patterns are helpful when different areas of the body require different sized patterns.
BACK VIEW ILLUSTRATIONS	The back of the pattern envelope shows a line drawing of the back of each garment. This allows you to see design details such as darts and zippers that cannot be seen on the front illustrations.
GARMENT DESCRIPTIONS	The pattern envelope gives a brief description of each of the garments that can be made with the pattern. This information will make you aware of design details that may be hard to see in the illustrations.
SUGGESTED FABRICS	Fabric weight, design, and hand (the way a fabric feels and drapes) affect the way a garment looks and fits. For instance, sporty shorts would not look or fit right if they were made from a sheer fabric. The pattern envelope tells what fabrics are appropriate for the garment being made. Using this information will help you select fabric for a finished garment that you will enjoy wearing.
KNIT GAUGES	When a pattern envelope suggests knit fabrics, you must be careful to select the right type of knit. There are basically two classifications of knit fabrics—stable knits and stretch knits. Stable knits have a limited degree of stretch. They generally require the same sewing techniques as woven fabrics. Stretch knits have greater stretch and require special sewing techniques.

(Continued)

With stable knit fabrics, you may use any pattern except one labeled for stretch knits. If you use a stretch knit pattern, your garment will be too small.

Stretch knit fabrics should be used only with patterns stating that they have been sized for stretch knits. Such a label indicates that, because the fabric will stretch, the pattern has been sized with less ease. If you do not use a stretch knit pattern with stretch knit fabric, your garment will be too large.

Most stretch knit patterns include a knit gauge on the envelope. This gauge allows consumers to measure the amount of stretch in knit fabrics. In this way, consumers can tell if the fabric they select has enough stretch for a given pattern design.

BODY MEASUREMENTS

The pattern envelope lists some basic body measurements for the different pattern sizes. This is to help you make sure you have selected the right size pattern for your body. You will notice that these measurements are given in centimeters as well as inches. This is because many American pattern companies sell their patterns in countries where metric measures are commonly used.

YARDAGE REQUIREMENTS

A chart on the pattern envelope tells you how much fabric is needed to make the garment. This is known as the yardage requirement. To read the chart, start by finding the garment view you wish to make. Under this heading, find the row labeled with the width of the fabric you are purchasing. Follow this row across to the column labeled with your size. This number is the number of yards of fabric you need to buy to make the garment.

(Continued)

Napped fabrics are those fabrics which have short fibers brushed up on the surface. Corduroy, velvet, and velveteen are examples of fabrics that have napped surfaces.

When using napped fabrics, all pattern pieces must be laid in the same direction. Otherwise, a variation in color will appear on the finished garment. This variation is due to the way light reflects off the brushed surface. For this reason, many pattern designs are inappropriate for napped fabrics. Generally, patterns with little detail are best. The pattern envelope will usually indicate if a napped fabric is suitable for the pattern selected.

Because all pattern pieces must be cut out in the same direction, more yardage is required when using napped fabrics. The envelope will usually use asterisks (*) to indicate which yardage requirements are for napped fabrics. These yardage requirements should also be followed when buying fabrics with a one-way design.

The envelope also gives the yardage required for interfacing. Always purchase your interfacing at the same time you purchase your fashion fabric. Interfacing is a necessity. You will not want to stop sewing to buy interfacing at a later time. Interfacing will be discussed further in Lesson 20, "Interfacing."

Like the body measurements, yardage requirements are given in metric measurements as well as measurements in inches and yards. For instance, most fabric is sold in widths of 35, 44/45, and 60 inches. In metric units, these same measurements would be 90, 115, and 150 centimeters, respectively. You may wish to familiarize yourself with metric measures. You will find them on patterns and some sewing equipment as well as pattern envelopes.

NOTIONS

The word notions refers to all the supplies that will be needed to complete a project. Elastic, thread, buttons, bias tape, zippers, and trims are all notions. All of the notions you will need are listed on the back of the pattern envelope.

(Continued)

Purchase all of the notions for your garment when you buy the fabric. In this way, you can make sure your thread, buttons, and other notions match your fashion fabric. You can also avoid making an extra trip to the store.

FINISHED GARMENT MEASUREMENTS

The pattern envelope will usually list certain finished garment measurements. You may be able to find out the length of a skirt or the width of pant legs. This information can help you visualize how a finished garment will look. It can also help you decide if you need to alter a pattern for better fit.

GARMENT DESCRIPTION   SUGGESTED FABRICS   FOREIGN LANGUAGE (FRENCH) TRANSLATION

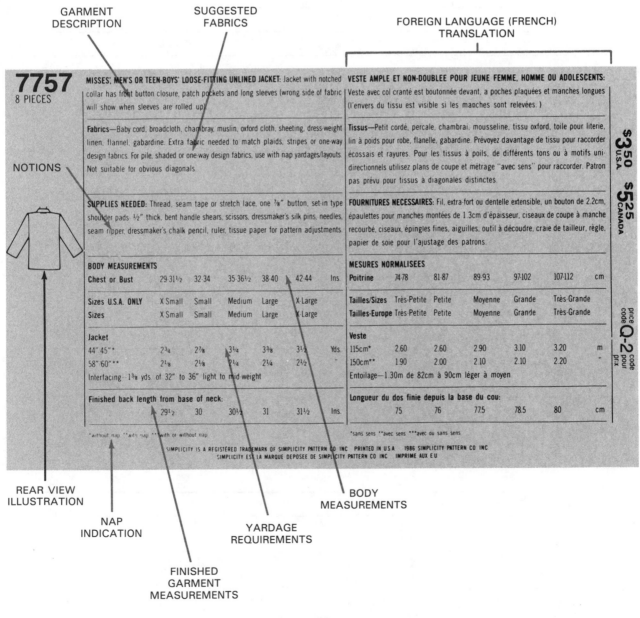

7757
8 PIECES

NOTIONS

MISSES', MEN'S OR TEEN-BOYS' LOOSE-FITTING UNLINED JACKET: Jacket with notched collar has front button closure, patch pockets and long sleeves (wrong side of fabric will show when sleeves are rolled up).

Fabrics—Baby cord, broadcloth, chambray, muslin, oxford cloth, sheeting, dress-weight linen, flannel, gabardine. Extra fabric needed to match plaids, stripes or one-way design fabrics. For pile, shaded or one-way design fabrics, use with nap yardages/layouts. Not suitable for obvious diagonals.

SUPPLIES NEEDED: Thread, seam tape or stretch lace, one ⅞" button, set-in type shoulder pads ½" thick, bent handle shears, scissors, dressmaker's silk pins, needles, seam ripper, dressmaker's chalk pencil, ruler, tissue paper for pattern adjustments.

BODY MEASUREMENTS

Chest or Bust	29-31½	32-34	35-36½	38-40	42-44	Ins.
Sizes U.S.A. ONLY	X-Small	Small	Medium	Large	X-Large	
Sizes	X-Small	Small	Medium	Large	X-Large	

Jacket

44" 45"*	2¾	2⅞	3¼	3⅜	3½	Yds.
58" 60"**	2⅛	2⅛	2¼	2¼	2½	"

Interfacing—1⅜ yds. of 32" to 36" light to mid-weight

Finished back length from base of neck:

	29½	30	30½	31	31½	Ins.

*without nap **with nap ***with or without nap

VESTE AMPLE ET NON-DOUBLEE POUR JEUNE FEMME, HOMME OU ADOLESCENTS: Veste avec col crânté est boutonnée devant, a poches plaquées et manches longues (l'envers du tissu est visible si les manches sont relevées.)

Tissus—Petit cordé, percale, chambrai, mousseline, tissu oxford, toile pour literie, lin à poids pour robe, flanelle, gabardine. Prévoyez davantage de tissu pour raccorder écossais et rayures. Pour les tissus à poils, de différents tons ou à motifs unidirectionnels utilisez plans de coupe et métrage ''avec sens'' pour raccorder. Patron pas prévu pour tissus à diagonales distinctes.

FOURNITURES NECESSAIRES: Fil, extra-fort ou dentelle extensible, un bouton de 2.2cm, épaulettes pour manches montées de 1.3cm d'épaisseur, ciseaux de coupe à manche recourbé, ciseaux, épingles fines, aiguilles, outil à découdre, craie de tailleur, règle, papier de soie pour l'ajustage des patrons.

MESURES NORMALISEES

Poitrine	74-78	81-87	89-93	97-102	107-112	cm
Tailles/Sizes	Très-Petite	Petite	Moyenne	Grande	Très-Grande	
Tailles-Europe	Très-Petite	Petite	Moyenne	Grande	Très-Grande	

Veste

115cm*	2.60	2.60	2.90	3.10	3.20	m
150cm**	1.90	2.00	2.10	2.10	2.20	"

Entoilage—1.30m de 82cm à 90cm léger à moyen.

Longueur du dos finie depuis la base du cou:

	75	76	77.5	78.5	80	cm

*sans sens **avec sens ***avec ou sans sens

$3.50 U.S.A $5.25 CANADA

price code Q-2 code pour prix

SIMPLICITY IS A REGISTERED TRADEMARK OF SIMPLICITY PATTERN CO INC   PRINTED IN U.S.A   1986 SIMPLICITY PATTERN CO INC
SIMPLICITY EST LA MARQUE DEPOSEE DE SIMPLICITY PATTERN CO INC   IMPRIME AUX E U

REAR VIEW ILLUSTRATION   NAP INDICATION   FINISHED GARMENT MEASUREMENTS   YARDAGE REQUIREMENTS   BODY MEASUREMENTS

Name _____

Date _____ Period _____

Activity 2-1: Investigating Pattern Classifications

Supplies needed:
   pattern catalogs

Each pattern company has its own classification labels to indicate the level of difficulty of a pattern. Using pattern catalogs, look up the classifications used by two different companies. List all the classifications with a brief description of each one.

   Pattern Company A _____

Classifications: (List in order from least difficult to most difficult.)

_____

_____

_____

_____

_____

_____

_____

_____

_____

_____

   Pattern Company B _____

Classifications: (List in order from least difficult to most difficult.)

_____

_____

_____

_____

_____

_____

_____

_____

_____

_____

_____

Name _____

Date _____ Period _____

Activity 2-2: Gathering Information About Special Fabrics

Napped fabrics. In the box below, mount a swatch of a napped fabric. Then answer the questions that follow. You may refer to the information in the "Yardage Requirements" box.

1. In your own words, give a definition of napped fabric.

   _____

   _____

   _____

2. How must pattern pieces be placed when using a napped fabric?

   _____

   _____

   Why? _____

   _____

3. What type of pattern designs are best suited for napped fabrics?

   _____

4. Why is it important to know if your fabric is napped when purchasing the required yardage?

   _____

   _____

Stretch fabrics. Obtain a sample of stretch fabric from your teacher. Place four inches of the fabric crosswise along the knit gauge below as indicated. The fabric should be in a relaxed state.

Hold the left edge of the fabric securely in place. Use your fingers to mark the other end of the four-inch strip. Gently stretch the fabric to the right. If the upper edge starts to curl, you have stretched the fabric too much. Mark on the gauge where the fabric reaches when you have stretched it to its farthest point. If the fabric stretches to the end of the gauge, it is appropriate for stretch knit patterns.

After determining the fabric's stretch, release the pressure to find its recovery characteristics. If the fabric springs back, it probably will not sag or bag when worn. If the fabric does not spring back, you will need to take special precautions during construction to prevent sagging.

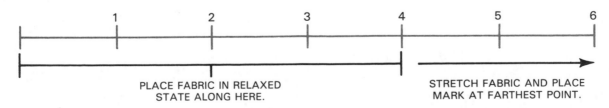

PLACE FABRIC IN RELAXED STATE ALONG HERE.

STRETCH FABRIC AND PLACE MARK AT FARTHEST POINT.

In the box below, mount a swatch of the knit fabric you tested with the knit gauge. Then complete the exercises and answer the questions that follow. You may refer to the information in the "Knit Gauges" box.

1. In your own words, give a definition of stable knit fabric.

   _____

   _____

   _____

2. Give a definition of stretch knit fabric.

   _____

   _____

   _____

3. What type of knit is the swatch you have mounted on this page?

   _____

4. What type of patterns should be used when sewing with stable knits?

   _____

5. What type of patterns should be used when sewing with stretch knits?

   _____

6. What problems might occur if the pattern is not correctly suited to the type of knit?

   _____

   _____

7. Explain, in your own words, how to use a knit gauge.

   _____

   _____

   _____

Name _____

Date _____ Period _____

Activity 2-3: Practicing Using a Pattern Envelope

For each problem below, you will be given a pattern envelope and specific data such as size, view, and type of fabric. You will also be given a list of information you are to find on the envelope based on this data. Record the given data and your answers in the spaces provided.

1. Use pattern envelope # _____

   Given data: _____

   _____

   Find the following information: Answers:

   _____   _____

   _____   _____

   _____   _____

2. Use pattern envelope # _____

   Given data: _____

   _____

   Find the following information: Answers:

   _____   _____

   _____   _____

   _____   _____

   _____   _____

3. Use pattern envelope # _____

   Given data: _____

   _____

   Find the following information: Answers:

   _____   _____

   _____   _____

   _____   _____

   _____   _____

4. Use pattern envelope # _____

   Given data: _____

   _____

   Find the following information: Answers:

   _____   _____

   _____   _____

   _____   _____

   _____   _____

Name _____

Date _____ Period _____

Activity 2-4: Evaluating Learning

Use the pattern envelope below to answer the following questions. Write your answer in the space following each question. Then place the appropriate letter in the blank before each question to indicate where on the envelope you found the information.

7757
8 PIECES

MISSES', MEN'S OR TEEN-BOYS' LOOSE-FITTING UNLINED JACKET: Jacket with notched collar has front button closure, patch pockets and long sleeves (wrong side of fabric will show when sleeves are rolled up).

Fabrics—Baby cord, broadcloth, chambray, muslin, oxford cloth, sheeting, dress-weight linen, flannel, gabardine. Extra fabric needed to match plaids, stripes or one-way design fabrics. For pile, shaded or one-way design fabrics, use with nap yardages/layouts. Not suitable for obvious diagonals.

SUPPLIES NEEDED: Thread, seam tape or stretch lace, one ⅞" button, set-in type shoulder pads ½" thick, bent handle shears, scissors, dressmaker's silk pins, needles, seam ripper, dressmaker's chalk pencil, ruler, tissue paper for pattern adjustments.

VESTE AMPLE ET NON-DOUBLEE POUR JEUNE FEMME, HOMME OU ADOLESCENTS: Veste avec col cranté est boutonnée devant, a poches plaquées et manches longues (l'envers du tissu est visible si les manches sont relevées.)

Tissus—Petit cordé, percale, chambrai, mousseline, tissu oxford, toile pour literie, lin à poids pour robe, flanelle, gabardine. Prévoyez davantage de tissu pour raccorder écossais et rayures. Pour les tissus à poils, de différents tons ou à motifs uni-directionnels utilisez plans de coupe et métrage "avec sens" pour raccorder. Patron pas prévu pour tissus à diagonales distinctes.

FOURNITURES NECESSAIRES: Fil, extra-fort ou dentelle extensible, un bouton de 2.2cm, épaulettes pour manches montées de 1.3cm d'épaisseur, ciseaux de coupe à manche recourbé, ciseaux, épingles fines, aiguilles, outil à découdre, craie de tailleur, règle, papier de soie pour l'ajustage des patrons.

$3.50 U.S.A. $5.25 CANADA

price code code Q-2 code pour prix

BODY MEASUREMENTS

Chest or Bust	29-31½	32-34	35-36½	38-40	42-44	Ins.
Sizes U.S.A. ONLY	X-Small	Small	Medium	Large	X-Large	
Sizes	X-Small	Small	Medium	Large	X-Large	

Jacket

44" 45" *	2¾	2⅞	3¼	3⅜	3½	Yds.
58" 60" **	2⅛	2⅛	2¼	2¼	2½	"

Interfacing: 1⅜ yds. of 32" to 36" light to mid-weight

Finished back length from base of neck:

29½	30	30½	31	31½	Ins.

MESURES NORMALISEES

Poitrine	74-78	81-87	89-93	97-102	107-112	cm
Tailles/Sizes	Très-Petite	Petite	Moyenne	Grande	Très-Grande	
Tailles-Europe	Très-Petite	Petite	Moyenne	Grande	Très-Grande	

Veste

115cm*	2.60	2.60	2.90	3.10	3.20	m
150cm**	1.90	2.00	2.10	2.10	2.20	"

Entoilage—1.30m de 82cm à 90cm léger à moyen

Longueur du dos finie depuis la base du cou:

75	76	77.5	78.5	80	cm

*without nap **with nap ***with or without nap

*sans sens **avec sens ***avec ou sans sens

SIMPLICITY IS A REGISTERED TRADEMARK OF SIMPLICITY PATTERN CO INC   PRINTED IN U.S.A   1986 SIMPLICITY PATTERN CO INC
SIMPLICITY EST LA MARQUE DEPOSEE DE SIMPLICITY PATTERN CO INC   IMPRIME AUX E.U.

a. Rear view illustration.
b. Garment description.
c. Suggested fabrics.
d. Knit gauge.

e. Body measurements.
f. Yardage requirements.
g. Notions.
h. Finished garment measurements.

_____ 1. What kind of closure is used on the front of this jacket? _____

_____ 2. What size pattern should someone with a 38-inch chest select?
            _____

_____ 3. How much 60-inch wide fabric should be purchased to make this jacket in size small? _____

_____ 4. List three kinds of fabric that are suggested for making this pattern.
            _____

_____ 5. Is the back of the jacket pleated? _____

_____ 6. How much interfacing is needed to make this jacket?_____

_____ 7. Is it necessary to purchase a zipper when making this pattern? _____

(Continued)

Name _____

_____ 8. When will it be necessary to purchase extra fabric? _____

_____

_____ 9. List four supplies that will be needed to construct this garment.

_____

_____

_____ 10. How much 44-inch wide fabric should be purchased to make this jacket in size large? _____

_____ 11. What will the finished back length of an extra large jacket be?

_____

_____ 12. What types of fabrics are not suitable for use with this pattern?

_____

Write the answers to questions 13 through 17 in your own words.

13. How would you find the difficulty level of a pattern before you purchased it?

_____

_____

14. Why are metric measures listed on pattern envelopes?

_____

_____

15. How do you determine the amount of yardage to purchase?

_____

_____

_____

16. When constructing a garment, explain how the following information found on the pattern envelope would be helpful.

Finished garment measurements: _____

_____

Suggested fabrics: _____

_____

Notions: _____

_____

Garment description: _____

_____

notes

Lesson 3 Making Fabric Choices

Objectives

This lesson will help you to:
1. Make generalizations about fiber and fabric characteristics from information provided.
2. Explain how fabric construction and applied finishes affect fabric characteristics.
3. Use the information provided to choose the best fibers and fabrics for various uses.

Words to Know

abrasion	hand	plain weave
absorbency	heat sensitive	resiliency
blend	knit fabric	satin weave
cellulosic	manufactured fibers	trade name
drapability	natural fibers	twill weave
fiber	noncellulosic	versatility
finish	nonwoven	woven fabric
generic name	pill	wrinkle recovery

Gathering Information

Knowing the basic types of fibers and fabrics and their general characteristics will help you to make wise choices when choosing fabrics for garment construction. In addition to the information below, charts on natural fibers, manufactured fibers, and fabrics are included on pages 55 through 57 of this lesson.

WHAT ARE FIBERS?

All fabrics are made from small, hairlike fibers. These can be less than an inch in length or long, continuous strands. These fibers are combined by twisting them together to form a yarn. Yarns are woven, knitted, or pressed into fabric.

Fibers can be separated into two major categories—natural fibers and manufactured fibers.

WHAT ARE NATURAL FIBERS?

Natural fibers come from animals and plants. Examples of natural fibers are cotton, linen, wool, and silk.

The natural fibers may be divided into protein fibers and cellulosic fibers. Protein fibers come from animals (wool, camel's hair, silk). Cellulosic fibers come from plants (cotton, linen).

Natural fibers are comfortable to wear and durable. They will not melt when pressed. Some of the natural fibers are expensive because of difficulty in collecting and processing them.

WHAT ARE MANUFACTURED FIBERS?

Manufactured fibers are formed from raw materials through manufacturing processes in factories. They do not occur as fibers in nature, but they may be made from some natural substances.

In 1910, Rayon became the first commercially produced manufactured fiber in the United States. It was made from a fibrous substance found in all forms of plant life. The first fiber produced completely from chemicals was nylon. Nylon was commercially produced in 1939. Since then a wide variety of manufactured fibers have been developed.

Manufactured fibers may be divided into two groups according to their composition and characteristics. The groups are cellulosic and noncellulosic. Cellulosic fibers are made from a fibrous substance found in plants. Noncellulosic fibers are made completely with chemicals.

Each group of fibers has a generic name or family name. Each fiber that belongs to the same family has the same general characteristics. The generic fiber name must appear on the label of any garment or fabric that is sold. When you know the generic name of a fiber you will know what to expect from the fiber in terms of performance and care requirements.

In addition to a generic name, a fiber will also have a tradename. Tradenames are used by companies to identify their fibers.

HOW IS FABRIC CONSTRUCTED?

PLAIN WEAVE

TWILL WEAVE

SATIN WEAVE

BASKET WEAVE

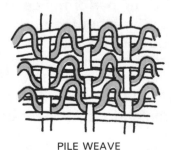

PILE WEAVE

Yarns may be woven, knitted, or pressed together to make a fabric. The method used affects the strength, appearance, feel, and care requirements of the fabric.

Woven fabrics. Woven fabrics are made by interlacing yarns together at right angles to each other. By varying the pattern in which the yarns are interlaced, fabrics with different qualities are made. The most basic weave is the plain weave. Plain weave fabric is often used for shirts and dresses. These fabrics are fairly strong and durable. They are easier to sew than many other types of fabric.

The twill weave is constructed in a manner that results in a pattern of diagonal lines in the fabric. Denim and many suiting fabrics are constructed in this way. Twill fabrics are generally stronger and more durable than other fabrics. They also resist wrinkles and hide soil.

Satin fabrics are woven in a way that produces a smooth, shiny surface. These fabrics are attractive and soft, making them popular for dressy blouses and dresses. However, satin fabrics tend to snag and pull easily. This makes them less durable and more difficult to sew than many other fabrics. Most satin fabrics do not resist wrinkles or hide stains very well.

Many variations of the above basic weaves are possible. For instance, a basket weave is a variation of the plain weave. It is created by weaving two or more yarns as one. Oxford and monk's cloth are examples of basket weaves.

A pile weave can be created by adding extra filling yarns to a plain or twill weave. The yarns project from the fabric surface. Pile fabrics generally have a nap and must be cut out with care. Otherwise, light reflecting from the surface of the fabric will create color variations among different pieces of a garment. Examples of pile weaves are corduroy, velvet, velveteen, and terry cloth.

(Continued)

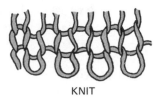

KNIT

Knit fabrics. Knit fabrics are made by interlocking loops of a continuous length of yarn to form a ribbed fabric. This produces a fabric which stretches and returns to its original shape. Stretch fabrics are especially good for active wear such as jogging suits and sport shirts.

The types of yarns and knitting methods can vary greatly in knit fabrics. Fabrics can be thin and smooth with a high amount of stretch as in T-shirt fabric. Or they can be more textured and stable as in double knit. Most knits are fairly wrinkle resistant. (Usually, the more textured the knit, the more it resists wrinkles.) Knits are fairly easy to sew, although care must be taken to allow for stretch.

Nonwovens. Nonwovens include felt, leather, and vinyl. Except for felt, which is made of short fibers which are pressed together, most nonwovens are not made of fibers or yarns. They do not have much stretch or give and they may require special sewing techniques. Nonwovens are most often used for craft or specialty items such as wall hangings, purses, and jackets.

FABRIC BLENDS

Often two or more fibers will be spun, woven, or knitted together. The fabrics that are made are called blends. Manufacturers blend fibers together to produce fabrics with the most desirable characteristics.

FABRIC FINISHES

Fabric finishes are treatments used to change the feel, appearance, or performance of the fabric. For instance, the manufacturer might want to make a fabric stain resistant by adding a special finish. Finishes can change fiber properties. So knowing which finishes have been added to the fabric is very important. The type of finish added to the fabric will appear on the label.

(Continued)

Fabric finishes can be permanent, durable, or temporary. A permanent finish will last the life of the garment. A durable finish lasts only through several launderings. A temporary finish lasts only until the fabric is washed or dry cleaned. There are hundreds of fabric finishes. Read labels carefully to determine the type of finish that has been added to the fabric and how it will change the care requirements.

The following are a few common finishes:

Permanent or durable press. This finish is heat-set onto the fabric. It will improve the fabric's resistance to wrinkling in wearing and laundering. No ironing should be needed if care instructions are followed. Stains may be difficult to remove.

Shrinkage resistant. Shrinkage is controlled by this finish. Garments can be laundered without excess shrinkage. In the case of wool garments, label directions must be followed to prevent shrinkage.

Soil release. This finish aids in removing oil, grease, and dirt during laundering.

Flame-retardant. Fabrics will resist burning. Special care may be needed to maintain the finish.

USING BOLT END LABELS

Today's fabrics are so carefully engineered that distinguishing various types can be impossible. The only way to determine fiber content of a fabric is to read the label on the bolt end. Since 1960, The Textile Fiber Identification Act has required that all fabrics be labeled by generic name. The law includes wearing apparel and household textile products. Each fiber that makes up 5 percent or more by total weight of a product must be named on the label. The fibers must be listed in order by weight, from the highest to the lowest.

On the charts included in this lesson, general care guidelines are given for the various fibers. Keep in mind that fabric construction, dyeing, and finishing affect the final performance of the

(Continued)

fabric and the care required. Always read labels for the fabric you select. Information about the fabric will be printed on the end of the fabric bolt. These bolt labels will tell you fiber content, brand name, fabric name, washability, and special finishes applied.

OTHER METHODS OF CHECKING FABRIC

Checking for fiber content and finishes won't tell you everything you need to know about a fabric. Use your senses of feel and sight to determine how the fabric will behave.

Check the hand of the fabric. The hand is the way a fabric feels. Will the texture be comfortable next to the skin? See how the fabric drapes. Hold up a length of the fabric and see how it falls. Does it fall in gentle folds, or is it stiff? Choose a fabric with a hand that fits the type of garment that you have chosen.

Crush a handful of fabric. Does the fabric wrinkle? Do the wrinkles disappear? The fabric will behave in the same way when you wear it.

Stretch the fabric. Check the amount of stretch. Check how quickly the fabric recovers its original shape.

Check the cut end of the fabric to see how much it ravels. Is the degree of ravel appropriate for the pattern you have chosen? Can the ravel be dealt with by using special techniques? Is the grain correct? Can the fabric be straightened?

Look at the surface quality of the fabric. Look for uneven streaks and imperfections in the weave. If it's a print, look for misprints or whether the print is off-grain.

Stand in front of a mirror and hold the fabric up to your face. Will the fabric look good on you?

Smell the fabric. Some fabrics have been treated with chemicals to impart wrinkle resistant properties. If the excess chemicals have not been washed out in the manufacturing process, you may detect a fish-like odor. Avoid any fabrics that have this unpleasant odor.

CHARACTERISTICS OF NATURAL FIBERS

FIBER NAME AND SOURCE	GOOD CHARACTERISTICS	POOR CHARACTERISTICS	CARE
Protein Fibers			
SILK (cocoon of silkworm)	Available in wide variety of weights and textures. Luxurious. Strong. Drapable, soft. Absorbent. Resists wrinkles. Resists mildew.	Damaged by perspiration, deodorants, perfumes, hairspray, bleach. Weak when wet. Sensitive to light. May water spot.	Dry cleaning is safest. Some fabrics may be hand washed, however, color loss can occur. Do not rub surface as damage to fibers can occur. Iron wrong side, moderate temperature.
WOOL (sheep)	Does not built up static. Strong, durable. Resilient and elastic due to natural crimp. Resists wrinkles. May be felted. Absorbent. Dyes well. Resistant to fading and perspiration. Warm.	Absorbs odors. Not moth resistant. Not washable unless treated. Weaker when wet. Undesirable felting can occur.	Usually dry-cleaned. May be machine washed if treated.
SPECIALTY HAIR FIBERS Mohair (Angora goat) Camel Hair (camel) Cashmere (Kashmir goat) Angora (Angora rabbit) Llama's Hair (Llama)	Warm. Soft, luxurious. Blend well with other fibers.	Expensive. Not as durable as wool. Tend to show wear in areas of strain or frequent abrasion. Sensitive to drycleaning chemicals.	Dry-clean. Inform dry cleaner of garment fiber content and areas that need spot treatment.
Cellulosic Fibers			
COTTON (cotton plant)	Strong, durable. Versatile. Comfortable. Absorbent. Does not build up static.	Mildews. Does not spring back into shape. Wrinkles easily without special finish. Shrinks unless treated or preshrunk.	Machine washable if colorfast. May shrink if washed or dried at high temperatures. Usually ironed at high temperatures.
LINEN (flax plant)	Cool, comfortable. Absorbent. Natural luster. Withstands high temperatures. Strong, durable. Resilient. Blends well with other fibers.	Wrinkles easily. Does not always dye well. Shows wear in areas of abrasion. Shrinks unless treated or preshrunk. Mildews.	May be machine washed and dried. Bleach weakens fibers; can yellow fabric. Check manufacturer's instructions due to shrinkage. Can be dry cleaned. Iron at high temperature.
RAMIE (plant similar to flax)	Dyes well. Absorbent. High luster. Blends well with other fibers. Cool, comfortable to wear.	Shrinks. Wrinkles easily.	Check manufacturer's instructions due to shrinkage variations.

CHARACTERISTICS OF MANUFACTURED FIBERS

GENERIC NAME AND TRADENAMES	GOOD CHARACTERISTICS	POOR CHARACTERISTICS	CARE
Cellulosic Fibers			

ACETATE
  Celebrate
  Chromspun
  Estron
  Loftura
	Excellent drapability.
	Dyes well.
	Luxurious feel and appearance.
	Shrink, moth, and mildew resistant.
		Poor resistance to abrasion.
		Wrinkles easily.
		Heat sensitive.
			Dry-clean for best results.
			Can machine wash but wrinkles difficult to remove.
			Iron at low temperature.

RAYON
  Avril
  Beau-Grip
  Coloray
  Durvil
  Fibro
  Zantrel
	Cool, comfortable.
	Highly absorbent.
	Good sheen.
	Soft drapability.
	Dyes well.
	Versatile.
		Lacks strength.
		May stretch or shrink.
		Heat sensitive.
		Poor resistance to soil and abrasion.
		Supports mildew growth.
		Wrinkles unless treated.
			Usually machine washable.
			Retains appearance better if dry-cleaned.
			Check care label.
			Iron at low temperature.

Noncellulosic Fibers			

ACRYLIC
  Acrilan
  Bi-Loft
  Creslan
  Fi-lana
  Orlon
  Remember
	Soft, warm, wool-like.
	Lightweight.
	Resists wrinkles.
	Resistant to sunlight, chemicals, oil.
	Quick drying.
	Retains shape.
		Surface tends to pill.
		Builds up static electricity.
		Does not absorb moisture.
			Machine washable and dryable.
			Use fabric softener to reduce static.

MODACRYLIC SEF	Quick drying. Good wrinkle recovery and shape retention. Abrasion resistant. Flame resistant. Soft. Accepts dyes well.	Heat sensitive. Does not absorb moisture. Tends to build up static electricity.	Check care instructions. Usually machine washable. Remove oily stains immediately. Use cool iron.

NYLON
  Antron
  Cantrece
  Crepeset
  Cumuloft
  Microsuplex
  Shareen
	Exceptionally strong.
	Abrasion resistant.
	Crease resistant.
	Soft, lustrous.
	Retains commercially heat-set pleats.
	Resists stretching and shrinking.
	Accepts dyes well.
		Builds up static electricity.
		Heat sensitive.
		Does not absorb moisture.
		May pill.
		White fabric may gray or yellow.
			Machine washable.
			Use fabric softener to reduce static.
			Iron at low temperature.

OLEFIN
(polypropylene)
  Avtex
  Eluster
  Herculon
  Marvess
	Abrasion Resistant.
	Strong.
	Durable
	Resists chemicals, stains, static, wrinkles.
	Lightweight.
		Heat sensitive.
		Poor dyeability.
		Nonabsorbent.
			Check care.
			Usually machine washable and dryable.

(Continued)

GENERIC NAME AND TRADENAMES	GOOD CHARACTERISTICS	POOR CHARACTERISTICS	CARE
POLYESTER Avlin Dacron Fortrel Golden Touch Kodel Trevira	Durable. Resists wrinkling. Versatile. Retains commercially heat-set pleats. Resists stretching, abrasion, shrinking. Resists heat, bacteria, most chemicals. Accepts dyes well.	Builds up static electricity. Does not absorb moisture. Absorbs oil and grease readily. May pill.	Usually machine washable. Use fabric softener to reduce static. Remove oily stains immediately with solvent or detergent solution.
SPANDEX Cleerspan Lycra	Elastic. Strong. Lightweight. Soft. Resists abrasion. Resists perspiration and body oils.	Heat sensitive. Chlorine bleach will cause loss of strength and yellowing.	Hand or machine wash and dry. Do not use chlorine bleach. Iron at low temperatures.

CHARACTERISTICS OF FABRICS

CONSTRUCTION METHOD	TYPICAL FABRICS	GENERAL CHARACTERISTICS
Plain weave	Batiste Broadcloth Chiffon Gingham Muslin Percale Poplin	Characteristics vary with tightness of weave. Fairly strong and durable. Easy to sew if weave is not too loose.
Twill weave	Denim Gabardine Herringbone	Surface has diagonal design. Very strong and durable. Resists wrinkles. Does not soil readily. Tends to ravel. Easy to sew if not too heavy.
Satin weave	Sateen Satin	Smooth, sometimes shiny surface. Surface snags easily. Not very durable. May be slippery and difficult to sew. May show soil.
Basket weave	Oxford Monk's cloth	Tends to ravel more than plain weaves. Wrinkles less than plain weaves.
Pile weave	Corduroy Velvet Velveteen Terry cloth	Surface color may vary when viewed from different directions. Loop pile may catch and snag. Cut pile may crush. Requires special sewing and pressing techniques. Strength and durability varies.
Knit fabric	Double knit Jersey Knit terry cloth Rib knit Velour	Amount of stretch and recovery will vary. Comfortable to wear due to stretch. Resists wrinkles fairly well. Care must be taken to allow for stretch with sewing. Some knits will run when torn; others may ravel.

Name _____

Date _____ Period _____

Activity 3-1: Interpreting the Information

As you select fabrics, you will need to look for relationships, interpret, and draw conclusions about the information in this lesson. To do this, answer the following questions and be prepared to discuss them. You may work with another person on this activity.

1. On the charts, a number of special words have been used as headings. What do these words mean to you?

    Natural fibers: _____

    _____

    Manufactured fibers: _____

    _____

    Cellulosic fibers: _____

    _____

    Noncellulosic fibers: _____

    _____

    Protein fibers: _____

    _____

2. In this lesson, you probably encountered a number of words with which you were unfamiliar. What do you think the following words mean in terms of fiber characteristics? Did you encounter any other words with which you were unfamiliar?

    Abrasion: _____

    _____

    Resilience: _____

    _____

    Absorbency: _____

    _____

    Crease recovery: _____

    _____

    Elasticity: _____

    _____

    Twill weave: _____

    _____

    Satin weave: _____

    _____

    Other words you may have encountered: _____

    _____

    _____

3. What characteristics do you find that are unique to natural fibers? To manufactured fibers? _____

_____

_____

_____

_____

4. Now that you have identified the basic characteristics of manufactured and natural fibers, how do you think this information might help you to know what to expect from a specific fiber? _____

_____

_____

_____

_____

5. How do the fiber content and fabric construction determine what types of garments are made from the fabric? _____

_____

_____

_____

_____

6. Explain how the characteristics of a fabric determine the way you would care for fabric while constructing the garment. Also explain how they affect the way you would launder the garment when it has been completed.

_____

_____

_____

_____

7. What similarities, if any, do you find between the care required for manufactured fibers and natural fibers? _____

_____

_____

_____

_____

8. How might finishes applied to fabrics change the characteristics of those fabrics?

_____

_____

_____

_____

Name _____

Date _____ Period _____

Activity 3-2: Determining Fabric Characteristics from Fiber Content

Below you will find a list of fabrics and the fiber content of each. Your task is to indicate the characteristics and care requirements that can be expected of each fabric. Use the fiber characteristic charts to help you with this activity. You will notice that some of the fabrics listed are fiber blends. Different fibers are often mixed together to make a fabric with more desirable characteristics. The type of fibers and the percentage of each fiber in the fabric give a clue to what can be expected from the fabric.

FIBER BLEND	EXPECTED CHARACTERISTICS AND CARE REQUIREMENTS
1. Calico Print 100% Cotton	
2. Ripstop Nylon 100% Nylon	
3. Corduroy 84% Polyester 16% Cotton	
4. Satin Face Crepe 87% Acetate 13% Nylon	
5. Velour 10% Polyester 90% Acetate	
6. Suit Fabric with Linen Look 55% Polyester 45% Rayon	
7. Velvet 65% Cotton 35% Rayon	
8. Stretch Solid 87% Nylon 13% Spandex	

Name _____

Date _____ Period _____

Activity 3-3: Choosing the Best Fibers for the Garments

Below is a list of garments. Your task is to select the fiber(s) and fabric(s) that you would consider using to construct this garment. Include reasons for your choice.

GARMENT	FIBER CHOICE	FABRIC CHOICE	REASONS FOR CHOICE
1. Summer Shirt			
2. Winter Coat			
3. Swimsuit			
4. Child's Play Outfit			
5. Party Dress			

Name _____

Date _____ Period _____

Activity 3-4: Evaluating Learning

Assess your understanding of this lesson by answering the questions below. Share your evaluation with your teacher.

1. Give several important differences between manufactured fibers and natural fibers regarding performance characteristics. _____
   _____
   _____

2. Explain how knowing the fiber characteristics, method of fabric construction, and finishes applied will help you during garment construction. _____
   _____
   _____
   _____

3. In your own words, give the meanings of the following words as they relate to fiber characteristics:
   Absorbency: _____
   _____

   Hand: _____
   _____

   Crease recovery: _____
   _____

4. Explain in your own words why it is helpful to know fiber characteristics when selecting fabric for specific types of garments. _____
   _____
   _____
   _____

5. Explain in your own words why it is helpful to know fabric construction characteristics when selecting fabric for specific types of garments. _____
   _____
   _____

6. What fiber characteristics would be most important when selecting fabrics for the following garments:
   Tennis clothes: _____
   _____

   Child's play clothes: _____
   _____

   School clothes: _____
   _____

Lesson 4 Fabric Preparation

Objectives

This lesson will help you to:
1. Identify grainlines in various types of fabrics.
2. State generalizations about cutting out pattern pieces on grain.
3. Determine whether or not fabric is on grain.
4. Identify when grainlines can be straightened.
5. Determine when fabric should be preshrunk.

Words to Know

bias	grain	rib
course	lengthwise grain	selvage
crosswise grain	preshrinking	warp
filling yarns	raw edge	weft

Gathering Information

Fabric must be prepared before cutting out pattern pieces. This preparation may involve two procedures. First, the fabric may need to be straightened. Second, the fabric may need to be preshrunk. If the fabric requires these procedures and they are not done, your finished garment will not fit properly.

WHAT IS GRAIN?

All woven and knitted fabrics and some non-woven fabrics have direction, or grain. The grain is determined by the position of the yarns and fibers in the fabric.

In woven fabrics, the grain must be made straight. Then pattern pieces must be cut out in the same direction as the grain if the garment is to hang properly.

Woven fabrics are constructed by interlacing yarns at right angles to each other. There are three grain directions.

Lengthwise grain. The lengthwise yarns, called warp yarns, form the lengthwise grain in woven fabric. This grain runs parallel to the selvage edges of the fabric. The selvage edges are the finished edges of the fabric as it comes off of a loom.

The lengthwise yarns are stronger than the crosswise yarns. They are used to pull the fabric through the loom. Therefore, the lengthwise grain is generally placed on the body in a vertical direction. This direction receives the greatest strain from sitting, bending, and moving.

Crosswise grain. The crosswise grain is perpendicular to the lengthwise grain. It is formed by the crosswise yarns which are also called weft or filling yarns. The crosswise grain tends to be weaker than the lengthwise grain. Therefore, it is usually placed going around the body.

Bias. The bias runs diagonally across the fabric. True bias forms a 45 degree angle with the lengthwise and crosswise yarns of the fabric. The bias has a great deal of give. On woven fabrics, the bias may be used when a pattern piece requires stretch.

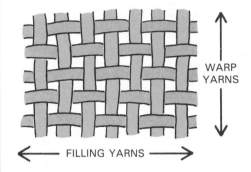

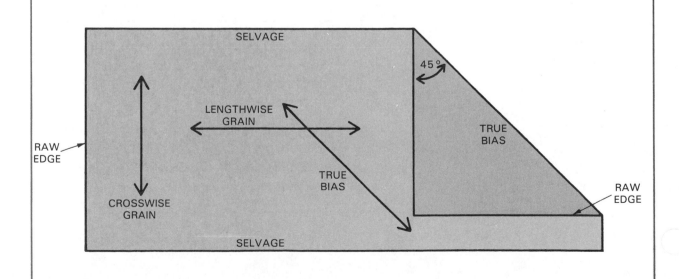

GRAIN IN KNIT FABRIC

Knit fabrics are made with a series of interlocking loops. These loops give knits their built-in abilty to stretch. They open out when subjected to stress and return to their original position when released. Grain in knit fabrics relates to the direction of the loops rather than to the direction of the yarns themselves.

Lengthwise grain. The lengthwise grain can be identified by ribs that run the length of a knit fabric. The lengthwise grain usually has less stretch than the crosswise grain.

Crosswise grain. The crosswise grain of knit fabrics is perpendicular to the ribs. It is identified by courses that run across the fabric.

The direction of greatest stretch, most often the crosswise direction, is usually placed around the body. The direction of the greatest stability, most often the lengthwise direction, is usually placed up and down the body.

Bias. Knit fabrics, like woven fabrics, have diagonal, or bias, stretch. The amount of stretch depends on the tightness of the knit and, therefore, varies from fabric to fabric. The bias stretch in knits tends to be unstable so pattern pieces are seldom cut in this direction.

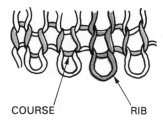

COURSE   RIB

GRAIN IN NONWOVEN FABRIC

Nonwoven fabrics are produced by bonding, knotting, or interlocking fibers together by chemical or mechanical means.

Three common types of nonwoven fabrics are:

1. Stretch: Fabrics having stability in the lengthwise direction and stretch in the crosswise direction.

2. Stable: Fabrics having equal stability in all directions.

3. All bias: Fabrics having equal stretch in all directions.

The direction of greatest stability is generally placed vertically on the body.

HOW TO CHECK STRAIGHTNESS OF FABRIC GRAIN

Fabric is on-grain when the crosswise and lengthwise threads (or in the case of knits, the ribs and courses) are at right angles to each other. Fabric may become off-grain during the finishing process at the factory. If pattern pieces are cut from fabric that is off-grain, the garment may not hang evenly when worn.

To check straightness of fabric grain, you must first straighten the cut ends of the fabric. These ends are often called raw edges. For woven fabrics, cut across an easily visible crosswise thread or a woven-in stripe. If crosswise threads are not easily visible, snip the selvage and lift a crosswise thread with a pin. Ease the gathers that form along the thread as you gently pull it. When you reach the other selvage, clip it and pull the thread out of the fabric. Cut along the space left by the pulled thread.

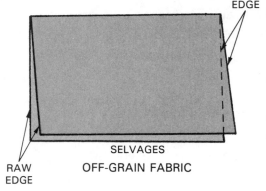

RAW EDGE

RAW EDGE

SELVAGES
OFF-GRAIN FABRIC

For jersey single knits, the ends may be straightened by cutting along a course or a knitted-in stripe. For other types of knits, deciding if the grain is straight may be difficult. You may use your eye to help you.

Once the raw edges have been straightened, fold the fabric lengthwise with the selvages even. If both edges match exactly and both layers of fabric lie smoothly, the fabric is on-grain. If the cut edges are not even and the corners do not match, the fabric is off-grain.

WHEN MAY FABRIC GRAIN BE STRAIGHTENED?

If fabric is off-grain, it may be straightened when:

- It is a woven or a jersey single knit fabric. (Jersey single knits are discussed in Lesson 3, ''Making Fabric Choices.'')

- It has no finish.

- It has a finish such as sizing that may be removed by laundering or dry-cleaning.

- It has a permanent finish such as a shrink resistant finish that does not affect the grain. (Finishes are discussed in Lesson 3, ''Making Fabric Choices.'')

(Continued)

If fabric is off-grain, it may not be straightened when:

- It is made from thermoplastic (heat sensitive) fibers such as polyester, acrylic, nylon, acetate, triacetate, or blends of these fibers. During stabilization and finishing, fabrics containing these fibers are subjected to heat, causing the fibers to become soft and pliable. If a fabric is pulled off grain during this process, it cannot be made straight again. Sometimes a fabric is pulled off-grain after this process. This could happen, for instance, when it is being wound on a bolt. In this case, the grain may be improved.

- It is a double knit, an interlock knit, a tricot knit, or any knit other than a jersey single knit.

- It is densely woven or heavily felted wool.

- It has a permanent finish such as crease resistance or stain resistance which does affect the grain.

HOW TO STRAIGHTEN FABRIC GRAIN

You have seen that the straightened ends of off-grain fabric do not match when it is folded lengthwise. To straighten an off-grain fabric, open it up and pull on the short corners. You may wish to ask another person to help you do this. Then, fold the fabric again, placing the selvages together. Check to see if the grain has been changed. Repeat this process until the raw edges of the fabric are even and the corners match.

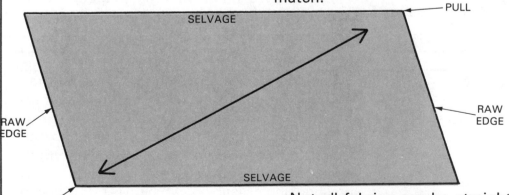

Not all fabrics can be straightened. If your fabric does not appear on-grain after several attempts, further effort may not bring success.

WHEN TO PRESHRINK FABRIC

Many fabrics require preshrinking before cutting out a pattern. If this step is not taken, the finished garment will shrink when it is washed. This will result in a garment that is too small.

You may wish to prewash a fabric even if it won't shrink. Prewashing helps remove fabric finishes that could later make the needle sticky and cause the machine to skip stitches. This is especially true for knit fabrics.

Use the following guidelines to help you decide when preshrinking is necessary.

- Preshrink fabric unless the label states that less than one percent shrinkage will occur.

- Fabric labeled wash and wear, crease-resistant, or stabilized finish usually does not need to be preshrunk.

- Fabric made of 100 percent synthetic fibers usually needs no preshrinking. Fabric containing a high percentage of rayon is an exception to this rule as rayon tends to shrink.

- If fabric has a high percentage of cotton, it should be washed several times. Cotton tends to have residual skrinkage.

- Preshrink all washable knits as they often shrink due to relaxation of the knit.

- Wool knits can shrink even when dry-cleaned. Be sure to steam press or dry-clean them before cutting out a pattern.

- If in doubt about whether or not to preshrink a fabric, test it. Cut two small, identical squares. Wash one square and steam press it dry. Place the two squares together and compare size for shrinkage.

HOW TO PRESHRINK MACHINE WASHABLE FABRICS

Preshrink fabric by using the same method that will be used to launder the finished garment. If the fabric was knitted in a tube, preshrink the fabric before cutting open the tube. If the fabric will ravel, machine stitch along the raw edges using a zigzag stitch before preshrinking. (Machine stitching is discussed in Lesson 11, ''Operating the Sewing Machine.'') Be sure not to machine dry any fabric that is labeled drip-dry, line dry, or dry flat.

HOW TO PRESHRINK FABRIC THAT MUST BE HAND WASHED OR DRY-CLEANED

This method straightens the grain while the fabric is drying.

Follow these steps:

1. Staighten the ends of the fabric.
2. Fold the fabric lengthwise, right sides together, matching selvages and straightened edges. (The fabric may not lie flat.)
3. Clip through the selvages every four inches. The selvages tend to shrink more and this relaxes the fabric.
4. Machine or hand baste the straightened ends together; then baste the selvages together.
5. Dampen the fabric. *For wool:* Spread the fabric on a damp sheet. Fold the sheet over the fabric. Use an additional sheet, if needed, to cover all the fabric. Fold the fabric and the sheet together in an accordian pleat style. Place folded fabric and sheet in a plastic bag and leave overnight to allow fabric to become thoroughly damp. *For other fabrics:* Fold the fabric carefully and place it in warm water for 30 minutes. Make sure the fabric is completely wet. Remove the fabric from the water. Press out excess water, being careful not to wring as this will wrinkle or even damage some fabric.
6. Lay the fabric on a flat surface that will not be damaged by moisture. (Do not let the fabric hang off the sides of the surface.) Smooth out the fabric so both ends are at right angles to the selvages.
7. When the top layer is dry, turn the fabric over. Allow the fabric to dry completely.

Dry-cleanable fabric may also be taken to a professional dry cleaner. Instruct the dry cleaner to:

1. Steam press the fabric if appropriate. This process is usually done with wool but is not advisable with silk and some specialty fibers. Your dry cleaner should be able to tell you whether or not this step is necessary.
2. Avoid pressing along the lengthwise fold to prevent permanently setting the crease.
3. Return the fabric folded, rather than draped over a hanger, to avoid stretching it.

Name _____

Date _____ Period _____

Activity 4-1: Identifying Grainlines

Your teacher will provide you with fabric pieces. The grains on each fabric piece will be labeled with a letter and an arrow indicating the grain in question. Identify the grainlines in each fabric piece as lengthwise, crosswise, or bias. Write your answers in the spaces below. You may refer to the fabric grain information sheets.

FABRIC #1 a. _____

b. _____

c. _____

FABRIC #2 a. _____

b. _____

c. _____

FABRIC #3 a. _____

b. _____

c. _____

FABRIC #4 a. _____

b. _____

c. _____

FABRIC #5 a. _____

b. _____

c. _____

Answer the questions below in your own words.

1. Why should fabric grain be straightened before pattern pieces are cut out?

_____

_____

_____

2. When using knit fabrics, which grain goes around the body? Why?

_____

_____

_____

3. Explain why grainline arrows usually run from top to bottom on pattern pieces. Also explain why pattern directions say, ''Place grainline arrow on the lengthwise grain.''

_____

_____

_____

Name _____

Date _____ Period _____

Activity 4-2: Determining if Fabric Is On-grain

You will be given various fabric pieces. Determine if each piece is on-grain or off-grain. Then decide whether the off-grain fabric pieces may be straightened. You may refer to the information sheets on straightening grainlines.

	Indicate if the fabric is on-grain or off-grain. Explain your answer.	Give your reason for thinking this fabric may be straightened.
FABRIC #1		
FABRIC #2		
FABRIC #3		
FABRIC #4		
FABRIC #5		

Name _____

Date _____ Period _____

Activity 4-3: Determining When Fabric Should Be Preshrunk

Your teacher will provide you with five fabric pieces and important information about each piece. Using this information and the information in this lesson, decide whether the fabric needs to be preshrunk. If the fabric is to be preshrunk, decide which method to use: (1) machine wash, (2) fold in a damp sheet and lay flat to dry, (3) place in a warm water bath and lay flat to dry, or (4) dry clean. If the fabric is to be machine washed, indicate if the raw edges need to be zigzagged to prevent raveling. Also indicate whether or not the fabric is to be machine dried.

	Indicate whether the fabric is to be preshrunk and the reason for your decision.	Preshrinking method to be used.
FABRIC #1 Fiber content- Knit or Woven- Finishes-		
FABRIC #2 Fiber content- Knit or Woven- Finishes-		
FABRIC #3 Fiber content- Knit or Woven- Finishes-		
FABRIC #4 Fiber content- Knit or Woven- Finishes-		
FABRIC #5 Fiber content- Knit or Woven- Finishes-		

Name _____

Date _____ Period _____

Activity 4-4: Evaluating Learning

Check your understanding of fabric preparation by answering the questions below. Do your own work.

1. Label the diagram with the following terms:
    Raw edge
    Selvage
    Lengthwise grain
    Crosswise grain
    True bias

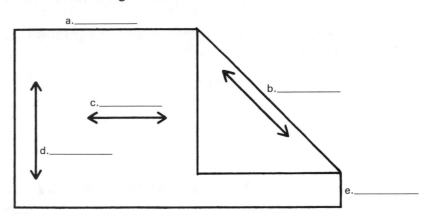

2. Label the knit fabric diagram with the following terms:
    Rib (lengthwise grain)
    Course (crosswise grain)

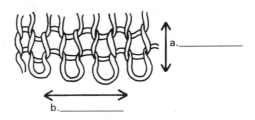

3. What unique characteristic do pattern pieces cut on the bias have?

    _____

4. In woven fabrics, the strongest yarns are used in the direction of the
    _____ grain. This grain is usually placed in a _____
    direction on the body because it receives the greatest strain.

5. Knit fabrics are cut so that the _____ (course, rib) goes around
    the body because it has the greatest degree of stretch.

6. Explain what happens if pattern pieces are cut from fabric that is off-grain.

    _____

    _____

    _____

    _____

(Continued)

Name _____

7. Explain, in your own words, how to determine if fabric is on-grain or off-grain.

_____

_____

_____

_____

8. If fabric is off-grain, can it always be straightened? _____
   Explain your answer.

_____

_____

_____

_____

9. Removing the finish on washable fabrics by laundering helps to avoid
   _____.

10. What synthetic fiber should be preshrunk? _____

11. Preshrinking dry-cleanable fabrics also helps to _____.

12. Explain how to straighten off-grain fabrics.

_____

_____

_____

_____

13. Explain how to preshrink a washable fabric.

_____

_____

_____

_____

14. What is one instruction you should give a dry cleaner when you are having a dry-cleanable fabric preshrunk?

_____

_____

_____

_____

Lesson 5 Reading the Instruction Sheet

Objectives

This lesson will help you to:
1. Identify the types of information found on the pattern instruction sheet.
2. Analyze and interpret the construction diagrams used on the instruction sheet.
3. Analyze and interpret the written directions given on the instruction sheet.

Words to Know

instruction sheet

Gathering Information

The pattern instruction sheet will tell you how to cut out and construct your garment. By following the instructions carefully, you will be able to make your garment quickly and easily. The diagrams and written instructions will be a valuable source of information. However, reading the instructions and diagrams is not always easy. This lesson will give you practice interpreting the information on the instruction sheet.

INSTRUCTION SHEET INFORMATION

There are many types of information provided on the pattern instruction sheet. You should be familiar with each type and where it is located. Following is a list of the types of information. Not all types of information will appear on every pattern instruction sheet.

1. Front and back view of each garment.
2. Pattern pieces required for each view.
3. Explanation of the various markings on your pattern pieces.
4. Instructions for preparing your pattern and fabric.
5. Layout key showing fabric and printed and unprinted sides of pattern.

(Continued)

6. Layout directions for each view. The layout diagrams show how to position the fabric and the placement of the pattern pieces on the fabric. Layout diagrams are given for each view, pattern size, and fabric width.
7. Layout directions for lining and interfacing fabrics.
8. Definitions of special sewing terms which are used in the instructions.
9. Suggested ways to transfer markings from the pattern pieces to the fabric.
10. Fabric key indicating right and wrong sides of fabric, interfacing fabric, and lining fabric.
11. Sewing directions and diagrams explaining how to construct each detail of the garment.

GARMENT CONSTRUCTION STEPS

After cutting out your garment as illustrated in the layout diagrams, you are ready to sew your garment together. Read through all of the steps pertaining to your garment before doing any sewing. This will give you an overall idea of the steps required to complete your project.

Diagrams and written instructions are given for each pattern view. You do not need to read the information which does not pertain to the view you are making. Scan the instructions until you reach a heading indicating your garment view. Begin at that point and complete each step given in the instructions. Occasionally the instruction sheet will refer you to another view and tell you to complete a certain number of steps. After completing those steps, return to your previous location in the instructions. Then continue working through the steps given.

Activity 5-1: Locating Types of Information

For this activity, you will need a pattern instruction sheet. You may use the instruction sheet for a pattern that you will be constructing. Or you may get one from your teacher. On your pattern instruction sheet, locate each of the types of information listed in the "Instruction Sheet Information" box. Remember, not all types of information can be found on every instruction sheet.

Activity 5-2: Using Instruction Diagrams and Written Information

The diagrams on the instruction sheet provide a fast and easy way to know what construction steps must be completed. The written instructions describe the diagrams and give additional information about the construction procedures. Understanding the diagrams and written information is very important if you are to complete your sewing project successfully.

In this activity, you will identify how specific sewing procedures are illustrated and described on the pattern instruction sheet. This activity will provide helpful information so that you will be able to complete Activities 5-3 and 5-4.

Using the pattern instruction sheet from the previous activity, identify how each of the items and procedures listed below is represented in the diagram and written instructions . Look over your instruction sheet until you find a diagram that illustrates each procedure. Examine the diagram closely. Then read the instructions beside the diagram so that you will have an idea how the procedure is described. Remember, not all procedures will be on every instruction sheet. Find as many of the procedures as you can. Your teacher may have you work with another individual on this activity.

bastestitching	hand stitching	seam
buttonholes	hem	staystitching
clean finished edge	interfacing	topstitching
clipping	reinforcement stitching	trimming
darts	right and wrong sides	tuck
ease stitching	of fabric	two layers of fabric

Name _____

Date _____ Period _____

Activity 5-3: Interpreting Diagrams

Given the following diagrams, write a brief description of what the diagram is show-ing you to do. You may refer to a pattern instruction sheet if it is helpful to you.

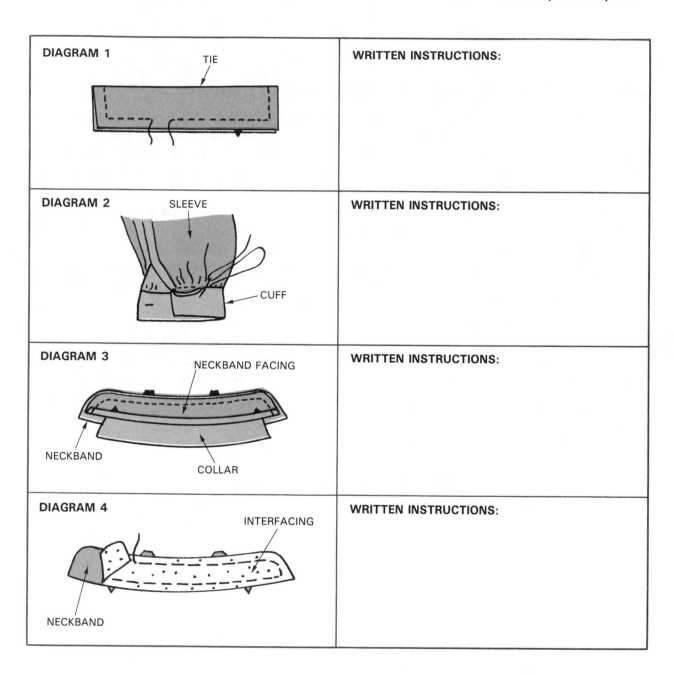

DIAGRAM 1 TIE	WRITTEN INSTRUCTIONS:
DIAGRAM 2 SLEEVE CUFF	WRITTEN INSTRUCTIONS:
DIAGRAM 3 NECKBAND FACING NECKBAND COLLAR	WRITTEN INSTRUCTIONS:
DIAGRAM 4 INTERFACING NECKBAND	WRITTEN INSTRUCTIONS:

Name _____

Date _____ Period _____

Activity 5-4: Interpreting Written Instructions

Given the following written instructions, try to sketch a diagram that illustrates what you need to do. Do not worry about how well you are able to draw. Do the best you can.

DIAGRAM	PIECE(S)	WRITTEN INSTRUCTIONS
	TIE 6	Fold the TIE (6) in half lengthwise, RIGHT SIDES TOGETHER. Stitch, leaving end nearest notch open. Cut corners diagonally.
	INTERFACING FOLD LINE CUFF 8	Position interfacing on notched half of CUFF (8). Machine baste in place on ends and notched side. Hand stitch along foldline. Press under 5/8″ on long UN-NOTCHED edge of CUFF (8).
	SLEEVE 10	To gather and ease cap of SLEEVE (10), machine baste 6/8″ and 1/2″ from raw edge between notches.
	SHIRT FRONT FACING RAW EDGE	Finish the lower edge of the shirt with a narrow hem. Press under raw edge 1/4″ and then press under again 1/4″.

Name _____

Date _____ Period _____

Activity 5-5: Evaluating Learning

Assess your understanding of the lesson by indicating how you feel about the statements below. Circle your response. Share your evaluation and activity sheets with your teacher.

1. Do you feel that you know where to find the information you need on the instruction sheet?   YES   NO   UNCERTAIN

2. Do you know where to begin reading the instruction sheet in order to construct the pattern view you will be making?   YES   NO   UNCERTAIN

3. Do you feel that you can analyze and interpret what the diagrams are showing?   YES   NO   UNCERTAIN

4. Do you feel that you can read and interpret the written instructions for each diagram?   YES   NO   UNCERTAIN

Lesson 6 Pattern Symbols

Objectives

This lesson will help you to:
1. Identify the meanings of various pattern symbols.
2. Demonstrate an understanding of pattern symbols by sketching symbols in the appropriate locations on several pattern pieces.
3. Show how pattern symbols are used to match garment pieces for stitching.

Gathering Information

Pattern symbols provide a great deal of sewing information. Some of the symbols will tell you how to adjust your pattern to make it fit. Others tell you how to lay your pattern on the fabric. Still other symbols will tell you how to construct details and sew the pieces together. Because pattern symbols give so much information, understanding what they mean is an important part of learning to sew.

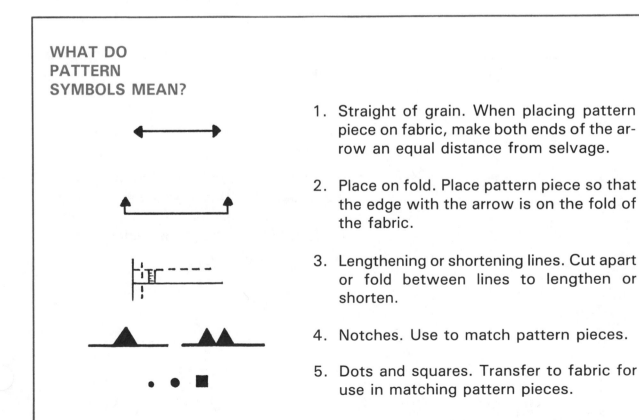

WHAT DO PATTERN SYMBOLS MEAN?

1. Straight of grain. When placing pattern piece on fabric, make both ends of the arrow an equal distance from selvage.

2. Place on fold. Place pattern piece so that the edge with the arrow is on the fold of the fabric.

3. Lengthening or shortening lines. Cut apart or fold between lines to lengthen or shorten.

4. Notches. Use to match pattern pieces.

5. Dots and squares. Transfer to fabric for use in matching pattern pieces.

(Continued)

6. Cutting line (solid) and stitching line (broken). The area between these lines is the seam allowance (usually 5/8 inch).

7. Dart placement. Transfer to fabric. Fold along solid line and stitch along broken line, using dots to match.

8. Sleeve placket placement. Transfer to fabric. Cut along solid line. Sew continuous lap to opening along dotted lines.

9. Tuck lines. Transfer to fabric. Bring solid lines to broken lines and baste in place along seamlines.

10. Welt pocket placement. Transfer to fabric. Cut along solid line. Sew welt to fabric at broken lines.

11. Patch pocket placement. Transfer to fabric. Match pocket piece to solid line.

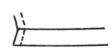

12. Button and buttonhole placement (may be used together or separately). Transfer to fabric to make placement of button and buttonhole.

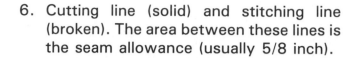

13. Hemline. Fold along inner solid line and hem.

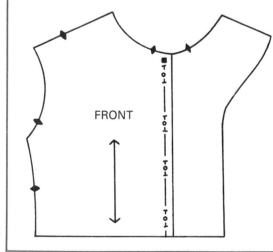

FRONT

14. Center front line and center front fold line. Use broken line to align the center fronts of the pattern pieces. Use solid line as a guide for folding back the facing portion of a pattern piece.

Name _____

Date _____ Period _____

Activity 6-1: Identifying Symbols

Match the following symbol names to the symbols used on the pattern pieces. Place the number of the name near the symbol on the pattern. Draw lines between the numbers and the symbols if it makes your labels more clear.

1. button and buttonhole placement
2. cutting lines
3. stitching lines
4. sleeve placket placement
5. patch pocket placement
6. small dots for matching
7. large dots for matching
8. square for matching
9. double notches for matching
10. single notches for matching
11. tuck lines
12. straight of grain
13. hem line
14. welt pocket placement
15. dart placement
16. place on fold
17. lengthening or shortening lines
18. center front line
19. center front fold line

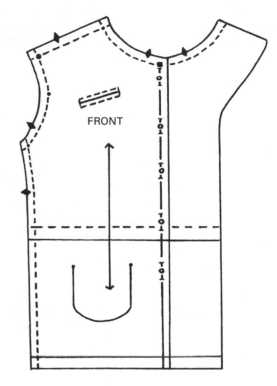

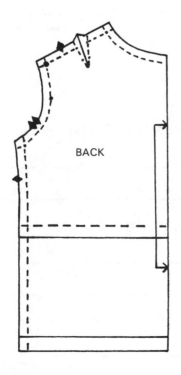

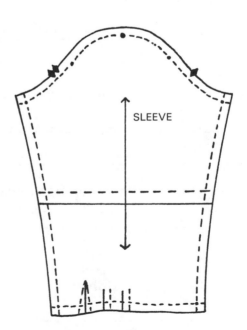

Name _____

Date _____ Period _____

Activity 6-2: Using Symbols to Match Pattern Pieces

When pattern pieces are connected, matching symbols are used to assure that pieces are joined in the right way. Draw lines connecting the symbols that need to be matched on the three pieces below. Then answer the questions that follow.

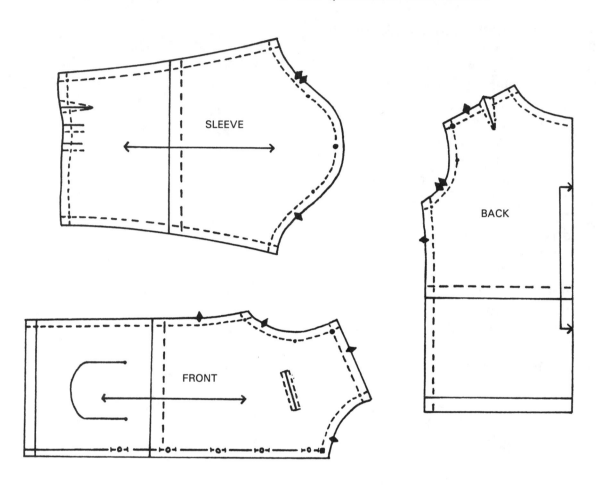

1. Does it matter into which armseye a sleeve is inserted? Explain your answer.

_____

_____

2. How can you tell the difference between the front and back of a sleeve?

_____

_____

3. With what do you match the top of the sleeve? Why is this important?

_____

_____

Name _____

Date _____ Period _____

Activity 6-3: Drawing Symbols

Below are the outlines of a jacket front and back. Also, there is a list of symbols required for these pattern pieces. Sketch the symbols on the pattern pieces in their proper location.

WHERE WOULD THE FOLLOWING SYMBOLS BE LOCATED?

One button hole and button located at the waist
One welt pocket located on the upper jacket front
One large patch pocket on the lower front
A small dart at the neckline on the back
Shortening or lengthening lines
Stitching lines
Straight of grain arrows
Hemlines
Single notches indicating shoulder matching and front sleeve matching
Double notches indicating side seam matching and back sleeve matching
Triple notches indicating back matching

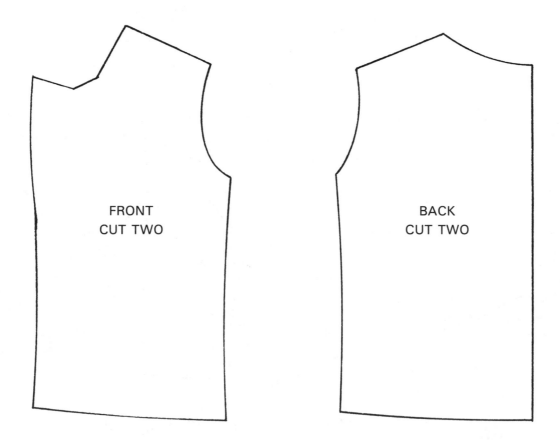

FRONT
CUT TWO

BACK
CUT TWO

Name _____

Date _____ Period _____

Activity 6-4: Evaluating Learning

Assess your understanding of pattern symbols by answering the following questions.

1. Give the meanings of the following pattern symbols:

2. Draw sketches of these pattern symbols:
    place on the fold
    place on straight of grain
    tuck
    patch pocket
    single notch

3. On a sleeve pattern, where would you expect to find the following symbols? You may either sketch the pattern symbols in the correct location or draw a line to the position that the symbols would be located.

    large dot
    small dots
    single notches
    double notches
    sleeve placket placement
    tucks

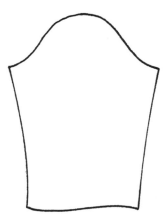

4. Explain briefly how pattern symbols are used to determine which garment pieces fit together.

_____

_____

86

Lesson 7 Pattern Adjustments

Objectives

This lesson will help you to:
1. Determine when to make pattern adjustments by comparing your measurements to those of the pattern.
2. Make a variety of pattern adjustments.

Words to Know

ease
swayback

Gathering Information

A perfect fitting garment should be the goal of everyone who sews. There is little point in making a garment that is uncomfortable or unattractive to wear. Perfect fit can best be achieved by taking a little extra time to compare your measurements to those of the pattern. The pattern should then be adjusted before cutting the pattern from the fabric. This will result in simple-to-make adjustments. It will also prevent time consuming alterations later.

PATTERN DESIGN AND FIT

Buying the same pattern size for each garment you construct will not always guarantee a perfect fit. Every new pattern will fit a little differently.

Two clues may be found on the pattern envelope to give you an idea of how the pattern will fit. First, the backview sketch will show the silhouette of the garment. This will help you see how the garment may be expected to fall on the body.

Second, the caption that describes the pattern design will give clues about the fit. You will find such words as loose fitting, fitted, semi-fitted, and close fitting.

HOW MUCH EASE?

The word ease refers to the amount of extra fabric allowed in the garment to make the garment comfortable to wear. In other words, extra room is needed for the body to sit, move, and bend. This wearing ease should never be removed in making adjustments in the pattern.

Minimum ease allowances:

Bust	3 to 4 inches
Waist	1/2 inch
Hips	1 inch for a snug fit 2 inches for a roomy fit
Back Waist Length	1/2 inch
Crotch Depth	1/2 inch for 35-inch hips 3/4 inch for 35-inch to 38-inch hips 1 inch for 38 inch plus hips

The ease allowances given above are not suitable for stretch knit fabrics. Less ease is provided in stretch knit patterns.

DETERMINING PATTERN MEASUREMENTS

Different garment designs allow varying amounts of ease. This makes determining the actual size of the finished garment and whether it will fit somewhat difficult. To solve this problem, the pattern may be measured. The most important areas of the pattern to measure are the crotch depth, hips, bust, shoulders, hem length, thigh, upper arm, and sleeve length.

To measure the pattern, simply lay the pattern pieces out flat, pin in any darts or tucks, and measure from seam line to seam line for those areas in question.

TO DETERMINE WHEN TO ADJUST THE PATTERN METHOD #1

Take your measurements and compare to those on the back of the pattern envelope. The measurements given on the envelope include an allowance for ease. If some measurements differ, you will want to make adjustments in those areas.

TO DETERMINE WHEN TO ADJUST THE PATTERN METHOD #2

Take your body measurements. Add to your measurements the amount of ease you wish to allow. If you like a tight fit use less ease. If you like a loose fit, allow for more ease.

Measure the pattern as described in the "Determining Pattern Measurements" box.

Compare your measurements (including ease) with the pattern measurements. Make adjustments accordingly.

FITTING AFTER THE PATTERN HAS BEEN CUT OUT

Major adjustments in the pattern should be made prior to cutting it out. However, fitting problems cannot always be foreseen at this early stage. For instance, all fabrics fit and hang differently. Therefore, even if the pattern is one that has been used before and resulted in a perfect fit, another fabric may give a totally different fit.

Fitting garments early in the construction process makes adjusting the garment easier. Do not wait until the garment is finished to try it on. The longer you wait the more difficult the adjustments will be to complete.

As you try on a garment, the fabric may fold, wrinkle, or pull over some of your body curves. This is a sign of poor fit. The folds indicate the area of the garment that needs alteration. For instance, when trying on a skirt, folds may form between the hip and the waist. This is a sign that more fullness is needed in the hip area.

There are many alteration books available. You can use them to work out procedures that will solve your personal fitting problems.

HOW TO LENGTHEN OR SHORTEN THE CROTCH

To lengthen, follow these steps:

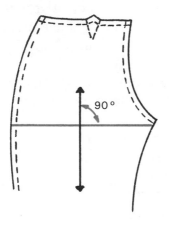

1. If your pattern does not already have one, draw in a crotch line. Be sure the line you draw forms a right angle to the grainline arrow.

2. To determine how much to lengthen the crotch depth, measure from the drawn line to the waist. Do not include the seam allowance in this measurement. Take this measurement on the hip side of the pattern. Compare this measurement to your crotch depth plus ease.

3. Cut the pattern on the lengthening lines. Spread the pattern the desired distance.

4. Place tissue paper under the area and tape in place.

5. Adjust pattern markings by drawing in new stitching lines and cutting lines.

6. Be sure to make the same change on the front pattern piece.

To shorten, follow the same procedure as given above except fold the pattern along the shortening and lengthening lines, taking up the necessary amount.

HOW TO SHORTEN OR LENGTHEN THE GARMENT

Follow these steps:

1. Fold or cut the pattern on the lengthening/shortening lines. Take up or add the necessary amount for the adjustment. Tape the pattern in place.

2. Draw new stitching and cutting lines.

HOW TO LENGTHEN OR SHORTEN THE SLEEVE

To lengthen, follow these steps:

1. The sleeve should be lengthened both above and below the elbow. Cut the pattern along both lengthening lines.

2. Spread the pattern one half the amount above the elbow; one half below the elbow. Place tissue paper under the pattern and tape in position. Draw new stitching and cutting lines.

To shorten, follow the same procedure given above except fold the sleeve along the lengthening and shortening lines, taking up the necessary amount.

HOW TO INCREASE OR DECREASE THE WAIST

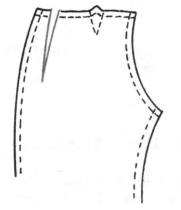

To increase, follow these steps:

1. Begin by determining how much you will increase the waist. You will need to add 1/4 of the total alteration at each side seam. You will make the same adjustment on front and back pattern pieces. Half the adjustment will be allowed on the front; half on the back pattern piece. Also, you are working with two layers of fabric—thus 1/4 of the total alteration is added to each side seam.

2. Slit the pattern piece close to the side seam. Spread the pattern the desired amount. Place tissue paper under the slit and tape in place.

3. Draw new seamlines and cutting lines.

4. When making this adjustment on your pattern, you will also need to increase the length of the waistband.

To decrease, follow the same procedure as given above except overlap the cut edges of the slit the necessary amount.

HOW TO INCREASE OR DECREASE THE HIP

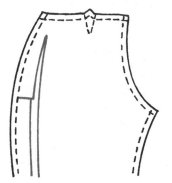

Follow these steps:

1. Begin by determining how much you will increase the hip. You will add 1/4 the total measurement (see explanation under increasing the waist.)

2. Slash the pattern from hemline to waist. Do not cut through the waist seam allowance.

3. Spread the pattern the desired amount. Tape tissue paper in place.

To decrease, follow the same procedure as given above except overlap the cut edges of the slit the necessary amount.

HOW TO TAPER OR INCREASE WIDTH OF PANT LEGS

To taper, follow these steps:

1. Begin by determining how much you will decrease the pant leg. Use 1/4 the total measurement on both sides of the leg pattern piece. You are working with two layers of fabric to get the total amount of the decrease.

2. Draw in new seamlines. Begin drawing at the hipline on the side seam and the crotch point on the inseam.

3. Trim off old seam lines.

To increase width, follow these steps:

1. Begin by determining how much you will increase the pant leg. Use 1/4 the total measurement on each side of the leg.

2. Tape tissue paper alone the edge of the pattern. Draw in new seamlines. Begin drawing at the hipline on the side seam and the crotch point on the inseam.

HOW TO ADJUST FOR A SWAYBACK

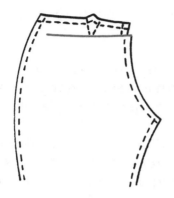

A swayback curves in at the waist more than other backs. People with this figure often have too much fabric in back.

To adjust for a swayback, follow these steps:

1. Slash the pattern across the upper back.

2. Overlap the pattern the desired amount.

3. Draw new center back line and dart.

4. When making this adjustment, it will also be necessary to adjust the waistband length.

FACTS FROM THE PAST

Garment patterns date as far back as the Roman Catacombs. These early patterns were made by cloistered monks. Since paper was practically unknown at that time, the patterns were made of slate and hung on the walls of the dark Catacombs. The patterns were for simple robes made from a one piece back and sleeve. The front and back were made from the same pattern piece. No provision was made for variations in the size and shape of the human body.

Before the development of patterns as we know them today, garments were designed by fitting muslin fabric to the body. The muslin then became the pattern for the fashion fabric.

The first paper patterns were displayed in 1850 in Philadelphia. By 1860, the first French inspired patterns could be ordered by mail. These early commercial patterns are very different from the ones we know today. As many as 15 different styles would be combined on one pattern. Using these patterns was very confusing to the home sewer. In 1863, Mr. & Mrs. Ebenezer Butterick introduced the first sized and graded paper patterns.

Name _____

Date _____ Period _____

Activity 7-1: Determining Pattern Adjustments

This activity will help you to determine what pattern adjustments to make. Follow these steps:

1. Take your body measurements (Review Lesson 1) and record below.
2. Record the measurements from the back of a pattern envelope in the correct column below. Or measure the corresponding places on the pattern pieces. Be sure to exclude seam allowances, darts, etc.)
3. Keeping ease in mind, compare your measurements with the pattern measurements. Record the amount to be added or decreased in the "Adjustment Needed" column.
4. If adjustments exceed 3 inches, consider purchasing a different sized pattern.

DETERMINING PATTERN ADJUSTMENTS

	YOUR MEASUREMENTS	PATTERN MEASUREMENTS	EASE TO ALLOW	ADJUSTMENT NEEDED
Bust			3 to 4 inches	
Waist			1/2 inch for fitted waist	
Hips			1 inch (snug fit) 2 inches (roomy fit)	
Back waist length			1/2 inch	
Length			3 inches	
Crotch depth			1/2 inch (35-inch hips) 3/4 inch (35-inch to 38-inch hips) 1 inch (38-inch plus)	
Sleeve length (with arm bent)				
Shoulders				

Activity 7-2: Practicing

Supplies needed:

ruler
scissors
tissue paper

transparent tape
T square

Cut out the pattern pieces from the following pages and alter as instructed. You may refer to the information provided earlier in this lesson. Attach the adjusted pattern pieces to a sheet of paper and label each one.

1. Lengthen the crotch to 2 1/4 inches. Then taper the pant legs. The total decrease for each pant leg will be 1 inch.
2. Lengthen the sleeve a total of 1/2 inch.

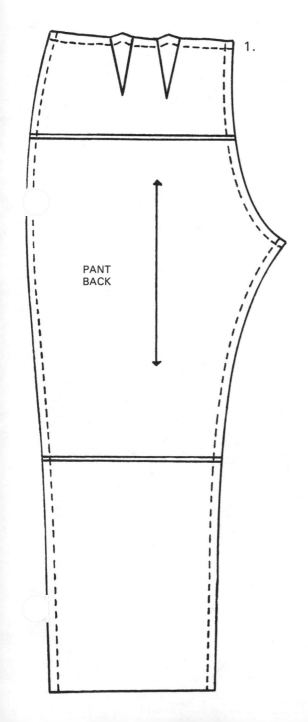

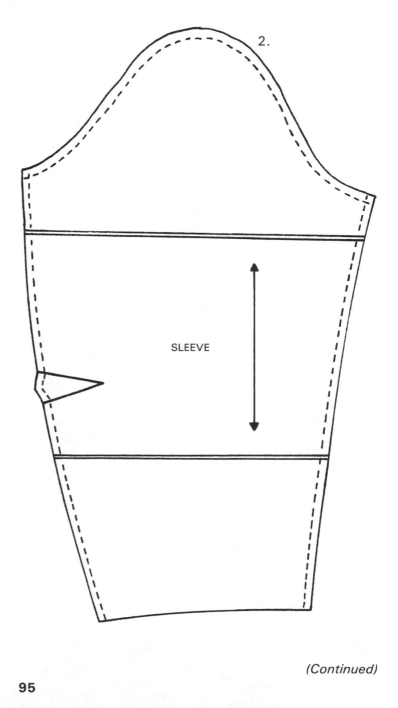

(Continued)

3. Add to the waist measurement of the shorts. The total waist increase will be 1 inch.

4. Increase the hip measurement of the pants. The total increase for the hip will be 1 inch.

5. Shorten the shirt length 1/4 inch.

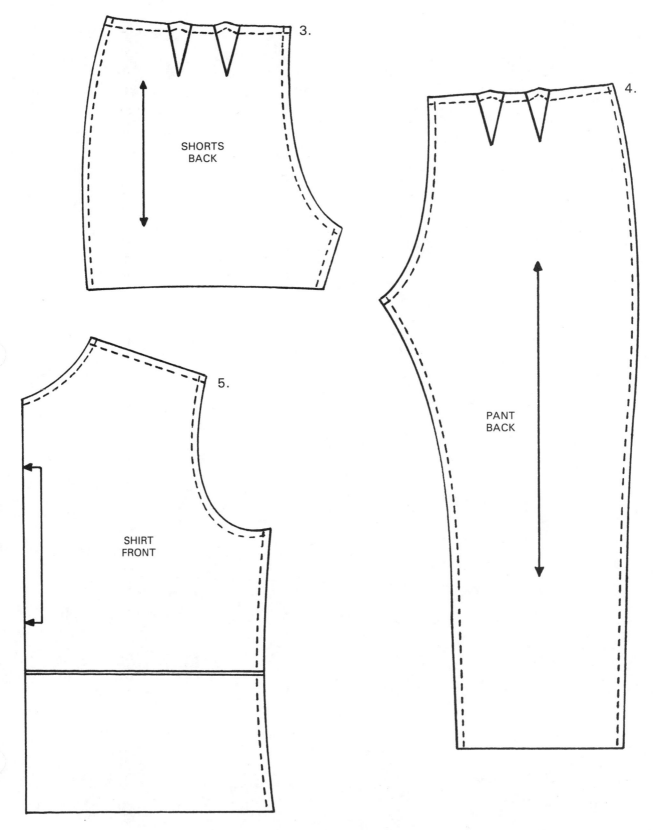

Name _____

Date _____ Period _____

Activity 7-3: Evaluating Learning

1. Explain how to determine when a pattern needs to be adjusted.

_____

_____

_____

_____

2. Explain the importance of ease allowances provided in patterns.

_____

_____

_____

_____

3. How much ease is generally allowed in the following pattern areas?

   Chest or bust: _____

   Waist: _____

   Hip: _____

   Crotch: _____

Do you feel that you understand how to lengthen and/or shorten a pattern?	YES	NO	UNCERTAIN
Do you feel that you understand how to increase or decrease the waist and hip areas of a garment?	YES	NO	UNCERTAIN
Do you feel that you understand pattern adjusting well enough that you are willing to attempt other pattern adjustments?	YES	NO	UNCERTAIN

notes

Lesson 8 Pattern Layout, Pinning, and Cutting

Objectives

This lesson will help you to:
1. Identify the various ways fabric may be folded in preparation for layout, pinning, and cutting.
2. Correctly lay out a pattern.
3. Give reasons for various layout, pinning, and cutting procedures.
4. Interpret layout, pinning, and cutting information found on the pattern instruction sheet.

Words to Know

crosswise fold	lengthwise fold	repeat
double fold	partial fold	uneven plaids and
even plaids and		stripes
stripes		

Gathering Information

Following the correct pattern layout will help assure that your garment is cut out on-grain. Pinning and cutting your garment carefully will avoid wasting fabric. This lesson will provide the information you need to lay out, pin, and cut out your pattern pieces.

FOLDING THE FABRIC

Fabric can be folded in a variety of ways before pattern pieces are positioned for cutting. The type of fold used depends on:

1. The number of pattern pieces that must be placed on a folded edge.

2. The fold that results in the most economic use of the fabric.

3. The width of the fabric.

4. The pattern size.

Pattern companies have already taken these factors into consideration for you. Therefore, you should fold your fabric as shown in the diagram found on your pattern instruction sheet.

(Continued)

101

Lengthwise fold. Most fabric is folded lengthwise on the bolt. Pattern instructions generally show that fabric should be folded in half lengthwise so that selvages match. But lengthwise folds can also be partial folds leaving some of the fabric extended as a single layer.

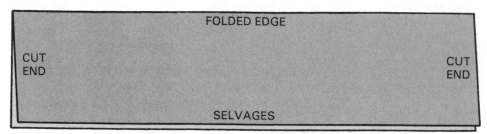

Crosswise fold. A crosswise fold is often used when pattern pieces are too wide to fit on fabric folded lengthwise. When fabric is folded crosswise, the cut ends usually match. But a crosswise fold can also be a partial fold.

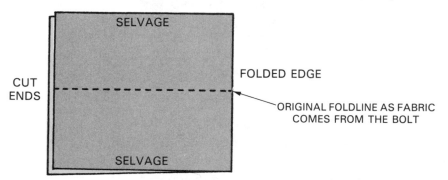

Double fold. You may use a double fold when you cannot press the original foldline out of the fabric. You may also use it when several pattern pieces are to be cut on a fold.

When making a double fold, be sure the full length of each folded side is the same width. Measure as shown. This will insure that the folded edges are straight with the grain.

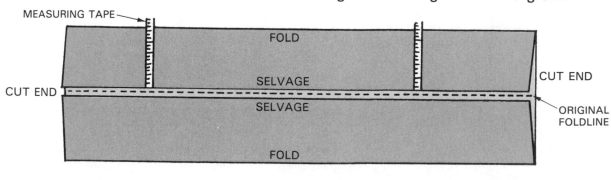

FOLDING KNIT FABRICS

Try to press out the lengthwise crease on knit fabrics before laying out pattern pieces. Often this crease is permanent in knit fabrics and, if used on the garment, may be unsightly. If you cannot press out the crease, you can avoid using it by folding your fabric with a double fold. Another possibility is to position the crease to work with the pattern design. For instance, place pattern pieces so that the crease will fall down the center of sleeves or pant legs.

GUIDELINES FOR PATTTERN LAYOUT

When laying out your pattern pieces on your fabric, follow these guidelines.

1. Circle the correct layout diagram on your pattern instruction sheet. Choose the correct diagram according to the pattern view, size, and fabric width.

2. Make any desired fit or design alterations to your pattern before laying it out. (Refer to Lesson 7, "Pattern Adjustments," for more information on alterations.)

3. Lay all pattern pieces on the fabric before pinning any of them in place. This will allow you to make sure that all pieces will fit on the fabric.

4. Follow the shading key shown on your instruction sheet. Black denotes fabric. White denotes pattern pieces to be placed with the printed side up. Lines denote pattern pieces to be placed with the printed side down.

5. Sometimes a layout diagram will show a pattern piece that is placed halfway off the fabric. This piece will usually be accompanied with a *. Find the star on your instruction sheet and follow the directions given. This generally means that there is not enough room to place the pattern piece on the folded fabric. The instructions will indicate that you should cut out all of the other pattern pieces. Then you should open out the fabric to accommodate the piece that was placed partially off the fabric.

(Continued)

6. Sometimes a layout diagram will show two pattern pieces with the same number. This indicates that the pattern piece will have to be cut out twice, such as when you need four cuff pieces. The pattern will only include one pattern piece. Therefore, simply relocate the pattern piece and cut it out a second time.

7. Avoid placing pattern pieces on the selvage edges of the fabric. Selvages do not give and can cause seams to pucker. If you must place a piece on the selvage, clip the selvage about every 1/2 inch to create more give.

8. When you are cutting two layers of fabric, the pattern pieces do not have to be placed printed side up. But if you are cutting one layer, the pattern pieces must be placed printed side up. They must also be placed on the right side of the fabric. Otherwise, you may find that pattern pieces fit the wrong side of your body.

9. Be sure to use the "with nap" layout when working with napped fabrics. (Refer to Lesson 2, The Pattern Envelope, for more information on napped fabrics.) Also use this layout when working with knits, as most knits tend to have shading in one direction. If this layout is not followed, differences in color may appear on the finished garment. You can also use this layout when working with fabrics that do not have nap. However, "with nap" layouts usually require more yardage.

PLACING PIECES ON THE FOLD

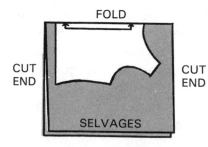

Check for pattern pieces that must be placed on the fabric fold. When cutting out these pieces, never cut along the folded edge.

PLACING PIECES ON-GRAIN

Accurate measuring will help you make sure your pattern pieces are cut out on-grain. Follow these steps:

1. Place each pattern piece so the grainline arrow runs lengthwise on the fabric. Grainline arrows should run parallel to the selvage edges regardless of the way the fabric has been folded.

2. Pin one end of the grainline arrow to hold it in place.

3. Measure from the pinned end of the arrow to the fabric selvage edge.

4. Now measure from the other end of the grainline arrow to the fabric selvage edge. Make sure it is the same distance from the selvage as the end you have already pinned in place. Adjust the distance if necessary and then pin the arrow in place.

5. Pin the edges of the pattern piece in place.

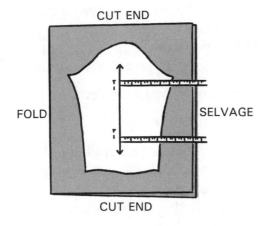

The lengthwise grain on knits is seen as a rib. Use this rib to place pattern pieces on the straight of grain.

Special techniques are used when placing pattern pieces on off-grain fabrics that cannot be straightened. For solid color fabrics or fabrics with an all-over design, lay the fabric so that the selvages are together. Make sure the lengthwise fold lies smoothly. (You will not be able to line up the cut ends of the fabric.) Then measure from the grainline arrows to the selvages as described above. For off-grain fabrics with a stripe, plaid, or obvious horizontal design, ignore the lengthwise grain. Instead, follow the print as much as possible. Cut the pattern pieces out of a single layer of fabric. Match the design of the second piece with the first.

PINNING PATTERN PIECES

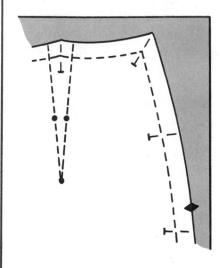

When pinning your pattern pieces to your fabric, follow these guidelines:

1. Pin with care to prevent inaccurate cutting. A cutting error of 1/8 inch on each side of a pattern piece can result in a 1/2 inch difference in the final garment.

2. Use only enough pins to hold down the pattern securely. Depending on the fabric and the size of the pattern piece, placing pins about six inches apart is usually enough.

3. Place pins completely inside the cutting line.

4. Place pins diagonally in corners.

5. Use pattern weights instead of pins to hold the pattern in position, if desired. However, be sure to pin grainlines in place first. Position weights, inside the cutting lines, on one pattern piece at a time.

CUTTING OUT PATTERN PIECES

When cutting out pattern pieces, follow these guidelines:

1. Use sharp shears or a rotary cutter to cut out your pattern pieces. Never use pinking shears. Pattern pieces cannot be cut out accurately with pinking shears.

2. Do not allow the fabric to hang over the edge of the table when you are cutting. This is especially true when working with knits and other stretchy fabrics. The weight of the fabric hanging over the table edge will pull the fabric and result in inaccurate cutting. Also, be careful to leave the fabric resting on the table as you cut. Lifting the fabric will result in inaccurate cutting.

3. Cut notches out away from the seam allowance. Cutting notches into the seam allowance will weaken the seam. This will also prevent you from letting the seam out if a looser fit is needed.

(Continued)

4. When using a rotary cutter, always be sure to place a protective plastic cutting mat beneath the fabric. Shift the cutting mat under your work as you proceed around the pattern. A metal ruler can be used as a guide for cutting straight edges. When cutting complex shapes, a small rotary wheel is easier to maneuver than larger ones. You will not be able to cut out the notches with a rotary cutter. Instead, cut off the notches and mark them using another technique, such as chalk or washable marking pen.

5. To cut out pattern pieces from a multisize pattern, begin by determining which lines you wish to follow. To do this, refer to the envelope size chart and compare your measurements with those on the chart. Identify which size you should use for different areas of your body. When cutting, taper from the cutting line for one size into the cutting line for another size as needed. Use a colored pen to trace along the lines you plan to follow before placing the pattern on the fabric. This will help you avoid confusion. You might also wish to cut out the pattern on the desired size lines before placing it on the fabric.

WORKING WITH STRIPED FABRICS

When working with striped fabrics, follow these helpful suggestions:

1. Stripes should be matched at seamlines to form a continuous line around the body. You may have to purchase extra fabric for matching.

2. Avoid using patterns that are labeled "not suitable for stripes." Matching stripes on these patterns will be difficult.

3. Interesting patterns may be created with stripes by cutting small pattern pieces on the bias.

4. When using stripes vertically, place the dominant stripe at the center of major garment pieces.

(Continued)

5. Make certain that stripes are on-grain before purchasing the fabric.

6. When cutting uneven stripes, use a "with nap" layout. To determine whether a stripe is even or uneven, fold the fabric lengthwise then fold back one corner. If the stripe is even, the stripes in one corner will match those in the other corner. If the stripes do not match, the stripe is uneven. Match uneven stripes using the same techniques you use for matching plaids.

WORKING WITH PLAID FABRICS

When working with plaid fabrics, follow these helpful suggestions:

1. You need to determine whether a plaid is even or uneven. To do this, fold the plaid diagonally through the center of a repeat. A repeat is one complete, four-sided design in the fabric. An even plaid has colored lines and spaces that are the same in both the lengthwise and crosswise directions. An uneven plaid has lines and spaces that will not match in either one or both directions.

2. Plaids should be matched at seamlines to form a continuous design around the body. To match plaids, pattern pieces need to be aligned on the fabric. Pattern notches having the same numbers should be placed on the same lines of the plaid.

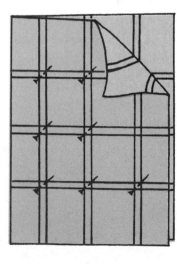

3. For even plaids, align the plaid in one layer with the plaid in the other layer of the folded fabric. Do this before laying any pattern pieces in place. To align the plaids, insert a pin in the plaid. Bring the pin through the bottom layer of fabric at the same point in the plaid. Repeat pinning in this manner at intervals that will hold the plaid in position. Leave the pins in place until the pattern pieces have been cut out.

4. For uneven plaids, follow the "with nap" layout. Cut each pattern piece from a single layer of fabric. When cutting the pattern piece for the second time, be sure to turn it over. This will give you both a left and right garment side. Also, place the notches at the same point in the plaid as they were placed for the first cutting.

Activity 8-1: Practicing Folding and Laying Out the Pattern

Supplies needed:

paper

scissors

pattern pieces 8A through 8K

glue or tape

This activity is made up of three problems. For each problem, cut out the specified pattern pieces found at the end of the lesson. Also cut a piece of paper the size of the dimensions given to represent fabric from which the garment is to be cut. Try various fabric folds—lengthwise, crosswise, partial, and double—and ways of placing the pattern pieces on the fabric. Decide on the best way to fold the fabric and lay out the pattern pieces. Then glue or tape the pieces in place. Attach your results to a sheet of paper. Be prepared to discuss your work.

Garment 1 — Knit Top

Use pattern pieces 8A and 8B.

Cut a sheet of paper 4 1/2 by 8 3/4 inches for the fabric.

Consider the lengthwise grain to run parallel to the 4 1/2-inch edge. A lengthwise crease runs through the center of the fabric.

Garment 2 — Skirt

Use pattern pieces 8C, 8D, and 8E.

Cut a sheet of paper 6 1/4 by 11 inches for the fabric. Consider the lengthwise grain to run parallel to the 11-inch edge.

Garment 3 — Shirt

Use pattern pieces 8F, 8G, 8H, 8I, 8J, and 8K.

Use a single 8 1/2 by 11 inch sheet of paper for the fabric.

Consider the lengthwise grain to run parallel to the 11-inch edge.

Name _____

Date _____ Period _____

Activity 8-2: Using the Instruction Sheet

You will be given a pattern instruction sheet. The instruction sheet and the information in this lesson will be your sources of information. Look over the instruction sheet and answer the questions below. Be prepared to discuss your answers.

1. Your instruction sheet shows a variety of pattern layout diagrams. Explain how to select the pattern layout to follow. What information do you need to know in order to make a decision about which layout to use?

   _____

   _____

   _____

   _____

2. What do the following shadings indicate:

   ▪ Black: _____

   ☐ White: _____

   ▨ Gray (Lined): _____

3. When using a crosswise fold, on which grain are the pattern pieces placed?

   _____

4. When using a lengthwise fold, on which grain are the pattern pieces placed?

   _____

5. The layout diagram shows two pattern pieces with the same number. But you have only one pattern piece in your envelope. What should you do?

   _____

   _____

6. Why is a crosswise fold sometimes used instead of a lengthwise fold?

   _____

   _____

7. What is meant when you see a layout diagram that has one pattern piece placed half way off the fabric?

   _____

   _____

8. Some layout diagrams may be labeled ''with nap'' or ''without nap.'' What do these words mean?

   _____

   _____

9. Can you use a ''with nap'' layout even if you do not have napped fabric? Explain.

   _____

   _____

(Continued)

Name _____

10. Can you use a ''without nap'' layout with napped fabric? Explain.

_____

_____

11. In your own words, explain why following the layout diagram on the instruction sheet is important.

_____

_____

12. How do you determine if pattern pieces are placed on the straight of grain?

_____

_____

13. What layout diagrams, other than for the main garment pieces, may be included on the instruction sheet?

_____

_____

14. Explain the reasons for the following procedures:
   a. Never cut out pattern pieces with pinking shears.

   _____

   _____

   b. Cut all notches out, away from the seam allowance.

   _____

   _____

   c. Do not use the selvage edges of the fabric. If it is necessary to do so, be sure to clip the selvage about every 1/2 inch.

   _____

   _____

   d. Pin all pattern pieces on the fabric before cutting them out.

   _____

   _____

   e. When cutting a single thickness of fabric, always place the pattern printed side up on the right side of the fabric.

   _____

   _____

15. Why should you follow the napped layout when sewing on knit fabric?

   _____

   _____

16. The crease line on knit fabric may not always disappear when pressed or washed. What must you do when cutting out pattern pieces if this is a problem?

   _____

   _____

Name _____

Date _____ Period _____

Activity 8-3: Evaluating Learning

Assess your understanding of layout, pinning, and cutting by completing the exercises below.

1. Sketch the three ways of folding fabric. On each sketch, draw lines indicating the lengthwise, crosswise, and bias grainlines. Be sure to label the sketches and the grainlines.

2. Briefly, explain how to select the correct pattern layout from those given on the instruction sheet.

   _____

   _____

   _____

3. Explain, in your own words, how to place a pattern piece on the straight-of-grain.

   _____

   _____

   _____

4. What is the meaning of the word "napped" and why is it important when laying pattern pieces on fabric?

   _____

   _____

   _____

5. Give three important suggestions for pinning pattern pieces to fabric.

   _____

   _____

   _____

6. Give three important suggestions for cutting out pattern pieces.

   _____

   _____

   _____

Pattern pieces for Activity 8-1.

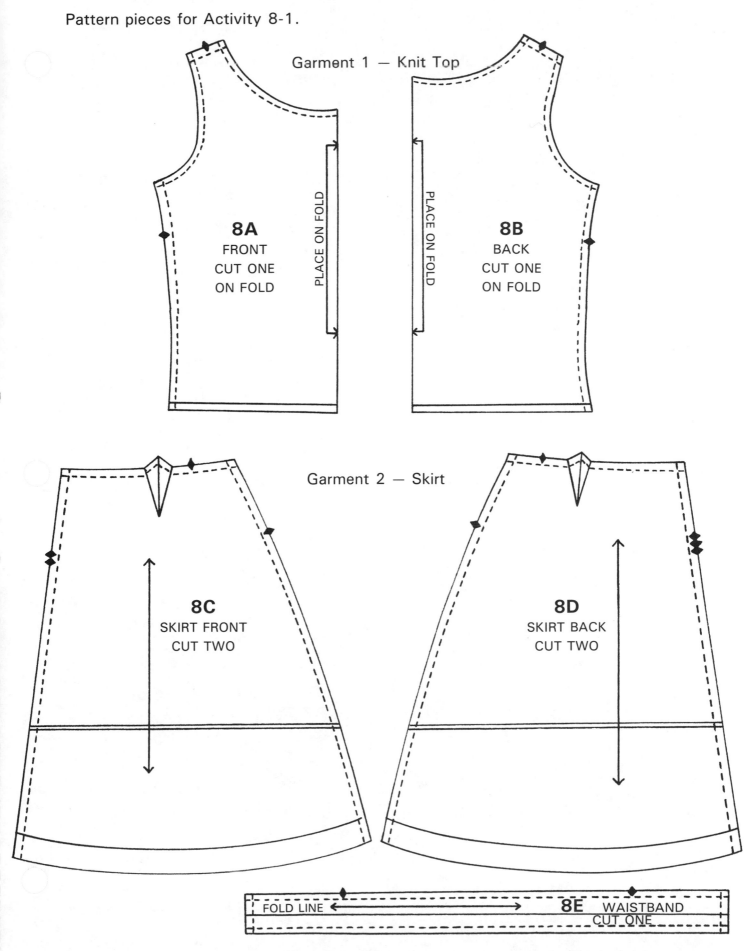

Garment 1 — Knit Top

8A FRONT CUT ONE ON FOLD

PLACE ON FOLD

8B BACK CUT ONE ON FOLD

PLACE ON FOLD

Garment 2 — Skirt

8C SKIRT FRONT CUT TWO

8D SKIRT BACK CUT TWO

FOLD LINE **8E** WAISTBAND CUT ONE

Pattern pieces for Activity 8-1.

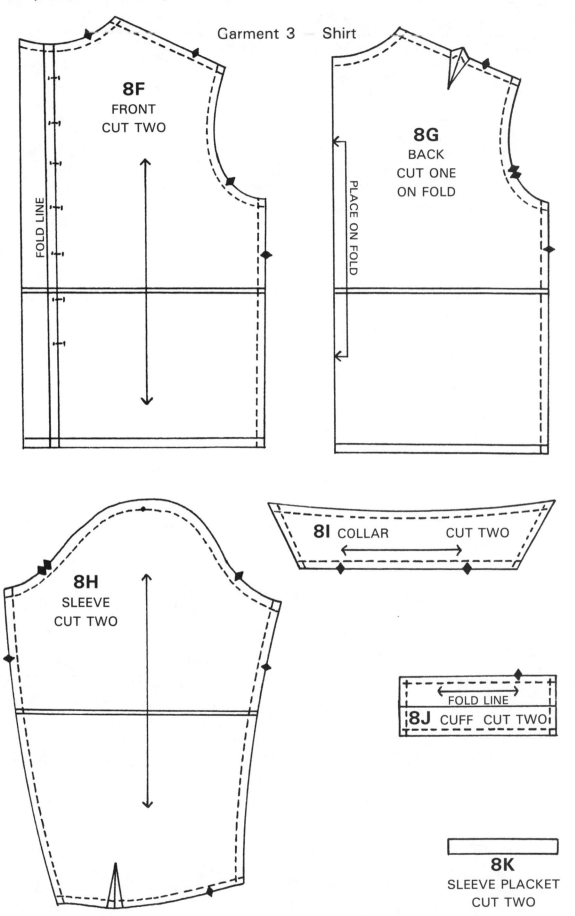

Garment 3 — Shirt

8F FRONT CUT TWO

FOLD LINE

8G BACK CUT ONE ON FOLD

PLACE ON FOLD

8H SLEEVE CUT TWO

8I COLLAR CUT TWO

FOLD LINE

8J CUFF CUT TWO

8K SLEEVE PLACKET CUT TWO

Lesson 9 Transferring Pattern Symbols to the Fabric

Objectives

This lesson will help you to:
1. Identify the various methods for transferring pattern symbols to fabric.
2. Select the method of marking that is most appropriate for various types of fabric and symbols.
3. Practice using the various marking methods.

Words to Know

tailor's tacks

Gathering Information

Lesson 6, "Pattern Symbols," illustrated and defined the use of various symbols that appear on pattern pieces. But for these symbols to be useful, you need to transfer them to the fabric pieces. This step is done after fabric pieces have been cut, before removing the pattern.

There is no single, correct method of transferring a specific pattern symbol. Several methods may serve the same purpose. For each marking situation, you will want to select the quickest and easiest of the methods. Your selection will depend on your fabric and the symbol you are marking. This lesson will provide the information you will need to make decisions about transferring pattern symbols.

| USING TRACING PAPER AND WHEEL | **Description of method.** Sheets of color-coated paper are placed between fabric layers. The colored side of the paper is always placed next to the wrong side of the fabric. Pattern symbols are then traced using a tracing wheel. Color is transferred from the tracing paper to the fabric where pressure is applied to the paper with the wheel.

Tracing wheels may be grooved or smooth. Grooved wheels work well for most fabrics. But the smooth wheel is preferred for delicate or napped fabrics. |

(Continued)

When using this method, keep the following suggestions in mind.

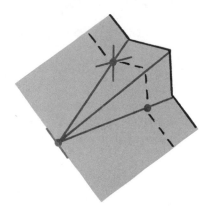

- Test this method on a scrap of fabric to be sure markings will show up clearly. Use this sample to also be sure that markings will wash out of the fabric.

- Select a color of tracing paper that contrasts with the fabric.

- Place a piece of cardboard under the area you are marking to avoid scratching the surface on which you are working.

- A ruler may be used as a guide when marking straight lines. Place the ruler along the line to be marked. Then run the wheel along the straight edge of the ruler.

- To mark dots, make an ''X'' with the tracing wheel over the center of the dot.

- To mark the ends of darts, mark a straight line across the point.

When to use this method. Use this marking method only with washable, smooth surfaced, light to medium weight fabric.

Shortcomings. The colored markings left by the tracing paper can have some drawbacks. Sometimes the markings will show through to the outside of white or sheer fabrics. The markings may not be visible on heavily textured or bulky fabrics. Also, the color from the tracing paper may not wash out of some fabrics.

One other shortcoming of this method is that the tracing wheel can damage the pattern. This limits the number of times the pattern can be reused.

USING TAILOR'S CHALK

Description of method. Chalk is available in pencil form or in small pieces. Some types of chalk are powdery and tend to brush off easily. Others are waxy and may be difficult to remove from some fabrics.

(Continued)

Chalk is used to mark the dots on a pattern. The dots are first marked by pins that are pushed through both layers of fabric. The pinheads are gently pushed through the pattern tissue and then the pattern is removed. Chalk marks are then made on the wrong sides of both layers of fabric where the pins are located. The dots may then be connected with the help of a ruler.

When to use this method. Tailor's chalk can be used on fabrics which allow the chalk to be visible yet easily brushed from the surface. Chalk does not show up well on heavily textured, bulky fabrics. Some tightly woven fabrics retain chalk. Therefore, another marking method would work better with these fabrics.

Chalk is a good choice for marking the wrong sides of fabric pieces that might easily be confused. You might mark pieces as being for the left or right side of a garment. You might draw arrows on napped fabric before cutting out a pattern to help you keep the nap running in the same direction. Chalk marks can also be used to help you distinguish between similar garment pieces such as under and upper collars.

Shortcomings. The accuracy of this method is reduced if the pins are not pushed straight through both layers of fabric. This prevents pattern symbols from being properly aligned. This method also damages the pattern tissue, limiting its reuse.

USING FABRIC MARKING PEN

Description of method. This is a special pen used to mark fabric. There are several types of these pens. Some make marks that can be removed by wiping with a water moistened cloth. Some make marks that eventually fade. And others make marks that are permanent.

When to use this method. Water soluble marking pens should be used on fabric that can stand the application of water. Permanent marking pens should be used only in hidden places.

Shortcoming. Only one layer of the fabric can be marked at a time. Marking cannot be removed from all fabrics.

USING TAILOR'S TACKS

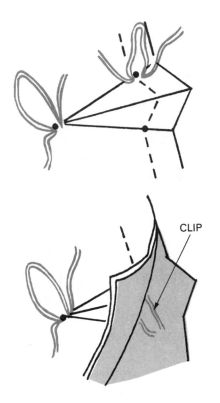

CLIP

Description of method. A thread loop is made through all layers of the fabric to mark the location of each pattern symbol.

Follow these steps:

1. Use a long, double thread in the needle.

2. Take a small stitch through the center of the pattern symbol and both layers of fabric. Do not pull the thread completely through the fabric—leave the end extend about two inches.

3. Take another small stitch through the dot. Draw the threads through, leaving a loop that is about two inches high. Clip the thread leaving another two-inch end. Continue making stitches in this way until the symbol has been marked.

4. Clip the loops and remove the pattern. Then separate the layers of fabric about half an inch. Clip the threads between the layers.

When to use this method. Use this method on white or sheer fabrics as well as napped, pile, thick, or rough surfaced fabrics. Also use it on any other fabrics on which other methods of marking are not visible.

Shortcoming. This method of marking is time-consuming.

USING CLIPPING

Description of method. A small clip is cut into the seam allowance at the location of the pattern symbol. Be sure not to cut into the seam allowance more than 1/4 inch.

When to use this method. This method is best used to mark foldlines, center front lines, and the tops of sleeve caps. This method is appropriate only for symbols that are located in or near the seam allowance.

Shortcomings. This method may weaken seam allowances and make alterations of marked seams no longer possible.

USING PIN MARKING	**Description of method.** Pins are positioned on the fabric where the pattern symbol is to be transferred. **When to use this method.** This method is best used as an occasional and temporary means of marking. **Shortcomings.** This method is not very accurate. Manipulating the paper pattern and positioning the pins on two layers of fabric is difficult. Pins tend to get in the way when stitching and may fall out of the fabric before stitching is completed.

USING BASTE MARKING	**Description of method.** With threaded needle, use long basting stitches to mark long straight lines. Use smaller stitches to mark smaller symbols such as buttonholes. **When to use this method.** This method is generally used to mark center front lines and grain lines. **Shortcoming.** As this method requires hand stitching, it is quite time-consuming.

Activity 9-1: Practicing Various Marking Methods

Supplies needed:

needle	pins	tailor's chalk
thread	fabric scraps	fabric marking pen
scissors	tracing paper	pattern piece 9A
ruler	and wheel	

Use pattern piece 9A to cut out one two-layer garment piece. Practice each of the marking methods discussed in this lesson—tracing paper and wheel, tailor's chalk, fabric marking pen, tailor's tacks, clipping, pin marking, and baste marking. Choose the best method for each type of symbol.

Name _____

Date _____ Period _____

Activity 9-2: Determining Which Marking Method to Use

Your teacher will give you seven numbered fabric samples. Mount a swatch or write a brief description of each fabric in the appropriate box in the first column of the chart below. In the second column, several types of pattern symbols are listed. Your task is to determine the best method of marking to use for each symbol on the given fabric.

FABRIC SWATCH	SYMBOL	MARKING METHOD	REASON FOR CHOICE
1.	Dart		
	Front Foldline		
2.	Dart		
	Buttonholes		
3.	Dart		
	Zipper Stitching		
4.	Top of Sleeve		
	Front Foldline		
5.	Buttonholes		
	Tucks		
6.	Pocket Location		
	Dart		
7.	Dots		
	Center Front Line		

Name _____

Date _____ Period _____

Activity 9-3: Evaluating Learning

The marking sample you have just finished will be evaluated using the chart below. Also, space is provided for you to list ideas, suggestions, or guidelines for marking pattern symbols.

TRACING PAPER AND WHEEL

	Poor	Fair	Good	Excellent
Markings are clearly visible.				
Markings are accurately placed.				
Color is appropriate for fabric.				

TAILOR'S CHALK

Markings are clearly visible.				
Markings are accurately placed.				

FABRIC MARKING PEN

Markings are clearly visible.				
Markings are accurately placed.				

TAILOR'S TACKS

Thread loops and ends were left long enough (about two inches) to allow for secure, visible markings.				
Threads clipped to extend on both sides of fabric.				
Markings are accurately placed.				

CLIPPING

Clipping did not cut into the seam allowance more than 1/4 inch.				
Markings are accurately placed.				

PIN MARKING

Pins are accurately placed.				

BASTE MARKING

Basting lines are straight.				
Markings are accurately placed.				
Stitch length is appropriate for symbol being marked.				

(Continued)

Name _____

In your own words, list five ideas, suggestions, or guidelines that might be considered most important for transferring pattern symbols to fabric.

1. _____

   _____

2. _____

   _____

3. _____

   _____

4. _____

   _____

5. _____

   _____

Pattern piece for Activity 9-2.

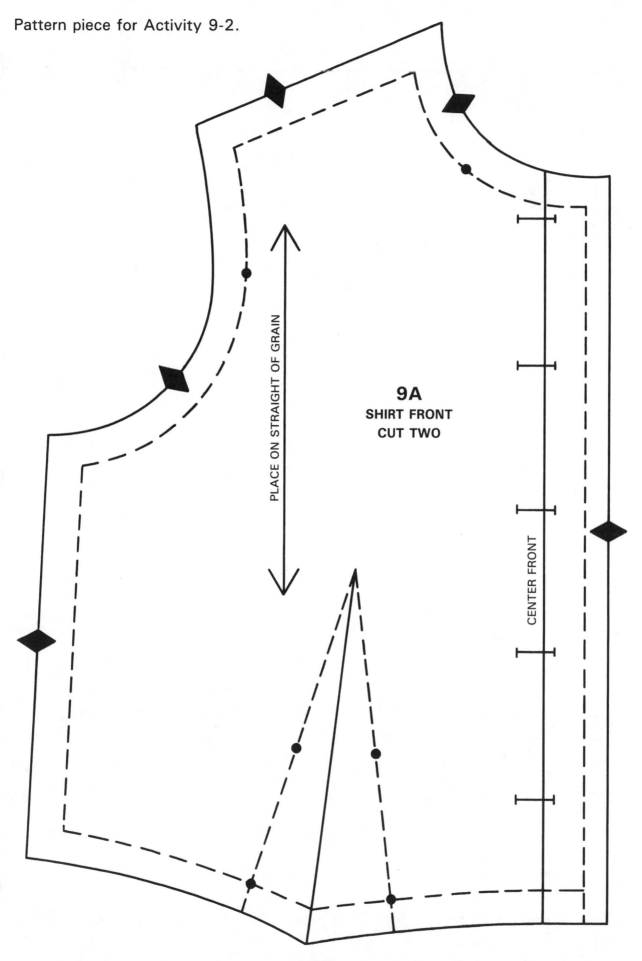

9A
SHIRT FRONT
CUT TWO

PLACE ON STRAIGHT OF GRAIN

CENTER FRONT

Lesson 10 Small Equipment and Notions

Objectives

This lesson will help you to:

1. List the notions, supplies, and small equipment you will need to construct your sewing project.
2. Identify the equipment in the classroom that is available for your use and its location.

Words to Know

awl	hem marker	rotary cutter
beeswax	hem tape	scissors
bias tape	interfacing	seam gauge
bobbin	long-handled tweezers	seam ripper
bodkin	loop turner	shears
dress form	needle threader	tape measure
emery bag	notions	tracing paper
fusible web	pinking shears	tracing wheel
hem gauge	point turner	twill tape

Gathering Information

Before you begin to sew, you must collect and organize your supplies and equipment. You will, of course, need to bring your pattern and fashion fabric to class. Be sure to check the pattern envelope to determine all of the fabrics required to complete your project. In addition to your fashion fabric, you may need to purchase lining, interlining, and interfacing fabrics. Also, you will need to bring notions and some small equipment items. Some equipment will be provided by your school. When you have finished this lesson, you will know what you must bring to class and what will be furnished.

> **NOTIONS**
>
> Notions are all of the extra items necessary to complete your project, such as trims, thread, zippers, buttons, lace, and elastics. You will find these items listed on the envelope back. When you shop for notions, take time to explore the wide variety of items available. Look for new products to make sewing fast and easy.

(Continued)

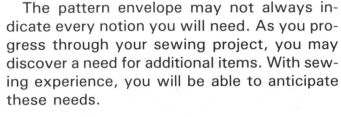

The pattern envelope may not always indicate every notion you will need. As you progress through your sewing project, you may discover a need for additional items. With sewing experience, you will be able to anticipate these needs.

Tapes and bindings. Tapes and bindings are among the items you will have to anticipate needing. There are many types of tapes and bindings. Twill tape is a sturdy polyester tape used to reinforce areas that may stretch or weaken.

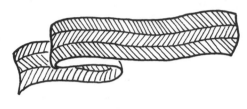

Double-fold bias tape is cut on the fabric bias and will stretch. Because of its stretch characteristic, it is good for binding curved edges. Never use it in areas requiring stability.

Hem tape and seam tape are used to finish hems. If you are working with medium to heavy fabric that will ravel, be sure to use this tape.

Sheer bias tricot tape is made of nylon and will blend with any fabric without adding bulk. This binding is used to encase seam edges and make casings. It comes in a limited range of neutral colors.

Elastics. There are a wide variety of elastics available. For waistbands, you might want to consider elastic with a drawstring running through the center. For knit sportswear, you could select specially made elastic with four-way stretch. Find the elastic just right for your purpose.

MEASURING EQUIPMENT

In order for garments and other sewing projects to turn out right, precise measurements are essential. A number of tools can be used to help you measure accurately.

Tape measure. A tape measure is made from fabric or flexible fiberglass. It is used to take body measurements and measure fabric and pattern pieces. Tapes should be sturdy and nonstretch.

Seam gauge. A seam gauge is a ruler with an adjustable marker for measuring seam allowances.

(Continued)

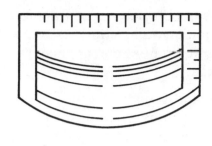

Hem gauge. A hem gauge is a multipurpose measuring tool. It has a curved, hem-shaped side that is used to mark standard hem depths. It also has a straight side that is used like a ruler.

Yardstick. As the name implies, a yardstick is one yard in length. It can be used for measuring skirt hems and other tasks that require a long, rigid measuring tool.

CUTTING EQUIPMENT

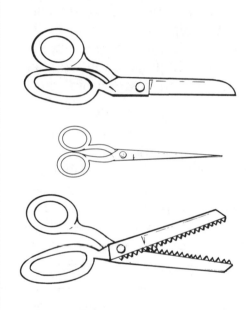

Sewing projects will include such cutting tasks as cutting out pattern pieces, snipping threads, and clipping seams. Sharp cutting equipment will help you make good, clean cuts.

Shears. Shears are used to cut fabric and should never be used on paper. The handles are different sizes so they will fit your hand.

Scissors. Scissors have shorter blades than shears and the handles have small, matching holes. They are used to trim seams, clip curves, and open button holes.

Pinking shears or scalloping shears. Pinking shears make zigzag shaped cuts and scalloping shears make scalloped cuts. These shears are used to finish raw edges.

Rotary cutter. A rotary cutter is a tool with a round blade attached to a handle. The blade turns and cuts the fabric as it is pushed along the pattern cutting line. Rotary cutters are available in a small size for most cutting needs, and a larger size for heavy fabrics. A special plastic mat is placed under the fabric to prevent damage to the table surface.

Pins. Pins are used to hold the pattern tissue on the fabric during cutting and marking. They are also used to temporarily hold layers of fabric together. For easy handling, use plastic headed pins. For knit fabrics, try ballpoint pins. Pleating pins are a finer pin used for delicate fabrics or easier insertion.

Pattern weights. Pattern weights are circular or shaped weights used to hold pattern pieces in place while cutting them out.

(Continued)

MARKING EQUIPMENT

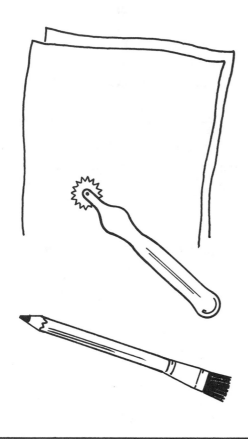

Some pattern symbols need to be transferred to the fabric to guide you as you sew. Various types of marking equipment can be used to accomplish this task.

Tracing paper and wheel. Tracing paper is coated paper that comes in an assortment of colors. The wheel is used to transfer the colored coating to the fabric.

Chalk pencil or fabric marking pen. Chalk pencils come in several colors. Choose one that is close to the color of your fabric while still remaining visible. Marking pens may be water soluble, permanent, or fading. To remove a water soluble mark, wipe the mark with a damp cloth. Do not use this type of pen on fabric that is damaged by water. Permanent markings, of course, can't be removed. Fading marking pens make a mark that will disappear within several days.

Heat transfer pencil. Heat transfer pencils are used to transfer designs to fabric surfaces. Trace the design with the pencil; then place the design, ink side down, on the fabric. Press with a dry iron to transfer a permanent, nonbleed design. The design can then be decorated with paint, embroidery, or other embellishments.

MACHINE STITCHING EQUIPMENT

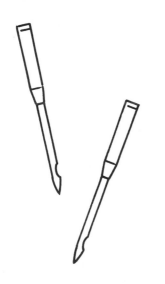

Several tools will be helpful when you begin to construct your project at the sewing machine.

Sewing machine needles. Select needles to fit your machine that are suitable for your fabric. For lightweight fabrics, use needle sizes 9 to 11. For medium fabrics, choose needle sizes 12 to 14. For heavy fabrics, select needle sizes 16 to 18.

Needles come in different types as well as different sizes. Regular point needles are used for most sewing needs. Ballpoint needles are excellent for knit fabrics. They gently separate yarns of the fabric without cutting or breaking them. Twin needles are special double needles used for pin tucking, decorative stitching, and stretch seams. Not all machines are capable of using twin needles.

(Continued)

Bobbins. A bobbin is a small spool used to hold the lower thread in a sewing machine. The size of bobbin will vary with sewing machine brand.

Topstitching guides. Topstitching guides are used to help you neatly place decorative machine stitching on the outside of sewn items. There are many types of stitching guides available. Some are plastic, see-through guides with short teeth on the underside that grip the fabric. Other guides are printed, adhesive-backed tapes.

Long-handled tweezers. Tweezers with long, bent handles are especially useful for threading the loopers on a serger.

Stabilizers. Stabilizers are nonwoven fabrics that provide support under areas to be stitched. Designs may be transferred to these fabrics and they can double as stitching guides. There are two varieties—tear away and water soluble. They are helpful for applique, cutwork, and machine embroidery.

HAND STITCHING EQUIPMENT

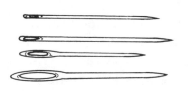

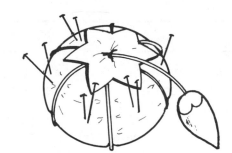

Not all sewing is done at the sewing machine. Securing hems and attaching buttons are just two of the hand stitching tasks that might require the following equipment.

Needles. An assorted package of needles is a good choice for handling a variety of sewing tasks.

Needle threader. A needle threader is a small disk with a loop of thin wire attached. The wire loop is inserted through the eye of the needle. Thread is passed through the loop. The thread is drawn through the eye of the needle when the threader is pulled back out of the eye.

Beeswax. Beeswax is used to coat sewing thread so it will not tangle as stitches are formed.

Pincushion with emery bag. A pincushion is convenient for storing pins so they can be quickly grabbed one at a time. The emery bag is usually attached to the pincushion. It is used to sharpen pins and needles by repeatedly jabbing them into the bag.

TIMESAVING TOOLS

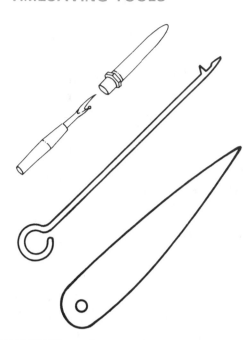

Some sewing tools are not essential. However, using them can save you time when working on a project.

Seam ripper. A seam ripper is a small tool used for ripping out stitching.

Bodkin. A bodkin is an instrument with a large eye or special teeth clamp at one end. It is used for inserting elastic or drawstrings in casings.

Loop turner. A loop turner is a long, slim wire with a latch hook at one end. It is used to turn tubing or cording to the right side.

Awl. An awl is a sharp, pointed tool used for making eyelets and round holes.

Point turner. A plastic or wooden point turner can be used to push out points, such as those on collars and cuffs.

FUSIBLE AIDES

A number of products are now available that can be fused with an iron rather than sewn. You may find these products to be real timesavers.

Glue stick. This is a solid glue that comes in a lipstick-like tube. It is used for pinless basting. Use the glue in small dots rather than long slashes.

Basting tape. This is a double-faced adhesive tape used for basting garment pieces together. You may stitch through the tape. The tape is usually water soluble and disappears when the garment is laundered.

Fusible web. This is a nonwoven material that may be used to bond two layers of fabric together. The webbing is available either in strips of varying widths or by the yard.

MISCELLANEOUS EQUIPMENT

Small boxes or containers. You may find boxes or plastic containers with lids convenient for storing fabric and equipment.

Dress form. A dress form is shaped like the torso of the body. Garments can be hung on it and checked for fit.

Name _____

Date _____ Period _____

Activity 10-1: Locating Materials

Find out which of the items listed in this lesson are provided in your classroom, and list them below. Then list those items which you must provide. Use these lists when gathering materials for projects.

Equipment found in class:

_____   _____

_____   _____

_____   _____

_____   _____

_____   _____

Equipment I must provide:

_____   _____

_____   _____

_____   _____

_____   _____

_____   _____

Name _____

Date _____ Period _____

Activity 10-2: Evaluating Learning

Assess your understanding of small equipment and notions by answering the following questions.

1. Define the following words:
   Bias tape: _____

   _____

   Emery bag: _____

   _____

   Fusible web: _____

   _____

   Pinking shears: _____

   _____

   Tracing paper: _____

   _____

2. Which of the following items would be considered notions? (Check the correct answers.)

   ____ Pins   ____ Hem tape

   ____ Fabrics   ____ Chalk pencil

   ____ Thread   ____ Rick-rack

   ____ Lace trim   ____ Buttons

   ____ Awl   ____ Seam ripper

   ____ Zipper   ____ Appliqués

Lesson 11 Operating the Sewing Machine

Objectives

This lesson will help you to:
1. Locate and explain the function of various sewing machine parts.
2. Wind the bobbin and thread the sewing machine.
3. Operate the sewing machine.
4. Compile a checlist to follow when resolving sewing machine problems.

Words to Know

bobbin	power and light	stitch length control
bobbin case	switch	stitch selector
bobbin winder	presser foot	stitch width control
drop feed button	presser foot lever	take-up lever
feed dog	pressure regulator	tension dial
hand wheel	reverse stitch control	thread guides
needle clamp screw	spool pin	throat plate

Gathering Information

The sewing machine is the most important piece of equipment you will use to construct your project. Correct use of the sewing machine is essential to trouble free sewing. This lesson will assist you in learning the basics of machine operation. It will also help you identify the causes and solutions to annoying sewing machine problems.

SEWING MACHINE PARTS

There are many different models of sewing machines. Each model operates a little differently. When unfamiliar with a sewing machine, always begin by reading the manual that comes with the machine.

Even though sewing machines vary, there are some similarities between all models. Following is a list of the names and functions of basic parts found on most sewing machines. As you read about each part, locate it on the machine diagram included in this lesson.

(Continued)

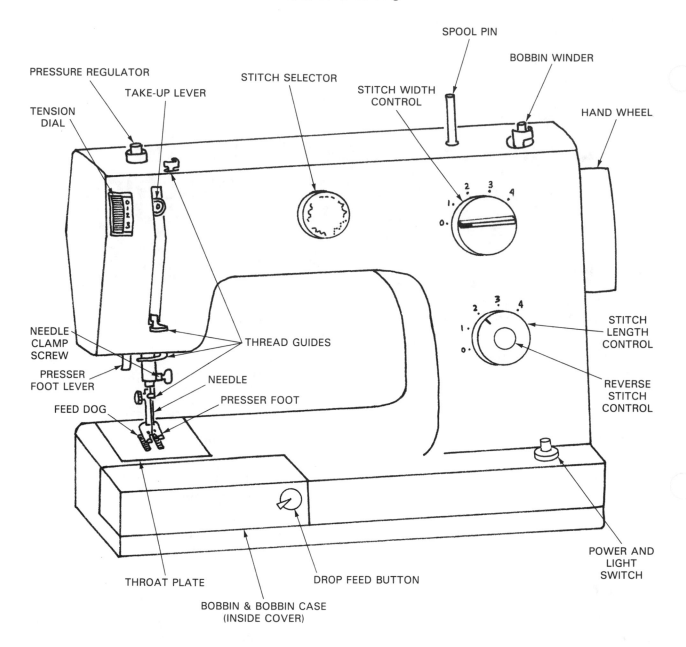

PRESSURE REGULATOR

TAKE-UP LEVER

TENSION DIAL

STITCH SELECTOR

SPOOL PIN

BOBBIN WINDER

STITCH WIDTH CONTROL

HAND WHEEL

NEEDLE CLAMP SCREW

PRESSER FOOT LEVER

FEED DOG

THREAD GUIDES

NEEDLE

PRESSER FOOT

STITCH LENGTH CONTROL

REVERSE STITCH CONTROL

POWER AND LIGHT SWITCH

THROAT PLATE

DROP FEED BUTTON

BOBBIN & BOBBIN CASE (INSIDE COVER)

Bobbin. Holds the thread that appears on the underneath side of the fabric.

Bobbin case. Holds the bobbin and applies tension to the thread.

Bobbin winder. Winds the thread onto the bobbin.

Drop feed button. Lowers the feed dog so that the fabric will not be fed under the presser foot. Generally used when making buttonholes or doing machine embroidery.

Feed dog. Moves the fabric under the presser foot.

Hand wheel. Turns to raise or lower the needle and thread take-up lever.

(Continued)

Needle clamp screw. Holds the needle in place.

Power and light switch. Turns on the machine.

Presser foot. Holds the fabric in place as the machine stitches.

Presser foot lever. Raises and lowers the presser foot.

Pressure regulator. Adjusts the amount of pressure applied to the presser foot and, in turn, to the fabric.

Reverse stitch control. Allows the machine to backstitch.

Spool pin. Holds the spool of thread.

Stitch length control. Adjusts the number of stitches per inch.

Stitch selector. Changes the type of stitches being sewn.

Stitch width control. Adjusts the width of zigzag and other two-dimensional stitches.

Take-up lever. Pulls the thread from the spool and through the tension regulator.

Tension dial. Applies tension to the thread so that it feeds at a constant rate.

Thread guides. Guide the thread from the spool to the needle.

Throat plate. Covers the area around the needle.

WINDING AND INSERTING THE BOBBIN

Check the machine manual for the correct method of winding the bobbin for the machine you will be using. The bobbin thread must be wound smoothly and snugly to prevent sewing problems. If the thread is loosely wound onto the bobbin, remove the thread and rewind the bobbin correctly.

Check your manual for the correct procedure for inserting the bobbin into the bobbin case. The thread generally should pull off the bobbin clockwise as it is dropped into the bobbin case. If the bobbin thread does not pull off in the correct direction, stitching problems can occur. Also check the manual for the correct procedure for inserting the bobbin case into the machine.

CHANGING THE MACHINE NEEDLE

The sewing machine needle can be damaged by sewing over pins or through thick, dense fabrics. If the needle is bent or blunt it can snag fabric, skip stitches, or cause other problems. Check the needle before you begin sewing. If it is damaged, insert a new needle.

To replace the needle, unscrew the needle clamp screw and remove the old needle. Insert the new needle into the needle clamp as far as it will go. The flat side of the needle is placed away from you. The long groove on the needle will be toward you. If the needle is not inserted correctly, the machine will not stitch properly. After correctly positioning the needle, tighten the needle clamp screw.

THREADING THE SEWING MACHINE

The sewing machine must be properly threaded or it will not stitch correctly. Follow the threading guide illustration in the manual for your sewing machine.

One common threading problem is an incorrectly threaded needle. Always thread the needle from the side of the last thread guide.

PULLING UP THE BOBBIN THREAD

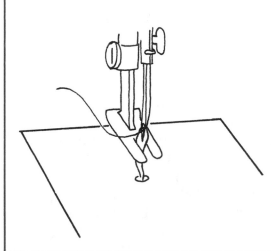

Always pull the bobbin thread through the needle hole before beginning to stitch. If the thread is not pulled up, it will knot as the first stitch is taken.

Pull the thread up through the needle hole by holding onto the top thread. Then lower the needle into the needle hole using the hand wheel. As you turn the hand wheel, the needle will enter the needle hole. As the needle comes back out of the hole, it will pull the bobbin thread up. Pull both the top thread and the bobbin thread to the back of the machine. Be sure the threads are between the toes of the presser foot.

MACHINE STITCHING

As you begin stitching, there are two important steps to follow that will prevent sewing problems. First, always start with the take-up lever at the highest point. This will prevent the thread from coming out of the needle as you begin to stitch. Second, hold on to the bobbin and top threads as you take the first stitch. This will prevent the threads from knotting under the fabric as you begin stitching.

To machine stitch, follow these steps:

1. Place the fabric under the presser foot. Line up the fabric edge with the desired seam guideline.

2. Using the hand wheel, lower the needle into the fabric.

3. Lower the presser foot onto the fabric.

4. Stitch by pressing lightly on the foot or knee control. As you make your first stitch, gently hold on to the bobbin and upper threads. Hold the fabric lightly and guide it with your right hand. The feed dog will move the fabric under the presser foot. When you stop stitching, stop with the needle and take-up lever at the highest position. You will then be ready for the next row of stitching.

BACKSTITCHING

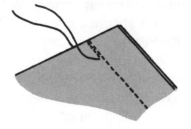

Backstitching is used to lock the stitches at the beginning and end of the row. Check your machine manual for the location of the reverse mechanism on your machine. To backstitch, lower the needle into the fabric 1/4 inch from the edge. Put the machine in reverse and make three or four backstitches. Take the machine out of reverse and sew forward. Sew to the end of the fabric. Put the machine in reverse and backstitch three or four stitches. Lift the presser foot. Clip the threads.

ADJUSTING MACHINE TENSION

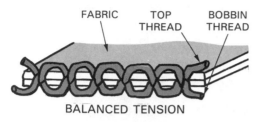

BALANCED TENSION

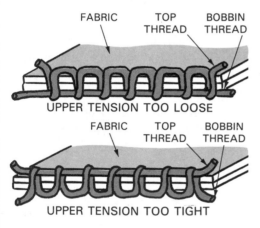

UPPER TENSION TOO LOOSE

UPPER TENSION TOO TIGHT

The tension regulator is used to adjust the thread tension so that a balanced stitch will be formed. A balanced stitch is important for a sturdy, long-wearing seam. If the stitch is not balanced, one thread will lay along the surface of the fabric. This thread can easily be pulled out.

Two thread tension regulators are found on the machine. The upper tension regulator applies tension to the top thread. Tension on the bobbin thread is applied by the bobbin case. Generally, you will not need to concern yourself with the bobbin case tension. But you should become familiar with adjusting the upper tension.

Locate the tension regulator on your machine. If the regulator is turned to a higher number, tension on the top thread is increased. If the regulator is turned to a lower number, tension is decreased.

When stitching, if the bobbin thread lies along the surface of the fabric, the upper tension is too loose. Turn the tension regulator to a higher number to increase the upper tension and form a balanced stitch.

If the top thread in a row of stitching lies along the surface of the fabric, the upper tension is too tight. Turn the tension regulator to a lower number to decrease the upper tension and form a balanced stitch.

ADJUSTING STITCH LENGTH

For most straight stitching, the machine should be set at 10-15 stitches per inch. This stitch length results in a sturdy, long wearing seam. However, stitch length may need adjusting depending on the weight and texture of the fabric. When sewing on heavy or highly textured fabrics, increase stitch length. For light, sheer fabrics decrease stitch length.

(Continued)

Other situations will require you to adjust stitch length. For instance, gathering stitches are made by using a lengthened straight stitch. You will also want to make length adjustments when using zigzag or serge stitches.

Before stitching on your garment, test stitch length on a scrap of garment fabric. Adjust the stitch length according to fabric needs.

ADJUSTING THE PRESSURE REGULATOR

The presser foot holds the fabric close to the feed dog. The feed dog, in turn, moves the fabric through the sewing machine. If the pressure on the presser foot is not adjusted correctly, the fabric will not feed through the machine properly.

Most sewing machines have a means of adjusting the pressure applied to the presser foot. This allows you to adjust the pressure for different fabrics. Sewing on heavy fabrics or through many layers of fabric requires a light pressure. Sewing on lightweight fabrics requires a firmer pressure.

Read the manual for your machine. Locate the pressure regulator. Set the regulator as recommended in the manual.

SEAM GUIDELINES

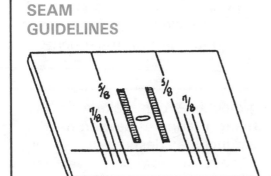

Most sewing machines have seam guidelines on the throat plate. If your sewing machine does not have these guides, you may make your own. Simply place tape on the throat plate at the desired location. The 5/8-inch guideline is used for stitching most seams. For stitching done 1/4 inch from the edge of the fabric, the presser foot can often be used as a stitching guide.

TURNING A CORNER

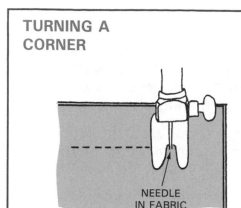

NEEDLE
IN FABRIC

Stitching a square corner is an important machine technique to learn. Begin by stitching to within 5/8 inch of the fabric edge. Stop with the needle inserted into the fabric. Lift the presser foot and pivot the fabric. Leaving the needle down prevents the fabric from shifting as the presser foot is lifted. If the fabric shifts, the corner stitch will be distorted. After pivoting the fabric, resume stitching in the new direction.

STITCHING BUTTONHOLES

Many sewing machines have a buttonhole mechanism built into the machine. Other machines have a buttonhole attachment. Check your machine manual for directions on how to make buttonholes.

The stitch length control adjusts the distance between the stitches. If the stitches are too close together, the thread will knot. To avoid this problem, adjust the stitch length control accordingly.

You will need to make several other adjustments to your machine when making buttonholes. You will need to use the drop feed button to lower the feed dog. The regular presser foot will need to be relaced with a special buttonhole presser foot. The stitch width control will also need to be adjusted.

Always make several practice buttonholes on fabric scraps that duplicate the fabric layers of your garment. This will allow you to make adjustments before stitching on the garment.

MACHINE STITCHES

Most sewing machines can make a variety of stitches to meet a range of sewing needs. The following list includes descriptions and illustrations of several common machine stitches.

Straight stitch. This is the most frequently used stitch. The length of the stitch can be adjusted using the stitch length control. For most fabrics, the machine will be set at 10 to 15 stitches per inch.

(Continued)

Baste stitch. The baste stitch is a long, straight stitch. It is used to temporarily hold several layers of fabric together. It is also used to make rows of gathering stitches. For machine basting, the stitch length control is generally set at six stitches per inch.

Zigzag stitch. The zigzag stitch is used to overcast seam edges and to make buttonholes. Check your machine manual for the correct settings for this stitch. The zigzag stitch can be adjusted by using both the stitch length and stitch width controls.

Pine (serge) stitch. This is an excellent stitch for overcasting seam edges. Adjustments can be made in stitch width as well as number of stitches per inch. Check your machine manual for the correct machine settings.

Stretch (multistitch) zigzag stitch. This stitch is used on stretch knit fabrics. The stitch forms a seam that will stretch as the fabric stretches. Check your machine manual for the correct machine settings for this stitch.

Stretch stitch. This stitch is used on stretch knit fabrics. It allows the seam to stretch as the fabric stretches. This stitch is almost impossible to remove without damaging the fabric. Use this stitch only if you are sure the stitching will not have to be removed.

Blind hem stitch. This stitch is used for making a machine blind hem. Adjust the machine controls as directed in your machine manual. Practice this stitch before using it on a garment. If the correct technique is not used, stitches will show on the right side of the garment. (See Lesson 23, "Hemming Methods," for a description of how to make a machine blind hem.)

Twin-needle stitch. This stitch is used to construct seams and hems on knits, make decorative topstitching, and make pin tucking. The stitch requires the use of a special twin needle. Twin needles are available in different sizes and with varying distances between the needles. Two spools of thread are used. The needles share one bobbin thread. As the stitches are formed, the bobbin thread is carried

(Continued)

from one needle to the other. A zigzag stitch is formed on the reverse side of the fabric. To prevent the two upper threads from tangling, place spools so they unwind in opposite directions. The left spool should unwind from behind and the right spool should unwind from the front. Not all machines are capable of using a twin needle. The machine must zigzag and thread from front to back (not from the side). Test your machine's ability to use a twin needle by carefully turning the hand wheel to see if the needles have sufficient clearance.

Decorative stitches. Some sewing machines can make a variety of decorative stitches. Check your machine manual to determine the stitch capability of your machine.

MACHINE CARE

Proper care of your sewing machine will result in fewer machine problems. Use a small brush to remove the lint around the bobbin area of the machine. Do this frequently. You should also oil the machine as recommended in the machine manual.

RESOLVING MACHINE PROBLEMS

Nothing can be more frustrating than a sewing machine that does not operate correctly. Most sewing machine problems are not serious. Problems can often be traced to incorrect threading, needle insertion, or bobbin and bobbin case insertion. The following chart will help you resolve these simple sewing machine problems for yourself.

PROBLEM	SOLUTION
Needle comes unthreaded when beginning a row of stitching.	Be sure the take-up lever is at the highest point when beginning to stitch.
Thread knots up on the underside of the fabric when beginning to stitch.	Hold thread ends under and to the back of the presser foot when beginning to stitch.
The bottom thread lies along the surface of the fabric. The stitches are not balanced.	Tighten the top tension.
The upper thread lies along the surface of the fabric. The stitches are not balanced.	Loosen the top tension.
When sewing with lightweight fabric, the fabric catches and is pulled down into the needle hole of the throat plate.	Use a straight stitch throat plate which has a smaller needle hole. When using this throat plate, be sure to straight stitch only.
Stitches are buried in the fabric.	Check stitch length on a fabric scrap before sewing on a garment. Stitch length will need to be adjusted from fabric to fabric. The thicker the fabric the longer the stitch length will need to be.
The sewing machine jams and makes a knocking noise. Thread is caught in the shuttle.	Remove the bobbin case and clean out any threads.
Machine does not sew.	Check to see if the machine is in gear and is plugged into an electrical outlet.
Machine skips stitches. Note: Knit fabrics may cause the machine to skip stitches. This is because the stretch and density of the fabric does not allow the needle to enter the fabric properly. Also, many knits have a chemical residue which leaves a sticky coating on the needle preventing it from penetrating the fabric properly.	Check to see if the needle is inserted correctly. Make sure the needle is the right size for the fabric. If sewing on knit fabrics: a. Use a ball point needle. b. Use a straight stitch throat plate. This will prevent the fabric from stretching as the needle penetrates it. c. Set pressure regulator at normal to heavy to hold fabric in place. d. Launder knits to remove any chemical residue. e. Balance machine tension.
Fabric does not move.	Be sure the feed dog is up. Be sure the presser foot is down. Increase the pressure on the presser foot. Check to see if thread is knotted under the fabric.
The upper thread breaks.	Make sure the machine is properly threaded. Loosen the upper tension.
The bobbin thread breaks.	Make sure the bobbin is threaded properly. Check to see if thread is caught in the shuttle.
Stitching puckers.	Make sure the needle is not bent or blunt. Check the thread tension. Check the pressure regulator.
The needle breaks.	Make sure you are using the correct needle size and that it is inserted correctly. Tighten the presser foot. Avoid pulling on the fabric as you sew. Avoid stitching over pins.

Name _____

Date _____ Period _____

Activity 11-1: Identifying Sewing Machine Parts

At the bottom of this page is a list of basic sewing machine parts. Notice the headings. They will help you learn the functions of the various parts.

Your teacher will give you a diagram of the sewing machine you will be using. Attach the diagram in the space provided below. Locate on the diagram each of the parts listed at the bottom of the page. To help you do this, refer to the section on "Sewing Machine Parts" in this lesson.

Note: Some machines may not have all of the following parts.

THREADING	NEEDLE	BOBBIN
thread guides	needle clamp screw	bobbin
take-up lever	throat plate	bobbin case
tension dial		bobbin winder
spool pin	FEEDING	
	feed dog	STITCH CONTROL
PRESSURE	drop feed button	reverse stitch control
pressure regulator		stitch length control
presser foot	MISCELLANEOUS	stitch width control
presser foot lever	power and light switch	stitch selector
	hand wheel	

In addition to the parts listed above, your teacher may help you locate the following:

bobbin case tension screw   seam guidelines
foot or knee control   sewing light
hand wheel knob   thread cutter
presser foot screw

Name _____

Date _____ Period _____

Activity 11-2: Practicing Basic Machine Operation

Supplies needed:

thread	sewing machine
scissors	bobbin
fabric swatches	machine needles
sewing machine manual	

The left-hand column of the following chart lists various tasks required in basic sewing machine operation. Where necessary, your teacher will tell you the correct machine settings to write in this column. Demonstrate your ability to perform each task. Then provide the sign of task performance requested in the right-hand column. This may require you to make a sample or answer a question. Or you may be required to obtain the signature of someone who observed you perform the task. In this case, your teacher will tell you who is to observe your task performance.

TASK	SIGN OF TASK PERFORMANCE
THREADING THE MACHINE Wind the bobbin and insert correctly in the sewing machine.	Signature of observer: _____
Thread the sewing machine. Be sure to pull up the bobbin thread.	Signature of observer: _____
THE NEEDLE Remove the needle. Inspect it for a blunt end and replace it correctly.	Signature of observer: _____
STRAIGHT STITCHING AND REVERSE For this stitch, set the machine at: _____ _____ _____ Find the reverse mechanism. Practice straight stitching, beginning and ending each row of stitching with several reverse stitches. Remember to: a. Start with the take-up lever at the highest point to prevent the thread from coming out of the needle when you begin stitching. b. Keep threads pulled to the back of the presser foot when beginning stitching to prevent the thread from knotting.	Make a straight stitching sample with reverse stitching at the beginning and end of your row of stitches.
SEAM GUIDELINES Find the seam guidelines on the throat plate.	
Most seams are stitched 5/8 inch from the edge of the fabric.	What do you use as a stitching guide? _____
Sometimes you will need to stitch 1/4 inch from the edge of the fabric.	What do you use as a stitching guide? _____

(Continued)

Name _____

TASK	SIGN OF TASK PERFORMANCE
TURNING A CORNER Stitch to a square corner on a fabric swatch. When you reach the corner, leave the needle down in the fabric. Lift up the presser foot and turn the fabric. Continue to sew.	Is the corner square?_____ What happens when you do not leave the needle in the fabric when you turn the corner? _____ _____
ZIGZAG STITCH /\/\/\/\/\/\/\ For this stitch, set the machine at: _____ _____ _____ Adjust the zigzag stitch by first changing the stitch length control and then the stitch width control.	Make a zigzag stitching sample. What happened with each adjustment? _____ _____ _____ _____
BASTE STITCH — — — — — — — For this stitch, set the machine at: _____ _____ _____ Adjust the stitch length control to a different setting.	Make a baste stitch sample. What happens? The larger the number, the _____ the stitches. What happens when you pull on the top thread of a baste-stitched row? _____ _____ _____

Name _____

Date _____ Period _____

Activity 11-3: Practicing Advanced Machine Operation

Supplies needed:

thread	sewing machine	buttonhole foot
scissors	bobbin	blind hem foot
fabric swatches	machine needles	decorative stitch
sewing machine manual		attachments

The left-hand column of the following chart lists various tasks required in advanced sewing machine operation. For each task, your teacher will tell you the correct machine settings to write in this column. Demonstrate your ability to perform each task. Then provide the sign of task performance requested in the right-hand column.

TASK	SIGN OF TASK PERFORMANCE
STRETCH (MULTISTITCH) ZIGZAG STITCH /\/\/\/\ For this stitch, set the machine at: _____ _____ _____	Make a stretch zigzag sample.
PINE (SERGE) STITCH _ΛΛΛΛΛΛ_ For this stitch, set the machine at: _____ _____ _____	Make a pine stitch sample.
STRETCH STITCH ⌐⌐⌐⌐⌐⌐ For this stitch, set the machine at: _____ _____ _____	Make a stretch stitch sample. When you stretch the fabric after stitching with this stitch, what happens? _____
BLIND HEM STITCH _Λ___Λ___Λ___ For this stitch, set the machine at: _____ _____ _____ Change to blind hem foot.	Make a blind hem stitch sample. (Your teacher may also ask you to refer to Lesson 23 to prepare a sample of an actual blind hem.)
BUTTONHOLE Change to buttonhole foot. Set machine at: _____ _____ _____	Make a sample buttonhole.
DECORATIVE STITCHES For decorative stitches, set the machine at: _____ _____ _____	Make samples of several decorative stitches.

Name _____

Date _____ Period _____

Activity 11-4: Practicing Machine Stitching

This exercise will give you practice in beginning and ending stitching, speed control turning corners, and stitching curved areas. Stitch on paper, without thread in the machine, following the lines as closely as possible. Be sure to stop at the corners with the needle down in the paper. This will enable you to turn corners without losing your stitching position.

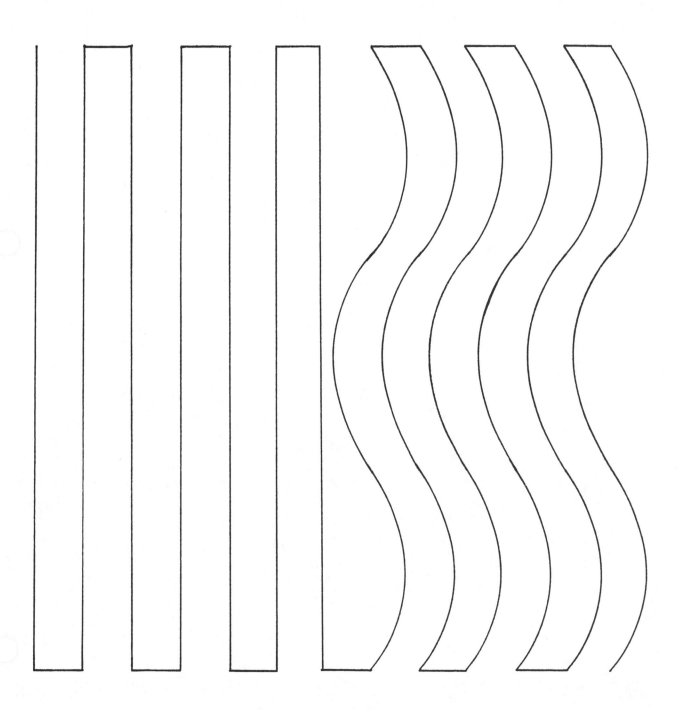

Name _____

Date _____ Period _____

Activity 11-5: Sewing Machine Problem Checklist

In the space provided below, list the points you would check if you were having trouble with your sewing machine. Try to list the points in the order you would check them. To help you complete this activity, refer to the "Resolving Machine Problems" section of this lesson.

1. _____

2. _____

3. _____

4. _____

5. _____

6. _____

7. _____

8. _____

9. _____

10. _____

11. _____

12. _____

Name _____

Date _____ Period _____

Activity 11-6: Evaluating Learning

Evaluate your learning by filling in the information requested in the first two sections on this page. Then evaluate your skill mastery by responding to the items in the third section.

1. In your own words, explain the function of the following sewing machine parts:

PART	FUNCTION
Tension dial	
Feed dog	
Drop feed button	
Presser foot lever	
Hand wheel	

2. For each of the sewing machine problems listed below, give a probable cause and/or solution.

PROBLEM	CAUSE/SOLUTION
The lower thread lies along the surface of the fabric, stitches are not balanced.	
The thread knots up when you begin a row of stitching.	
Stitches are not forming at all.	
The needle comes unthreaded every time you start to sew.	

3. Answer the following questions by circling yes or no.

    a. Do you feel you know how to wind the bobbin and thread the sewing machine?   Yes   No

    b. Can you replace the sewing machine needle?   Yes   No

    c. Do you know how to set the machine for straight stitching without asking?   Yes   No

    d. Do you feel comfortable doing all of the stitches listed in activities 11-2 and 11-3? If not, which ones are giving you trouble? List them below.   Yes   No

    _____

    _____

    _____

Lesson 12 Pressing as You Sew

Objectives

This lesson will help you to:
1. Identify the meaning of pressing and its importance when sewing.
2. Describe the uses of various pieces of pressing equipment.
3. Select the iron temperature and pressing techniques to use with various types of fabrics.
4. Identify the direction to press various seams and darts and select the pressing equipment to use.

Words to Know

iron cover	point presser	seam roll
ironing	press cloth	sleeve board
needle board	pressing	tailor's ham
pounding block	press mitt	

Gathering Information

Pressing is one of the most important procedures you will use as you sew. Pressing can make the difference between a garment that looks homemade and one that looks professionally constructed. To achieve a store-bought look, remember to apply the sewing motto ''Press as you sew.'' This means pressing each construction detail immediately after stitching. You will be pleased with the results.

Many pressing decisions must be made when you sew. For instance, iron temperature, equipment to use, use of moisture, and special techniques to follow are all important considerations. These decisions are based upon fiber content and fabric construction. This lesson will help you make these decisions.

PRESSING OR IRONING?

Pressing and ironing do not mean the same thing. Pressing requires an up and down motion of the iron. A light pressure is used. Generally, moisture is applied either by a steam iron or dampened press cloth. Ironing requires a back and forth motion of the iron. This motion can cause the fabric to stretch and should not be used during the construction of a sewing project.

WHY PRESS AS YOU SEW?

Pressing is needed from the start of each sewing project. By pressing fabric before a pattern is cut out, fabric grainlines can be improved or straightened. This will help the garment hang straight when it is completed. Removing creases and wrinkles from the fabric before cutting also insures that garment pieces are cut to the right size.

Pressing as you sew makes the construction process easier after you cut out your pattern. The need for basting and pinning can be decreased. Details that are pressed do not always need to be basted or pinned in place. Also, when construction details are pressed flat and smooth, garment pieces are easier to join. You are less likely to get an unintended tuck of fabric caught in the stitching.

The need for pressing continues until a project is complete. During construction, desired shaping can be created in different areas of a garment such as around darts and curves. Pressing these areas as you sew will give your finished garment a more professional look.

PRESSING EQUIPMENT

The iron is your most important pressing tool, and you will want to take the best possible care of it. Avoid pressing over pins, zippers, and other metal objects that will scratch the bottom. You will also need to keep the soleplate clean. If it should become dirty, clean it immediately. Many commercial cleaners are available. See your teacher for instructions.

By filling the iron with water, it can become a source of steam. Use a measuring glass to pour water into the filling hole of the iron.

Most fabrics will require moisture in the form of steam. However, some fabrics water spot so be sure to check your fabric for this characteristic. Also, too much moisture may cause an overpressed look or destroy the texture of the fabric. Always try pressing a fabric scrap before pressing garment pieces.

(Continued)

Many other pieces of equipment are available to aid you with specific pressing tasks. You should become familiar with the uses of various pieces of pressing equipment. This will help you choose the best tool for giving your garment a professional look. Information about pressing equipment is summarized in the following chart.

EQUIPMENT	DESCRIPTION	USES
Tailor's Ham	Firm, oblong cushion.	Pressing curved areas of a garment such as darts.
Seam Roll	Firm, cylindrical cushion with rounded ends.	Pressing small curves or long seams in narrow areas.
Press Mitt	Padded mitt that fits on the hand.	Pressing hard to reach places.
Sleeve Board	Two small, connected ironing boards.	Pressing garment parts that will not fit on a regular ironing board.
Point Presser	Wooden tool with pointed end and narrow extended surface.	Pressing points and corners.
Pounding Block or Clapper	Wooden block.	Pounding seams to flatten them.
Needle Board	A bed of needles attached to a stiff backing.	Preventing pile fabrics from being crushed while pressing.
Paper	Strips of paper, index card, envelopes, etc.	Preventing impressions of seams from being pressed through to the right side of a garment.
Press Cloth	Any cloth used between fabric and iron. Cheese cloth is recommended.	Preventing shine or iron marks on fabric.
Iron Cover	A cover which slips over the bottom of iron; usually coated with a nonstick finish.	Preventing matting, shine, or melting of fabric.

SETTING THE IRON TEMPERATURE

Most irons have a chart that indicates the correct temperature settings for various fibers. To use the chart, you must know the fiber content of your fabric. If you do not know the fiber content of your fabric, test the iron temperature on a scrap before pressing garment pieces. For fiber blends, use the temperature suited to the most heat sensitive fiber in the fabric.

Iron temperatures for a few fibers are given in the following chart.

FIBER	RECOMMENDED SETTING	PRESSING CONSIDERATIONS
Wool	Moderate	Extreme heat and moisture will cause wool fabric to mat or shine.
Silk	Low	Silk is a delicate fiber and should be pressed carefully. Care must be taken to prevent water spotting and unwanted shine from the iron.
Cotton Linen	High	These fabrics wrinkle badly and can withstand high temperatures.
Rayon Polyester Nylon Triacetate	Moderate	These fibers are less heat sensitive than the other manufactured fibers.
Acrylic Spandex Acetate Modacrylic	Low	These fibers are heat sensitive and will glaze, melt, pucker, or shrink from higher temperatures.
Vinyl	No heat	This fiber is extremely heat sensitive. Finger press seams.

APPLYING PRESSURE TO THE IRON

Light pressure is satisfactory for most pressing. Use a press cloth to help prevent shining, matting, and iron impressions. On some fabrics, placing strips of paper between the fabric and the seam allowances is helpful. This will prevent impressions of the seam allowances from showing through to the outside of the garment.

Special care must be taken when pressing fabrics with nap, luster, texture, or a raised design. When using these fabrics, always test a scrap to be sure of the pressing technique to use.

(Continued)

Too much pressure on the iron can destroy the texture of some fabrics. Covering the ironing board with a towel can help prevent flattening fabrics with nap or a raised design. Use light pressure when pressing these fabrics. Or if the fabric can withstand steam, hold the iron slightly above the fabric and allow the steam to do the work.

The impression of the iron may be left on the surface of napped fabrics like corduroy or pile fabrics like velvet. Therefore, these fabrics should always be pressed on the wrong side. Placing these fabrics right side down on a towel (or a needle board for pile fabrics) will help preserve their texture. Again, use light pressure or allow the steam to do the work.

PRESSING SEAMS AND DARTS

Pressing over seams and darts in the direction they were stitched helps to set the stitching. Most seams, such as side, sleeve, and center back seams, are then pressed open. This gives them a smooth, flat appearance on the outside of the garment.

Some exceptions for pressing seams and some guidelines for pressing darts are given below.

- Armhole seams are pressed toward the bodice of a garment.

- Waistline seams are generally pressed up toward the bodice of a garment.

- Seams that attach small pieces to a garment and will eventually be enclosed are generally pressed toward the small piece. Seams used to attach collars and cuffs would fall into this group.

- Seams used to assemble collars and cuffs are first pressed open over a point presser. Then they are pressed toward the under collar or the cuff facing, respectively.

- Horizontal darts are pressed down toward the hem of a garment.

- Vertical darts are pressed toward the center of a garment.

Name _____

Date _____ Period _____

Activity 12-1: Selecting Iron Temperature

Indicate the iron temperature to use with each of the fabrics listed below. Also describe points you should consider when pressing each fabric and any special techniques you should use. To help you complete this activity, your teacher may provide fabric samples to examine and possibly try pressing. Try to complete this activity without referring to the information given earlier. Then check your answers with the information in the lesson and correct them as needed.

FABRIC	IRON TEMPERATURE	PRESSING CONSIDERATIONS AND SPECIAL TECHNIQUES
Fabric #1: Shirting fabric, light weight, textured surface. 100% Cotton		
Fabric #2: Velvet, pile surface. 65% Cotton 35% Rayon		
Fabric #3: Stretch fabric, suitable for swimwear. 87% Nylon 13% Spandex		
Fabric #4: Flannel, napped surface. 100% Wool		
Fabric #5: Lightweight, wool-like fabric. 81% Acrylic 19% Wool		
Fabric #6: Corduroy, napped surface. 60% Cotton 40% Polyester		
Fabric #7: Knit fabric, suitable for warm ups. 50% Acrylic 50% Polyester		
Fabric #8: Smooth, satin-like surface. 87% Acetate 13% Nylon		

Name _____

Date _____ Period _____

Activity 12-2: Pressing Garment Details

Below is a list of various garment details. Give the direction in which each detail should be pressed. Also list the pressing equipment that should be used to make the task easier. To complete this activity, you will be using information given in the sections on pressing equipment and pressing seams and darts. Try to complete this activity without referring to the information given earlier. Then check your answers with the information in the lesson and correct them as needed. After filling in the chart, answer the questions at the bottom of the page.

GARMENT DETAIL	DIRECTION TO PRESS	PRESSING EQUIPMENT TO USE
Curved side seam (hip)		
Center back seam		
Armhole seam		
Shoulder darts		
Pant leg seam		
Waistline seam		
Bust darts		
Collar points (involves seam used to assemble collar pieces)		
Neckline seam (seam that attaches collar to garment)		

1. What type of iron motion is used when pressing?

   _____

2. What type of iron motion is used when ironing?

   _____

3. Why should ironing not be used during the construction of a sewing project?

   _____

   _____

4. Explain why pressing as you sew is such an important sewing step.

   _____

   _____

Name _____

Date _____ Period _____

Activity 12-3: Evaluating Learning

Demonstrate your understanding of this lesson by answering the following questions. Complete this activity without referring to information given in the lesson.

1. In your own words, describe the difference between pressing and ironing.

   _____

   _____

   _____

2. In your own words, explain why pressing as you sew is such an important sewing step.

   _____

   _____

   _____

3. Other than the iron and the ironing board, list three pieces of pressing equipment and describe their uses.

   EQUIPMENT   USES

   a. _____

   b. _____

   c. _____

4. Match the following fibers with the recommended iron setting for pressing each one.

   _____ Linen.   a. No heat.

   _____ Vinyl.   b. Low.

   _____ Polyester.   c. Moderate.

   _____ Nylon.   d. High.

   _____ Silk.

   _____ Cotton.

   _____ Acrylic.

   _____ Wool.

   _____ Acetate.

   _____ Rayon.

(Continued)

Name _____

5. What type pressure should be applied to the iron when pressing most fabrics?

_____

6. What should you do when you are uncertain about the iron temperature or pressing techniques to use when working with a fabric?

_____

_____

_____

7. Explain how most seams should be pressed.

_____

_____

_____

8. Give a guideline for pressing darts.

_____

_____

_____

notes

Lesson 13 Staystitching

Objectives

This lesson will help you to:
1. Explain the meaning of the sewing term staystitching.
2. Staystitch a garment piece.

Words to Know

directional stitching
staystitching

Gathering Information

Handling garment pieces made from stretchy or loosely woven fabrics can cause them to lose their shape. Even pieces cut from sturdier fabrics can stretch along curved edges. Staystitching before construction can be used to avoid this problem.

WHAT IS STAYSTITCHING?	Staystitching is used to stabilize edges that might otherwise be stretched out of shape during the construction process. This step is completed prior to the construction of all other garment details. Staystitching is directional stitching because it is done with the grain of the fabric.

WHEN IS STAYSTITCHING NEEDED?	Staystitching is needed on: 1. Curved or bias cut edges. 2. Edges of knit fabric where stretching needs to be controlled, such as shoulder seams. 3. Curved edges of any fabric piece that will be clipped during the construction process. Staystitching will prevent weakening of the seam due to the clipping.

HOW TO STAYSTITCH

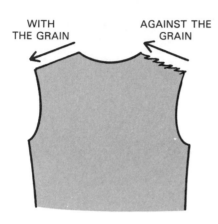

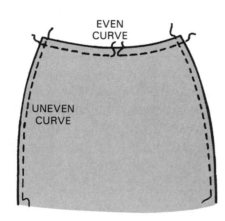

Follow these steps:

1. Adjust the sewing machine to a regular stitch length. Be sure to use matching thread, as this stitching will not be removed.

2. Stitch 1/2 inch from the cut edge of the garment piece through a single layer of fabric.

3. Be sure to stitch with the grain. If you stitch against the grain you will stretch the area being stitched.

You can use a number of methods to help you stitch with the grain. Pattern pieces often have arrows printed on the seamlines to indicate which direction to stitch. As a general rule, stitch from the wide to the narrow part of a garment piece. Sliding your fingers along the edge of the garment piece can also tell you the direction of the grain. If the edge stays smooth, you are going with the grain—stitch in that direction. If threads are raveled free, you are going in the opposite direction of the grain—stitch from the other direction.

Stitch even curves such as waistlines from both directions toward the center. Stitch uneven curves such as skirt or pant side seams from the direction that stays with the grain longest.

For knit fabrics, determining the staystitching direction may be difficult. Follow the above guidelines whenever possible. Staystitch those seams that will eventually be sewn together in the same direction.

Activity 13-1: Practicing Staystitching

Supplies needed:

thread	sewing machine
shears	bobbin
fabric	pattern piece 13A

Cut out the pattern piece from a fabric scrap. Be sure to cut the pattern out with the grain of the fabric. To staystitch, follow the directions in the "How to Staystitch" box. Be sure to stitch with the grain.

Name _____

Date _____ Period _____

Activity 13-2: Evaluating Learning

The staystitched sample you have just finished will be evaluated using the chart below. Also, space is provided for you to answer questions that will help you demonstrate your understanding of staystitching.

	Poor	Fair	Good	Excellent
A regular stitch length has been used.				
All stitching is 1/2 inch from the cut edge.				
Even curves have been stitched to the center from each direction.				
Uneven curves have been stitched from the direction that goes with the grain for the longest length.				
All edges that require staystitching have been stitched.				

In your own words, answer each of the following questions.

1. What purpose does staystitching serve?

   _____

   _____

2. When is staystitching completed in the sewing process?

   _____

   _____

3. Where is staystitching done on a garment?

   _____

   _____

4. Explain how staystitching is done with the grain of the fabric.

   _____

   _____

   _____

   _____

notes

Pattern piece for Activity 13-1.

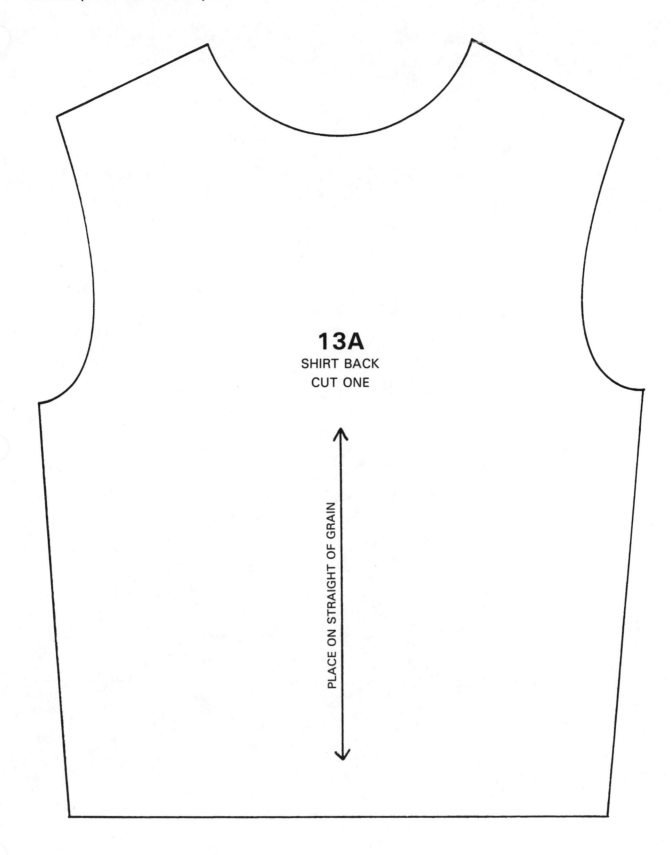

13A
SHIRT BACK
CUT ONE

PLACE ON STRAIGHT OF GRAIN

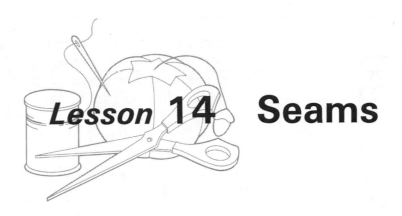

Lesson 14 Seams

Objectives

This lesson will help you to:
1. Identify methods for constructing seams.
2. Select the appropriate seam to use for various types of fabrics.
3. Practice making a number of seams.

Words to Know

double-stitched seam
flat-felled seam
French seam
hand basting

pin basting
plain seam
seam

slot seam
topstitched seam
welt seam

Gathering Information

A seam is a row of stitching that joins one or more garment pieces together. There are many methods of constructing seams. Some seams have raw edges that may need to be finished to provide a neater appearance and prevent raveling. (Seam finishing techniques are discussed in Lesson 16, ''Seam Finishes.'') Other seams are self-finished as they are constructed and require no further finishing. In addition to holding the garment together, some seams provide a decorative touch. Some seams are designed to be extra sturdy or to give the garment a tailored appearance.

The type of seam you use on a given garment will depend on garment design, durability desired, and fabric characteristics. The pattern instruction sheet will give you an indication of the type of seam to use. You will still need to make the decision based on your fabric and needs. This lesson will help you decide which type of seam to use. It will also tell you how to construct different types of seams.

PIN BASTING SEAMS	Before a seam is stitched, garment pieces should be pinned together. If the seam is stitched without pinning, the layers of fabric might stretch or slip. This could cause the seam to be crooked, puckered, or uneven.

(Continued)

Unless your pattern instruction sheet states otherwise, seams are always stitched with the right sides of the garment pieces together. When pinning garment pieces, match seam edges, notches, and the ends of the pieces. Place a pin at each end of the seam and at the notches. Add additional pins, adjusting the fabric so that it lays flat. Place pins about four inches apart. Do not over-pin.

Pins should be placed at a right angle to the seam with the pinheads toward the edge. This will make removing them easier. Remove the pins before stitching over them. Stitching over pins can cause uneven stitching and damage the machine needle.

HAND BASTING SEAMS

For some seams, pins can be awkward to handle while maneuvering the fabric under the machine needle. This may be true when stitching some eased or curved seams and narrow areas such as set-in sleeves. In these cases, you may wish to pin baste first. Then hand baste close to the seamline and remove the pins. Your garment pieces will be held together securely until you replace the basting with machine stitching.

USING THE STITCHING GUIDES

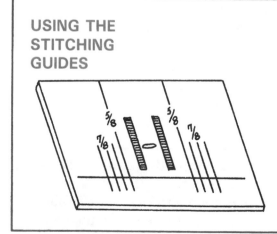

Most sewing machines have stitching guidelines on the throat plate at either side of the presser foot. Place the edge of the fabric along one of these lines as you stitch. This will give you an even seam allowance of the desired width.

Most seams are stitched at 5/8 inch. Occasionally, the pattern instruction sheet will tell you to stitch at a different width. Always read your instruction sheet.

STITCHING WITH THE GRAIN

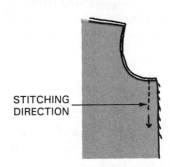

STITCHING DIRECTION

In Lesson 13, the importance of stitching with the grain of the fabric was discussed in terms of staystitching. Stitching with the grain of the fabric is also important when stitching seams. This prevents garment pieces from stretching as they are being stitched.

To determine the direction of the grain, run your fingers along the edge of the garment pieces. The threads will be smoothed down in the direction of the fabric grain. Stitch in that direction.

STITCHING PLAIN SEAMS

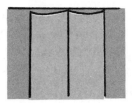

The plain seam is the most widely used seam. It is also the basis for constructing other types of seams.

Procedure:

1. Place the pin basted garment pieces under the presser foot of the sewing machine. Position the pieces so that the bulk of the fabric is at the left of the machine foot.

2. Line up the edge of the fabric with the 5/8 inch line on the throat plate of the machine.

3. Lower the presser foot and insert the machine needle into the fabric about 3/8 inch from the top edge of the seam. The machine threads should be pulled to the back of the presser foot.

4. Take one or two stitches while holding onto the machine threads.

5. Reverse the machine and stitch to the top edge of the seam.

6. Release the stitch reverse and stitch the seam. Be careful to keep the fabric edge on the correct guideline.

7. Backstitch at the end of the stitching row.

8. Press the seam open unless the pattern instruction sheet states otherwise.

STITCHING CURVED SEAMS

Stitching curved seams can be difficult. For best results, stitch slowly but at an even speed. If you must stop stitching to adjust the fabric, be sure to stop with the needle down in the fabric. This will prevent the fabric from slipping as you adjust it.

TURNING CORNERS

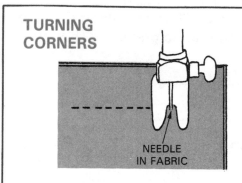

NEEDLE IN FABRIC

Turning corners can also be difficult. You may find marking the corner helpful. This will prevent you from stitching too far into the seam allowance.

Stitch to the corner marking. Leave the needle in the fabric and lift the presser foot. Pivot the fabric. Lower the presser foot and continue stitching.

TOPSTITCHED SEAM

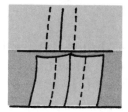

This seam is a variation of the plain seam and is used to achieve a decorative effect.

Procedure:

1. Make a plain seam and press open.

2. From the outside, stitch 1/4 inch (or desired distance) from each side of the seamline. Catch the seam allowances in the stitching.

WELT SEAM

This seam gives the finished garment a tailored look.

Procedure:

1. Make a plain seam.

2. Press both seam allowances in the same direction.

3. Trim the under seam allowance to 1/4 inch.

4. From the outside, stitch 1/4 inch from the seamline, catching the wider seam allowance in the stitching.

SLOT SEAM

This seam will help prevent stretching in the seamline. It will also add a decorative touch to the finished garment.

Procedure:

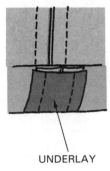

UNDERLAY

1. Baste seam together along the seamline. Press open.

2. Cut a 1 1/2-inch wide strip of fabric to use as an underlay. (You may wish to use a contrasting fabric as a decorative detail.)

3. Center underlay beneath the seam.

4. From the right side of the garment, topstitch 1/4 inch on each side of the seamline.

5. Remove basting.

FLAT-FELLED SEAM

This seam is self-enclosed and requires no additional seam finishing technique. Use it where durability is needed or a tailored appearance is desired.

Procedure:

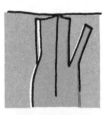

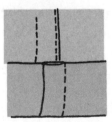

1. With the wrong sides of the fabric together make a plain seam. Press seam allowances in one direction.

2. Trim the under seam allowance to 1/4 inch.

3. On the remaining seam allowance, turn under 1/4 inch and press. Fold this side over the trimmed edge. Pin in place.

4. Stitch very close to the folded edge of the seam allowance.

DOUBLE-STITCHED SEAM

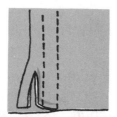

This seam is excellent for sheer fabrics or lightweight knits.

Procedure:

1. Make a 5/8-inch plain seam.

2. Stitch the two seam allowances together, stitching 1/4 inch from the seamline. Trim the seam to 3/8 inch.

3. Press seam to one side.

TWIN-NEEDLE SEAM

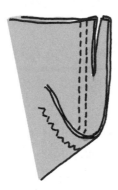

This seam is a variation of the double-stitched seam. It provides stretch and is excellent for seams on knit garments.

Procedure:

1. Place right sides of fabric together. Stitch the seam using a twin needle and two spools of thread.

2. Trim the excess seam allowance.

3. Press seam to one side.

FRENCH SEAM

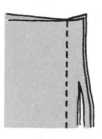

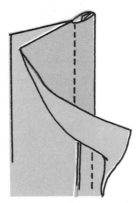

This durable, self-enclosed seam is excellent for sheer fabric when you want to conceal the seam allowances.

Procedure:

1. With the wrong sides of the fabric together, stitch a 3/8-inch seam.

2. Trim seam allowances to slightly less than 1/4 inch.

3. Press seam open.

4. Fold the right sides of the fabric together, with the seam exactly on the fold line.

5. Press and pin in place.

6. Stitch on the original pattern seamline, which is 1/4 inch from the fold.

7. Press seam to one side.

Name _____

Date _____ Period _____

Activity 14-1: Matching Seams to Fabric

Your teacher will be giving you six different fabric swatches. Attach the swatches in the spaces provided. Indicate under each fabric swatch which seam would be most appropriate for the fabric. Also indicate the criteria on which you based your decision such as fabric weight or tendency to ravel.

SEAMS

Seam _____

Criteria _____

Seam _____

Criteria _____

Seam _____

Criteria _____

Seam _____

Criteria _____

Seam _____

Criteria _____

Seam _____

Criteria _____

Name _____

Date _____ Period _____

Activity 14-2: Practicing Making Seams

Supplies needed:

thread   bobbin
fabric scraps   shears
sewing machine

Cut twelve pieces of fabric 6'' x 2''. You will be using two fabric pieces for each seam you sew. Construct samples of the following seams:

Plain seam   Flat-felled seam
Welt seam   Double-stitched seam
Slot seam   French seam

To construct the seams, follow the procedures given in this lesson.

Name _____

Date _____ Period _____

Activity 14-3: Evaluating Learning

The seam samples you have just finished will be evaluated using the chart below. After completing the chart, answer the question at the bottom of the page.

		Good	Fair	Poor	Excellent
Correct procedure followed.	Plain				
	Welt				
	Slot				
	Flat-felled				
	Double-stitched				
	French				
Stitching is straight and an even distance from the edge.	Plain				
	Welt				
	Slot				
	Flat-felled				
	Double-stitched				
	French				
Threads are neatly clipped.	Plain				
	Welt				
	Slot				
	Flat-felled				
	Double-stitched				
	French				
Seam is neatly pressed.	Plain				
	Welt				
	Slot				
	Flat-felled				
	Double-stitched				
	French				

What factors should you consider when selecting the type of seam to use in constructing your garment?

_____

_____

_____

_____

_____

_____

notes

Lesson 15 Clipping, Notching, Trimming, and Grading

Objectives

This lesson will help you to:
1. Explain the meaning of the sewing terms clipping, notching, trimming, and grading.
2. Determine when to clip, notch, trim, and grade.
3. Practice clipping, notching, trimming, and grading.

Words to Know

clipping   notching
grading   trimming

Gathering Information

Some seamlines tend to pucker or look bulky. For seams on a finished garment to appear smooth, they may require special attention after stitching. This lesson discusses when and how to use various techniques to achieve neat, smooth seamlines.

WHAT IS CLIPPING?

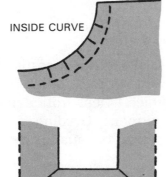

INSIDE CURVE

CLIP HERE

Clipping means to cut slits into the seam allowance. Clipping is needed on all seams with an inside curve. This will make the seam turn over smoothly. If curved seams are not clipped, they will pucker when turned.

Clipping is usually done at 1/2 inch intervals at a 90 degree angle to the seamline. Be sure not to cut the seam stitching.

On occasion, an instruction sheet will ask that a single clip be made. For instance, you might clip to a dot on the corner of a placket opening. In these instances, it is important to clip only to the dot. Again, be careful not to cut through the stitching.

WHAT IS NOTCHING?

OUTSIDE CURVE

Notching means to cut wedges into the seam allowance. Notching is done on seams with an outside curve. It removes excess fabric that would otherwise cause the seam to be bulky when turned. As with clipping, it is important not to cut through the stitching when you notch.

WHAT IS TRIMMING?

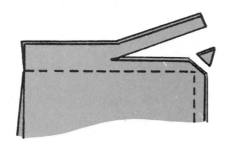

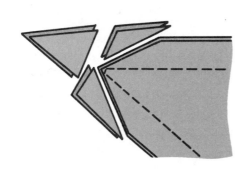

Trimming means to cut off part of the seam allowance to reduce bulk. Trim away 3/8 of an inch of fabric along the full length of the seam. This will leave a 1/4-inch seam allowance.

Corners of garment pieces are trimmed by cutting diagonally across the corner. Tighter angles, such as the points of collars, require more bulk to be removed. Trim excess fabric from the sides of a point at an angle. Then trim diagonally across the end of the point, being careful not to cut through the stitching.

WHAT IS GRADING?

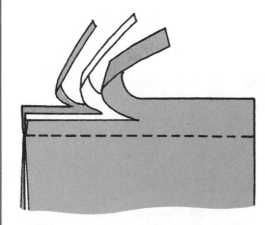

Grading means to trim each layer of the seam allowance to a different width. Grading results in a layered seam which is less noticeable on the outside of the garment. Grading is often done instead of trimming because it reduces bulk more smoothly.

Name _____

Date _____ Period _____

Activity 15-1: Practicing Clipping, Notching, Trimming, and Grading

Supplies needed:

thread	medium- to heavy-	bobbin
shears	weight fabric scraps	pattern piece 15A
pins	sewing machine	

Cut out four fabric pieces using the pattern provided. With right sides together, sew together two of the pieces following the stitching lines for the inside curve sample. Sew the other two pieces together following the stitching lines for the outside curve sample.

1. Try to turn and press each sample. Explain what happens.

   Inside curve sample: _____

   _____

   _____

   Outside curve sample: _____

   _____

   _____

2. **Trim** the seam allowance and the stitched corner of the inside curve sample. Also, clip the seam allowance. Then turn and press the sample. Explain the results.

   _____

   _____

   _____

3. **Grade** the seam allowance and trim the stitched corner of the outside curve sample. Also, notch the seam allowance. Then turn and press the sample. Explain the results.

   _____

   _____

   _____

Name _____

Date _____ Period _____

Activity 15-2: Evaluating Learning

The clipping, notching, trimming, and grading samples you have just finished will be evaluated using the chart below. Also, space is provided for you to write an explanation of these four sewing terms.

	Poor	Fair	Good	Excellent
INSIDE CURVE SAMPLE				
Corners trimmed diagonally to reduce bulk. Seam has not been weakened by trimming too close.				
Seam trimmed to 1/4 inch. Seam has not been weakened by trimming too close.				
Seam allowance has been clipped close to stitching, but stitching has not been cut.				
OUTSIDE CURVE SAMPLE				
Corners trimmed diagonally to reduce bulk. Seam has not been weakened by trimming too close.				
Seam graded to varying widths to reduce bulk.				
Seam allowance has been notched close to stitching, but stitching has not been cut.				

In your own words, explain the meaning of the terms given below. Include in your explanation when you would need to use each of the techniques and how each is completed.

Clipping: _____

_____

Notching: _____

_____

Trimming: _____

_____

Grading: _____

_____

Pattern piece for Activity 15-1.

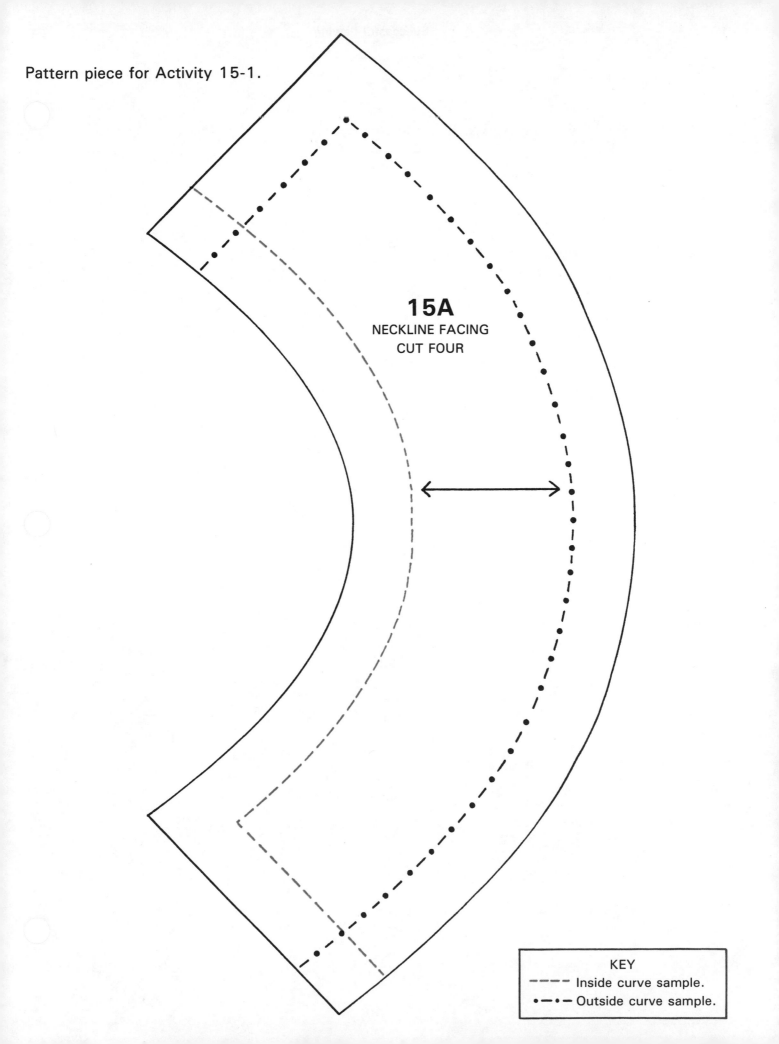

15A
NECKLINE FACING
CUT FOUR

Lesson 16 Seam Finishes

Objectives

This lesson will help you to:
1. Identify various seam finishes.
2. Select the appropriate seam finish for various types of fabric.
3. Practice making a number of seam finishes.

Words to Know

bound	stitched and pinked
seam finish	turned and stitched
serge stitched	zigzagged

Gathering Information

Raw seam edges of a garment can look unattractive and may ravel during laundering and wearing. This can result in weakened seams and will reduce the life of the garment. Therefore, raw seam edges generally need to be finished in some way. A seam finish is a technique used to keep the raw edges of seam allowances from raveling. Seam finishes also make raw edges look more attractive.

A number of techniques can be used to finish seams. The method you select will depend on the weight of your fabric and the degree to which it ravels. If your fabric does not ravel, you may not need to finish the raw edges. Seam finishes are also unnecessary on self-enclosed seams such as the flat-felled seam and the French seam.

PINKED OR STITCHED AND PINKED

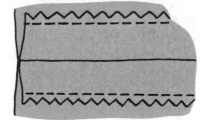

Use these finishes on firmly woven fabrics or fabrics that ravel only slightly. Stitching and pinking is a sturdier finish and more effectively prevents raveling than pinking alone.

To make these finishes, use pinking shears and pink close to the edge of the seam allowance. Or, stitch 1/4 inch from the edge of the seam allowance. Then pink close to the edge. Be careful not to cut through the stitching.

TURNED AND STITCHED

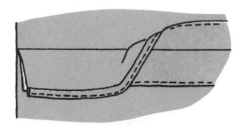

Use this finish for lightweight or medium weight fabrics.

To make this finish, turn under the edge of each seam allowance 1/8 inch and press. Stitch close to the fold.

ZIGZAGGED OR SERGE STITCHED

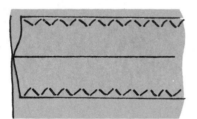

Use this finish for fabrics that ravel.

To make this finish, zigzag or serge stitch close to the seam allowance edge. (See Lesson 11, "Operating the Sewing Machine," for more information about these stitches.)

BOUND

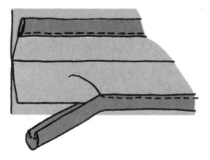

Use this finish for fabrics that ravel easily. It is an especially good choice for finishing the seams in unlined jackets and coats.

To make this finish, wrap double-fold bias tape around the seam allowances. Make sure the wider side of the tape is underneath. Stitch close to the fold of the tape. Be sure to catch the underneath side of the tape in the stitching.

Sheer tricot bias binding may also be used to enclose seam edges. Fold the tricot strip in half lengthwise and encase the edge of the seam allowance. Stretch strip slightly as you sew. It will curl over the seam edge. Stitch using a straight stitch or medium zigzag.

Name _____

Date _____ Period _____

Activity 16-1: Matching Seam Finishes to Fabric

Your teacher will be giving you six different fabric swatches. Attach the swatches in the spaces provided. Indicate under each fabric swatch which seam finish would be most appropriate for the fabric. Also indicate the criteria on which you based your decision such as fabric weight or tendency to ravel.

SEAM FINISHES

Seam Finish _____   Seam Finish _____

Criteria _____   Criteria _____

Seam Finish _____   Seam Finish _____

Criteria _____   Criteria _____

Seam Finish _____   Seam Finish _____

Criteria _____   Criteria _____

Name _____

Date _____ Period _____

Activity 16-2: Practicing Seam Finishes

Supplies needed:

thread	shears
fabric scraps	pinking shears
sewing machine	double-fold bias tape or
bobbin	tricot bias binding

Cut eight pieces of fabric 6″ x 2″. For each sample, place two pieces right sides together and make a 5/8 inch plain seam. Construct samples of the following seam finishes:

Stitched and pinked
Turned and stitched
Zigzagged or serge stitched
Bound

To construct the seam finishes, follow the procedures given in this lesson.

Name _____

Date _____ Period _____

Activity 16-3: Evaluating Learning

The seam finish samples you have just finished will be evaluated using the chart below. After completing the chart, answer the question at the bottom of the page.

		Poor	Fair	Good	Excellent
Correct procedure followed.	Stitched & pinked				
	Turned & stitched				
	Zigzagged or serged				
	Bound				
Finish applied close to edge of seam allowance. (Bound finish should be stitched close to the fold of the bias tape.)	Stitched & pinked				
	Turned & stitched				
	Zigzagged or serged				
	Bound				
Appropriate stitch length and tension used.	Stitched & pinked				
	Turned & stitched				
	Zigzagged or serged				
	Bound				
Threads clipped and seam pressed open.	Stitched & pinked				
	Turned & stitched				
	Zigzagged or serged				
	Bound				
Stitching is straight.	Stitched & pinked				
	Turned & stitched				
	Zigzagged or serged				
	Bound				

What factors should you consider when selecting the type of seam finish to use when constructing a garment?

_____

_____

notes

Lesson 17 Clean Finishing

Objectives

This lesson will help you to:
1. Explain the meaning of the sewing term clean finishing.
2. Determine when to clean finish an edge.
3. Prepare a clean finished edge.

Words to Know

clean finishing
raw edge

Gathering Information

An important sewing step is to "finish" the raw edges of a garment piece. Raw edges are edges that have not been pinked, zigzagged, bound, or treated with any other technique. Finishing raw edges leads to longer wear and neater appearance of the garment. Clean finishing is one technique for treating raw edges.

WHAT IS CLEAN FINISHING?	Clean finishing is a means of finishing raw edges of a garment piece by turning under the edge and stitching.

WHY IS CLEAN FINISHING NECESSARY?	Raw edges are generally clean finished for two reasons.
	1. To prevent them from raveling during wearing and laundering.
	2. To provide a neat, finished appearance to a garment piece that would otherwise have a raw, unfinished edge.

WHERE IS CLEAN FINISHING NEEDED?	Most often, clean finishing is needed on the long, unnotched edges of facings. It is also used to finish the edge of some hems.
	Clean finishing may be used with light to medium weight fabrics. This technique is not used with heavy fabrics as it increases the bulk along the finished edges.

HOW TO CLEAN FINISH

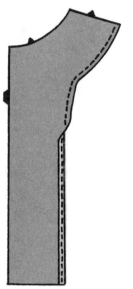

To clean finish a garment piece, follow these steps:

1. Using a regular stitch length, stitch 1/4 inch from the raw edge of the garment piece. (The sewing machine presser foot will be close to the edge of the fabric as you stitch.)

2. Press under 1/4 inch along the line you have just stitched.

3. Stitch again close to the folded edge.

Name _____

Date _____ Period _____

Activity 17-1: Determining When to Clean Finish an Edge

Below are a number of pattern pieces. Under certain circumstances and with specific fabric weights, each piece may need to be clean finished. With a pen, trace over the line(s) of each pattern piece that should be clean finished.

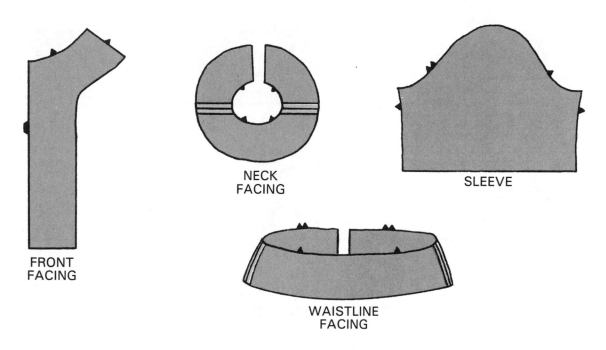

FRONT
FACING

NECK
FACING

SLEEVE

WAISTLINE
FACING

Activity 17-2: Practicing Clean Finishing

Supplies needed:

thread	bobbin
shears	sewing machine
fabric scrap	pattern piece 17A

Fold the fabric scrap in half, keeping the grainline straight. Pin the pattern piece on the fabric scrap, placing the fold line on the folded edge. Cut out the pattern piece. Open it flat and clean finish the unnotched edge.

Name _____

Date _____ Period _____

Activity 17-3: Evaluating Learning

The clean finished edge that you have just completed will be evaluated using the chart below. Also a space is provided for you to write an explanation of clean finishing. Be prepared to discuss your work and your explanation.

	Poor	Fair	Good	Excellent
Edge is smoothly curved.				
Edge has been evenly turned under 1/4 inch.				
All stitching is straight and an even distance from the edge.				
The correct procedure has been followed.				
All threads have been clipped.				

In your own words, write an explanation of the term clean finishing. Include in your explanation under what circumstances you might need to clean finish an edge.

_____

_____

_____

_____

_____

_____

_____

_____

_____

_____

_____

Pattern piece for Activity 17-1.

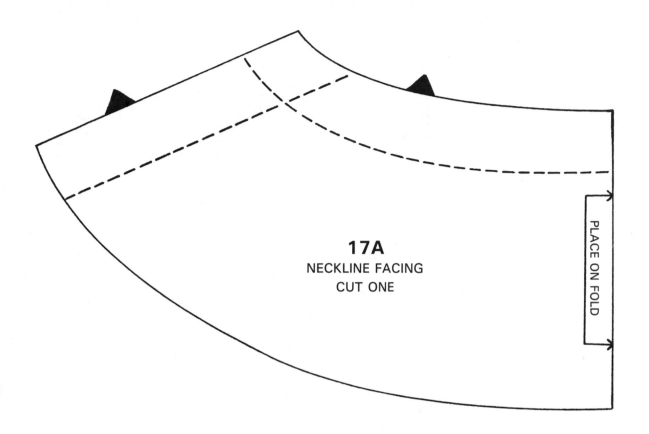

17A
NECKLINE FACING
CUT ONE

PLACE ON FOLD

Lesson 18 Understitching

Objectives

This lesson will help you to:
1. Explain the meaning of the sewing term understitching.
2. Prepare an understitched seam.

Words to Know

understitching

Gathering Information

You may have purchased a shirt with a facing that keeps rolling to the outside of the garment. Such construction can make clothing seem annoying and unattractive. Understitching can be used to avoid this problem.

WHAT IS UNDERSTITCHING?	Understitching is a row of stitching that holds a seam allowance to one of the fabric pieces joined by the seam. It is mainly used on facings. The purpose of understitching is to keep the facing from rolling to the outside of the garment.

HOW TO UNDERSTITCH	Follow these steps: 1. Stitch the facing to the main garment piece. 2. Grade and clip the seam as required. 3. Press the seam allowance toward the facing.

FACING

(Continued)

199

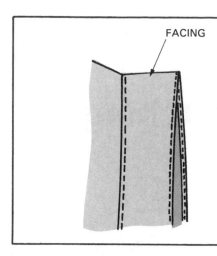

FACING

4. From the outside of the garment, stitch close to the seam. You will be stitching through the facing and the seam allowance. Do not stitch on the garment side of the seam.

5. Press work when finished stitching.

Activity 18-1: Practicing

Supplies needed:

thread	sewing machine
shears	bobbin
fabric	pattern pieces 18A and 18B

Cut out the pattern pieces from a fabric scrap. One piece represents the main garment section. The other represents a facing. Place the stitching lines of the two pieces together and stitch a seam. To understitch, follow the directions in the ''How to Understitch'' box.

HELPFUL SEWING HINTS

The pattern instruction sheet may tell you to understitch the seam allowance of the collar or cuffs to the facing pieces. As you understitch, you will find that you are unable to stitch to the points of the collar or cuffs. Begin and end the stitching approximately 1/2 inch from the points. Be sure to secure the stitching at the beginning and ending of the stitching row.

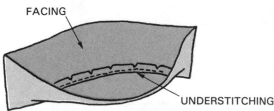

FACING

UNDERSTITCHING

Name _____

Date _____ Period _____

Activity 18-2: Evaluating Learning

The understitched seam that you have just finished will be evaluated using the chart below. Also, a space is provided for you to write a brief definition of understitching. Write the definition in your own words—what the term understitching means to you. Be prepared to discuss your work and your definition.

	Poor	Fair	Good	Excellent
Seam clipped and trimmed as needed.				
Seam pressed toward facing.				
Understitching attaches seam allowance to facing.				
Understitching is very close to seam.				
Stitching is secured.				
Threads have been clipped.				
All stitching is straight and even.				

In your own words, write a definition of understitching. Include in your definition how, why, and where understitching should be done.

_____

_____

_____

_____

_____

_____

_____

_____

_____

_____

_____

_____

notes

Pattern pieces for Activity 18-1.

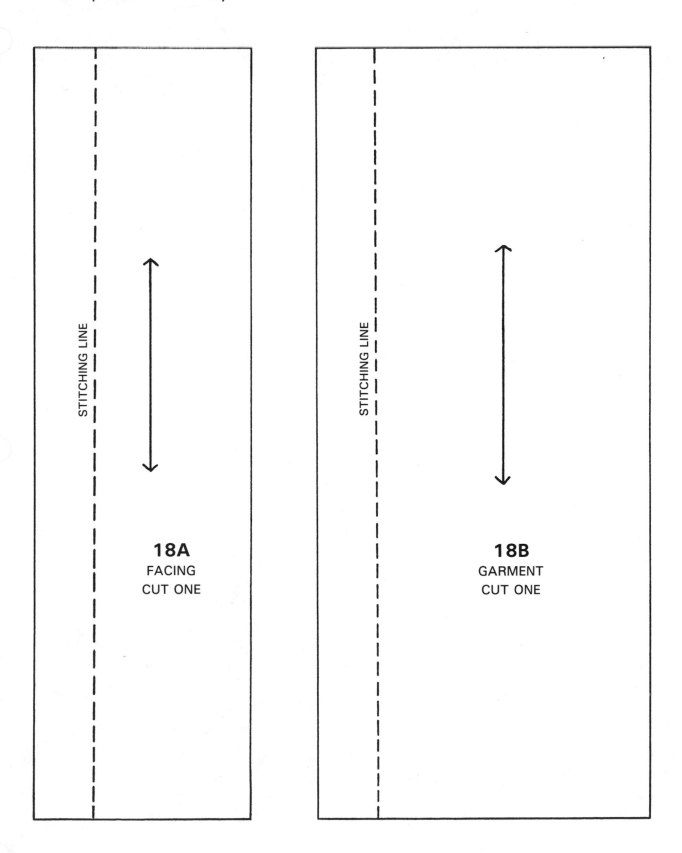

Lesson 19 Easing and Gathering

Objectives

This lesson will help you to:
1. Explain the meanings of the sewing terms easing and gathering.
2. Practice easing and gathering.

Words to Know

easing
gathering

Gathering Information

Imagine a garment made only of straight pieces of fabric. It wouldn't be very comfortable—or very interesting. To give clothes a better fit and to add interest, fullness is often worked into a garment. Easing and gathering are the two main ways to add fullness.

WHAT IS EASING?	Easing is making a larger piece of fabric fit with a smaller piece of fabric as a seam is sewn. It allows extra fabric to be provided at certain points on the body. For instance, extra fabric is allowed in the back shoulder to make room for the shoulder bone. The front shoulder does not need to have the same fullness. Therefore, the extra fabric in the back shoulder must be eased in with the lesser fabric of the front shoulder.

HOW TO EASE 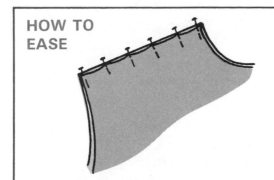	The easiest way to do easing is by pinning the two ends of the pieces together first. Then distribute the rest of your fabric evenly across the seam, pinning as you work.

| WHAT IS GATHERING? | Gathering means to work in fullness. Generally, gathering is used to work in a greater fullness than easing. |

HOW TO GATHER

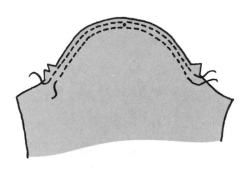

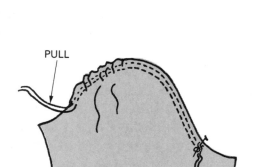

PULL

To gather, sew two rows of large stitching (6-8 stitches per inch) across the area to be gathered. Stitch one row on 1/2 inch and one row on 3/4 inch. The 3/4 inch stitching will be removed later because it will appear on the outside of the garment. Do not backstitch. Also, leave "tails" on the thread at each end of the stitching row.

Never try to take a short cut by using only one row of stitching. The two rows are needed if even gathers are to be achieved.

After stitching, place a pin at one end of the stitches. Wrap the ends of the two threads around the pin securely. This will prevent pulling the threads completely through the fabric as you pull on the threads from the opposite end.

Now pull on the two top threads at the opposite end. With your other hand, help the fabric "gather up" along the threads. Adjust the gathers to the required length. Make sure the gathers are evenly distributed. Pin the gathered fabric to the flat piece. Pin and stitch seam. Remove the 3/4 inch row of basting stitches.

Activity 19-1: Practicing Easing

Supplies needed:

thread	sewing machine
shears	bobbin
fabric	pattern pieces 19A and 19B

Cut out the pattern pieces from a sewing scrap. One piece represents a front shoulder. The other represents a back shoulder. To ease, follow the directions in the "How to Ease" box.

Activity 19-2: Practicing Gathering

Supplies needed:

thread	sewing machine
shears	bobbin
fabric	pattern pieces 19C and 19D

Cut out the pieces from a fabric scrap. Gather fabric piece 19C to fit fabric piece 19D. Follow the directions in the "How to Gather" box.

HELPFUL SEWING HINTS

If you have a problem with threads breaking as you gather, you might want to consider using one of the following methods:

- *Try using heavy duty or buttonhole thread on the bottom. The threads will not break as easily as they are pulled to gather the fabric.*

- *Zigzag over thread. With the wrong side of your fabric up, take one stitch with the sewing machine. Pull the bobbin thread up through the fabric. Next pull both the bobbin thread and the top thread until they extend the length to be gathered. Stitch over the two threads with a medium zigzag being careful not to catch the threads in the stitching. Pull on the threads to adjust the gathers. (A small cord or heavy duty thread may be placed along the surface to be gathered instead of using thread from the sewing machine.)*

Name _____

Date _____ Period _____

Activity 19-3: Evaluating Learning

Your gathering and easing activity will be evaluated using the form below. Also, in the space provided at the bottom of this page, write definitions of easing and gathering. Write the definitions in your own words—what easing and gathering mean to you.

EASING

	Poor	Fair	Good	Excellent
There are no tucks or puckers.				
Seams fit together (ends of seams match).				
Threads are clipped.				
Seam is pressed.				

GATHERING

	Poor	Fair	Good	Excellent
Two rows of gathering stitches were used—1/2 inch and 3/4 inch from the seam edge. (This can be seen by whether or not gathers are even.)				
The 3/4 inch row of stitching has been removed.				
Stitching is straight and even.				
Gathers are uniform and neat.				
Threads are clipped.				
Seam has been pressed.				

In your own words, write definitions of easing and gathering. Include in your definitions how each is done.

Easing: _____

_____

_____

_____

Gathering: _____

_____

_____

_____

Pattern pieces for Activity 19-1.

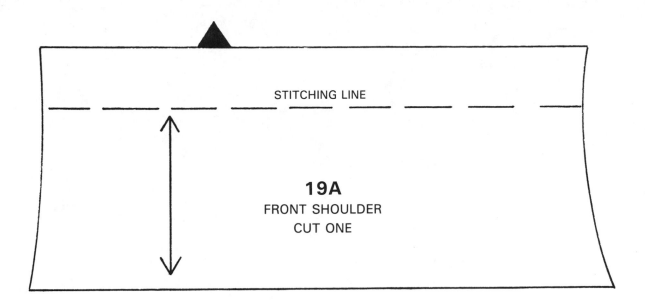

STITCHING LINE

19A
FRONT SHOULDER
CUT ONE

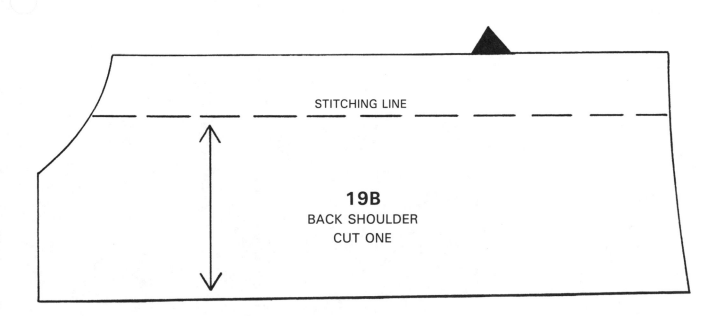

STITCHING LINE

19B
BACK SHOULDER
CUT ONE

Pattern pieces for Activity 19-2.

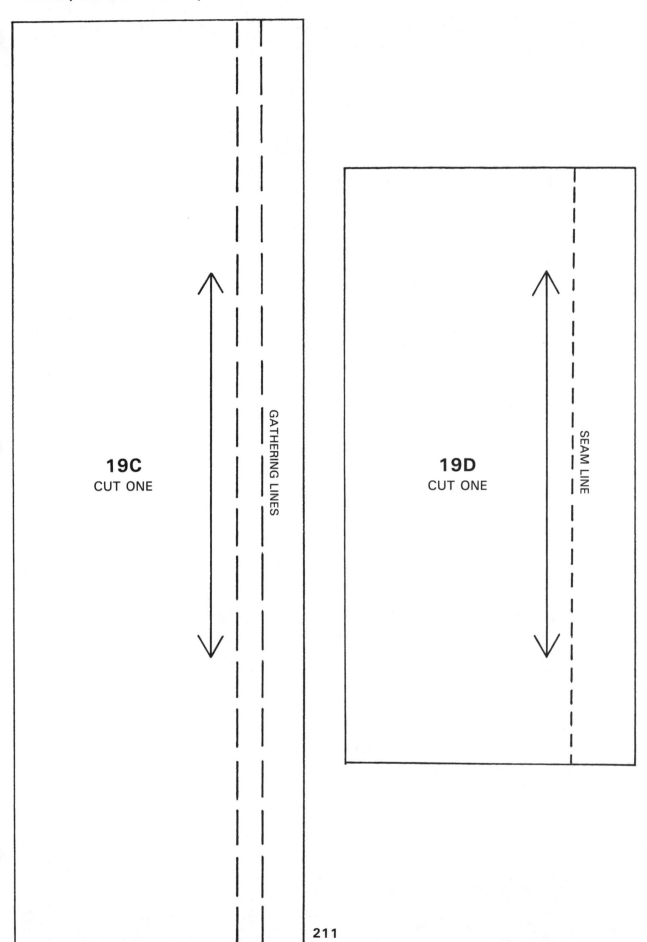

19C
CUT ONE

GATHERING LINES

19D
CUT ONE

SEAM LINE

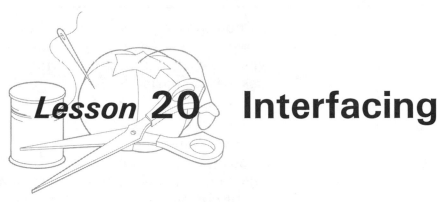

Lesson 20 Interfacing

Objectives

This lesson will help you to:
1. Identify the various types of interfacing and when to use each type.
2. Select interfacing application techniques used for special results.
3. Determine where to use interfacing in a garment.

Words to Know

bubbling	interfacing	woven interfacing
fusible interfacing	nonwoven interfacing	stretch interfacing
fusible knit interfacing	weft-insertion interfacing	

Gathering Information

Before interfacing fabrics were available, items such as metal hoops, corsets, and girdles were worn to achieve garment shape. Today, garments are shaped by a layer of interfacing fabric. Interfacing is placed in the areas where additional support is desired. Interfacing fabrics have the added value of comfort. This was never possible with corsets and metal hoops.

The earliest interfacings were woven from linen, burlap, horse hair, or goat's hair. Modern interfacing fabrics are largely constructed from manufactured fibers that are chemically bonded together.

WHAT IS INTERFACING?

Interfacing is a layer of fabric placed between the facing and the fashion fabric. It is used to achieve one or more of the following purposes:

1. To create a fashion image or silhouette.
2. To increase the life of the garment.
3. To add support to stress areas.
4. To emphasize detail areas of the garment.

The following areas of a garment should almost always be interfaced: collars, cuffs, plackets, waistbands, and under buttons and buttonholes. Sometimes hems, yokes, pockets, hatbands, and craft projects require interfacing as well.

TYPES OF INTERFACING

Choosing interfacing can be very confusing. However, by knowing the classifications into which the many types of interfacings fall, the task will be easier.

WOVEN INTERFACING

Woven interfacings are constructed by interlacing yarns at right angles. These interfacings have a grainline, and pattern pieces must be cut out on the grain. This type of interfacing is usually non-fusible, though a few fusible wovens are available.

Uses. Woven interfacings are very versatile. They are especially good for tailored garments and for places where fusible interfacings are not appropriate.

Characteristics. Stable control, crisp finish, available in a variety of weights, generally more pliable than nonwovens or fusibles.

NON-WOVEN INTERFACING

These interfacing fabrics are constructed by making use of chemical binders. Some non-woven interfacings have what appears to be a grain. If a grain is apparent, pattern pieces will need to be cut out on grain. Nonwovens may be either fusible or nonfusible.

Uses. A wide variety of uses is possible.

Characteristics. Stable control, crisp finish, available in a wide variety of weights. If non-fusible, may crease inside collars and other large areas.

FUSIBLE INTERFACING

A bonding material has been applied to one surface of this interfacing. Therefore it may be fused rather than basted to the fashion fabric. This interfacing may be woven or nonwoven. It may or may not have a grain.

Uses. A wide variety of uses is possible.

Characteristics. Easy to apply, available in a wide variety of weights, tends to stiffen slightly once applied. May bubble on lightweight fabric, corduroy, or velvet.

(Continued)

FUSIBLE KNIT INTERFACING

This is a knit interfacing with a fusible backing. As with any knit fabric, this interfacing has a grain. All pattern pieces must be cut out on the straight of grain. Generally, this type of interfacing is fused to the fashion fabric and treated as one piece with it.

Uses. Fusible knit interfacings are used as underlining for knits and lightweight wovens. They may be used to strengthen stress areas such as knees, seats, or elbows.

Characteristics. Fusible, provides for soft shaping, stretchable.

STRETCH INTERFACING

Stretch interfacings may stretch in one of three ways. One type stretches in one direction. It should be cut out as if there is a grainline. A second type, called all-bias interfacing, stretches in all directions. It may be cut out in any direction. A third type stretches in two directions. This should be cut out as if there is a grainline.

Uses. Good for knit fabrics.

Characteristics. Stretches, may be fusible or non-fusible.

WEFT-INSERTION INTERFACING

This interfacing has knitted warp yarns with weft yarns woven in. It does have a grain and pattern pieces must be cut out on grain.

Uses. May be used where soft tailoring is desired.

Characteristics. Has a flatter finish, eliminates bulk, preshrunk.

HOW TO SELECT INTERFACING

Choosing the right weight. Interfacings come in many different weights to suit many purposes. To determine which weight to use for your fabric, test the hand, or feel. Place the interfacing fabric and the fashion fabric together. In most cases, the interfacing should be slightly lighter in weight than the fashion fabric. You may use different weights in various parts of the same garment depending upon the results you want.

(Continued)

Knit fabrics. When sewing with a stable knit, always use interfacing where called for on the pattern instruction sheet.

Patterns designed for stretch knits generally do not call for interfacing. If interfacing is desired, use a fusible knit or stretch interfacing.

Woven interfacings may be used on knits where soft shaping is desired and there is no need to stabilize. Use woven interfacings by cutting them on the bias so that there is lots of stretch.

Sheer fabrics. When interfacing sheer fabrics, organza or chiffon may be used as the interfacing. Apply these fabrics just as you would any other interfacing fabric.

PRESHRINKING INTERFACING FABRICS

In most cases, interfacing fabrics do not require preshrinking. But there are exceptions. Check the end of the interfacing bolt when you make your purchase.

Always be sure that the fashion fabric has been preshrunk, if necessary, before applying the interfacing.

HOW TO APPLY INTERFACING

To apply fusible interfacing, follow these steps:

1. Always pretest fusible interfacing on a scrap of fabric. Fusible interfacings cannot be used on all fashion fabrics.

2. Trim off 1/2 inch on all edges of the interfacing piece. This decreases the bulk in the seam allowance. Also, trim the corners diagonally.

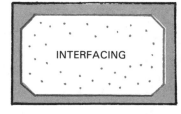

3. Position interfacing on the garment piece and cover with a damp press cloth.

4. Press by lifting the iron up and placing it down on the interfacing. Count to 10 slowly each time you put the iron down.

5. Check for bonding. You may have to repeat the process.

(Continued)

Bubbling. After applying a fusible interfacing to certain fabrics, small bubbles may appear on the surface of the fabric. This is especially common on corduroy, velvet, velveteen, and lightweight fabric. Bubbling may be caused by any of the following reasons: 1. Steam was insufficient. 2. Fashion fabric was not preshrunk. 3. Interfacing was ironed rather than pressed on to the fabric. 4. Interfacing is too heavy for the fabric. 5. Interfacing is too spongy for the fabric.

To prevent this problem for corduroy, velvet, and velveteen fabrics, try cutting along the crosswise grain instead of the lengthwise grain of interfacing. This is called reversing the grainline. This may help because the fabrics will not shrink on the crosswise grain, but the interfacing fabric will have slight shrinkage.

To apply non-fusible interfacing, follow these steps:

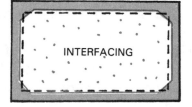

1. Pin the interfacing to the fashion fabric. Trim corners diagonally.

2. Stitch the interfacing to fabric.

3. Trim the interfacing close to the stitching line.

HOW TO USE INTERFACING

Pockets. To eliminate sagging pockets, the entire pocket may be interfaced. Trim away seam allowances on the interfacing. Fuse the interfacing to the pocket piece. For even greater stability, the grainline of the interfacing may be reversed.

Collar stays. A convenient way to secure collar stays is to place the stay between the collar piece and the interfacing. Fuse the interfacing over the top of the stay.

Zippers. Applying a zipper to a bias cut edge or to knit fabric may result in rippling. To prevent this, apply a strip of interfacing along the seam where the zipper is to be inserted.

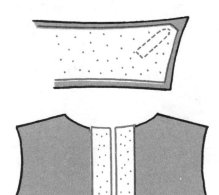

(Continued)

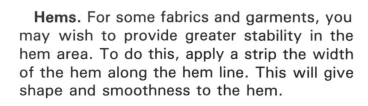

Hems. For some fabrics and garments, you may wish to provide greater stability in the hem area. To do this, apply a strip the width of the hem along the hem line. This will give shape and smoothness to the hem.

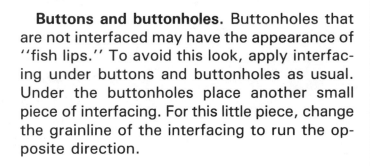

Buttons and buttonholes. Buttonholes that are not interfaced may have the appearance of "fish lips." To avoid this look, apply interfacing under buttons and buttonholes as usual. Under the buttonholes place another small piece of interfacing. For this little piece, change the grainline of the interfacing to run the opposite direction.

Collar roll line. Interface the collar using a collar interfacing piece that is on the bias. To find the bias of the interfacing fabric, fold the selvage at a 90 degree angle. Place the grainline arrow of the collar on the bias edge.

Cut an additional piece of interfacing to fit from the roll line to the neckline. Change the grainline for stability. The grain should run from the neck to the roll line. Press on top of the first interfacing. This process will allow the collar to roll rather than crack.

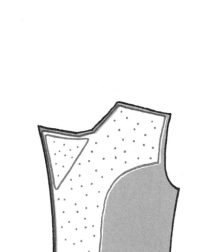

Lapel roll line. Cut a piece of interfacing from the point of the lapel to the roll line. Fuse this piece of interfacing on top of the interfacing piece called for by the instruction sheet. The second piece of interfacing should be cut out on the same grainline as the main lapel interfacing. Fold the lapel and pin to the pressing ham. Steam and let dry before removing.

Name _____

Date _____ Period _____

Activity 20-1: Practicing

Your teacher will provide you with fabric swatches for each of the garments illustrated below. Attach the swatch to the space in the fabric column. Then fill in the information requested.

GARMENT	FABRIC	TYPE OF INTERFACING	AREAS TO BE INTERFACED	SPECIAL APPLICATION TECHNIQUES REQUIRED
1. 				
2. 				
3. 				
4. 				
5. 				
6. 				
7. 				

Name _____

Date _____ Period _____

Activity 20-2: Evaluating Learning

Read over the following situations and respond to the questions asked.

Situation #1 You have just applied a lightweight interfacing to a lightweight fabric. You have done this on a scrap of fabric. Small bubbles have appeared on the surface of the fabric.

What may have caused the problem?

_____

_____

_____

_____

What will you do now?

_____

_____

_____

_____

Situation #2 You are making a shirt from a medium weight cotton/polyester fabric. The instruction sheet does not tell you to use interfacing.

Will you use interfacing anyway?

_____

If so, what areas of the shirt will you interface?

_____

_____

Situation #3 A friend is making pants from a medium weight fabric. Your friend does not want to bother interfacing the waistband.

What reasons could you give your friend for not skipping this step?

_____

_____

_____

(Continued)

Name _____

Situation #4 You are purchasing the interfacing to go with your fashion fabric. The sales clerk has shown you a number of fusible and non-fusible interfacings of varying weights.

How will you make your decision as to which one to purchase?

_____

_____

_____

_____

Situation #5 You have borrowed a piece of interfacing from another person. It appears to be the correct weight for your fabric, so you have decided to go ahead and use it. You are ready to cut out your interfacing pieces.

How do you tell if the interfacing has a grain?

_____

_____

What guidelines would you use to determine which direction to place the pattern pieces on the interfacing fabric?

_____

_____

_____

 *SHORTCUTS* _____

Save time sewing by making wise use of your time when it comes to buying and using interfacing. Begin by purchasing an assortment of interfacings to have on hand. A single garment may require more than one type or weight of interfacing. By having a variety of interfacings on hand you will be ready for any interfacing need that may arise.

Further time savings can be made by cutting out all interfacing pieces at one time. And save needless interruptions by fusing all of the interfacing pieces in a batch. Do your fusing before you take a stitch.

notes

Lesson 21 Topstitching

Objectives

This lesson will help you to:
1. Identify various topstitching techniques.
2. Make decisions about topstitching on various types of fabrics.
3. Practice topstitching on various types of fabrics.

Words to Know

buttonhole twist
edge stitching
topstitching

Gathering Information

Topstitching is a line of stitching on the outside of the garment generally for the purpose of decoration. Topstitching usually gives the garment a more tailored appearance.

There is much variation in how topstitching can be done. For instance, variation can occur in the number of rows of stitching, the distance of the stitching from the edge of the garment, and the stitch length. This lesson will help you to make choices about how to topstitch.

SELECTING THREAD	
	A single thread, double thread, or buttonhole twist may be used when topstitching.
	To use a double thread, place two thread spools on your machine. Thread your machine as usual, holding the two threads together as you bring them through the guides and needle eye.
	Buttonhole twist is thicker than standard thread. It is generally used only as the top thread in the sewing machine.
	If you decide to use a double thread or buttonhole twist, you may need to use a size 16 needle and increase the stitch length to 8 stitches per inch. Do not attempt to backstitch. Instead, pull the beginning and ending stitches through the fabric so that both threads are on one side. Tie a knot in the threads by hand.

MAKING STITCHING CHOICES

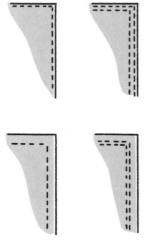

Topstitching is varied by changing the number of rows of stitching used, the distance of stitching from the edge of the garment, and the size of stitch length. Your instruction sheet may give you suggestions about how and where to topstitch your garment. But, do not hesitate to make your own topstitching decisions.

The stitch length you select will depend upon the weight and texture of your fabric. It will also depend on the look you want. Generally, heavier or more textured fabrics require a larger stitch length. Practice on a scrap of your garment fabric to determine the stitch length that will look the best.

The number of stitching rows and the distance you stitch from the garment edge will depend upon your fabric and the garment design. There are no rules for making these choices. Use your own sense of good design.

An excellent source for topstitching ideas is professionally designed garments. As you look at clothing, analyze the garments for style, fabric design and weight, and topstitching techniques. By trying to imitate techniques used by clothing designers, you can have a more professional looking garment.

STITCHING GUIDES

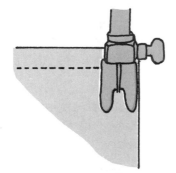

To achieve straight topstitching try one of these methods:

Method 1. Use the sewing machine foot as a guide. Do this by placing the machine foot along the edge of the garment piece.

(Continued)

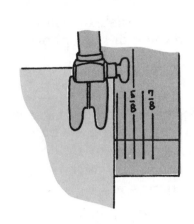

Method 2. Use the lines on the throat plate as a guide. If your machine does not have a guide, make your own with tape.

Method 3. A special topstitching tape can be applied to the garment. Lines on the tape indicate where to stitch.

Method 4. Draw your own line with a chalk pencil or removable marking pen. Test the marking method on a fabric scrap before using it on your garment. You will want to be sure the marking is not permanent.

Method 5. Use clear, plastic topstitching guides. These guides have small projections on the underside that grip the fabric and prevent them from slipping. Plastic guides are available in various shapes and are marked for different seam widths. There is even one in the shape of a front curved zipper fly.

DIRECTIONAL STITCHING

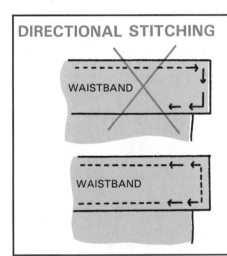

When topstitching, follow the general guidelines for directional stitching. (See Lesson 13, ''Staystitching,'' and Lesson 14, ''Seams.'') For instance, stitch both rows of a zipper from the bottom of the zipper to the top. Or stitch both topstitching rows on a waistband in the same direction. Directional stitching will prevent puckering which is caused by stretching the fabric in opposite directions. If the fabric puckers when stitched from one direction, try stitching from the opposite direction.

EDGE STITCHING

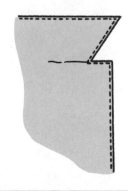

Your pattern instruction sheet may tell you to edge stitch. Edge stitching is a form of topstitching. Edge stitching always means to stitch close to the finished edge of the garment piece.

HOW TO TOPSTITCH

Follow these steps for attractive topstitching:

1. Decide whether topstitching will add to the appearance of your garment.

2. Decide whether you wish to use a single thread, double thread, or buttonhole twist.

3. Adjust the tension and stitch length as needed to get the look you want.

4. Always practice topstitching on a scrap of fabric from the garment you are constructing. Use as many layers of fabric in your practice sample as you will be sewing through on the garment.

5. As you topstitch, stitch slowly but at an even pace. Starting and stopping can cause uneven stitching. If you must stop stitching, be sure to leave the needle down in the fabric. This will keep the fabric from slipping. This procedure should also be followed when turning a corner. Stitch to the corner and stop with the needle down in the fabric. Pivot the fabric and begin stitching in the new direction.

Name _____

Date _____ Period _____

Activity 21-1: Making Topstitching Choices

Supplies needed:

scrap of medium weight suiting	shears
scrap of shirt weight fabric	thread
scrap of single knit fabric	sewing machine
	bobbin and case

In Activity 21-2, you will be topstitching on three types of fabric. But first you must make choices about the best topstitching technique to use on each fabric. This activity will help you make those decisions by giving you a chance to experiment on the fabric scraps.

Practice topstitching on half of the scraps given to you. (Save half of your scraps for Activity 21-2.) Experiment by adjusting the stitch length, using thread variations, and using variations in number of rows and stitching distance from the edge. Stitch on the same number of fabric layers that you would normally find when topstitching on a garment. After you have experimented, record your topstitching decisions in the space provided below. As you make your choices, don't forget to consider the garment design for which the fabric will be used.

	TOPSTITCHING CHOICES				
	Thread	Tension	Stitch length	Number of rows	Location of rows from edge
FABRIC #1 Garment: jacket Fabric: medium weight suiting					
FABRIC #2 Garment: shirt Fabric: medium shirt weight					
FABRIC #3 Garment: shirt Fabric: single knit					

Name _____

Date _____ Period _____

Activity 21-2: Practicing

Supplies needed:

fabric scraps from   thread
  activity 21-1   pins
sewing machine   bobbin and case
shears

Cut two 3 by 5-inch pieces of fabric from each of the three fabrics used in your last activity. Place the right sides of each two pieces together and stitch a 5/8-inch seam along one side. Grade the seam, fold over and press along the seamline. Topstitch each seam according to your decision made in activity 21-1.

Name _____

Date _____ Period _____

Activity 21-3: Evaluating Learning

Your topstitching samples will be evaluated using the following scale: E—Excellent, G—Good, F—Fair, P—Poor. The appropriate letter will be placed in the spaces provided below. Also answer the question at the bottom of the page.

	Fabric 1	Fabric 2	Fabric 3
Topstitching is an even distance from the edge.			
Appropriate stitch length was used.			
Correct machine tension for fabric was used.			
Threads are clipped.			

What factors should be considered when determining when and/or how to topstitch a garment? List as many ideas as you can.

_____

_____

_____

_____

_____

_____

_____

_____

_____

_____

_____

_____

_____

notes

Lesson 22 Hand Stitching

Objectives

This lesson will help you to:
1. Identify various hand stitches and when to use each.
2. Tie a knot in the thread.
3. Fasten off the thread at the end of a row of hand stitching.
4. Make four different hand stitches.

Words to Know

basting stitch	hemming stitch	slip stitch
buttonhole stitch	overcast stitch	
catch stitch	rolled-hem stitch	

Gathering Information

There are many hand stitches. Sometimes more than one stitch will work for your need. Other times, a specific stitch will work best for a certain purpose. This activity will help you to make decisions about which hand stitch to use.

HOW TO BEGIN AND END HAND STITCHING

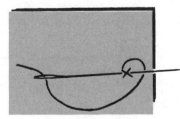

A fastening stitch can be used to secure the thread either at the beginning or ending of a row of stitching.

Procedure: Take a small stitch but leave a thread loop rather than pulling the stitch tight. Run the needle through the loop. Then pull the stitch tight. Repeat several times in the same position.

(Continued)

Knotting the thread can be used to secure the thread at the beginning of a row. To knot, follow these steps:

1. Wrap thread around the index finger once. For a larger knot, wrap thread around two or three times.

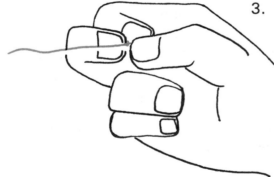

2. Roll thread between fingers until it rolls off the end of the finger. However, do *not* let loose of the thread.

3. Place the middle finger over the thread. Pull on the thread to form the knot.

HOW TO HAND STITCH

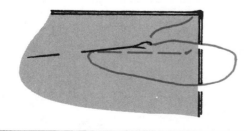

Basting stitch. Used to temporarily hold layers of fabric together.

With a knotted thread, weave the needle in and out of the fabric. The length of the stitch may vary depending on the fabric being used.

(Continued)

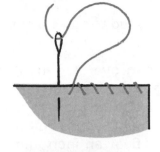

Overcast stitch. Used to prevent a flat, raw edge from raveling.

Bring the needle through the fabric about 1/4 inch down from the top edge. Pull thread through. Move 1/4 inch to the left and repeat the stitch. Keep stitches evenly spaced.

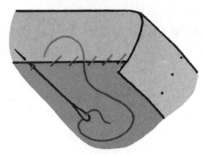

Hemming stitch. Used to stitch down an edge that has been turned under. May also be used on a flat edge.

Pick up one or two threads of the garment fabric close to the hem. Push the needle up through the hem. Pull the thread through. Moving 1/4 inch to the left. Repeat the stitch.

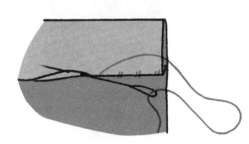

Slip stitch. Used for a hem edge that has been turned under.

With a knotted thread, pick up one or two threads of the garment fabric close to the hem. Just above this stitch, slide the needle through the folded edge of the fabric for about 1/4 inch. Repeat. This stitch should not be visible.

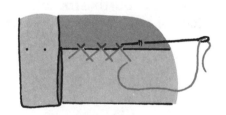

Catch stitch. Used to stitch a flat edge (one that has not been turned under.)

Work from left to right. Pick up one or two threads on the garment directly above the hem. Pull the thread through the fabric. Move 1/4 inch to the right. Take a small stitch in the hem only, 1/8 inch down from the edge of the hem. Pull thread through. Move to the right and repeat stitch.

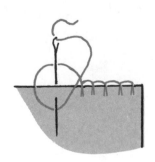

Buttonhole stitch (blanket stitch). Used to bind a raw edge.

Place the needle through the fabric about 1/4 inch below the raw edge. Do not pull the needle through. Loop the thread around the needle as shown. Pull the needle through the fabric. Move to the left and repeat the stitch. The distance the needle is inserted from the raw edge and the distance between stitches will depend on the sewing task.

(Continued)

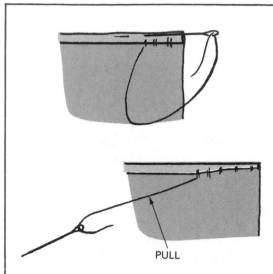

PULL

Rolled-hem stitch. Used to make a small hem on sheer fabric.

With the hem turned over 1/8 inch, take a stitch 1/4 inch long in the hem. Pull the stitch through. Take another stitch picking up one or two threads on the main fabric. Pull through. Move to the left 1/16 of an inch and repeat stitch. After repeating the stitch for about an inch, pull on the thread and the fabric will roll over on itself forming a very small rolled hem.

Activity 22-1: Practicing

Supplies needed:
    four 3 by 4-inch squares of fabric
    needle
    pins
    shears

On each of three of the fabric strips, press under 1/4 inch on a long edge. Then fold up one inch on the same long edge. Fold up one inch on the fourth strip also.

Hand stitch along the folded edge using a different stitch for each of the fabric strips. As you do each stitch, you will practice making a knot and fastening off the row of stitching. Make the following four stitches:
    heming stitch
    slip stitch
    basting stitch
    catch stitch (For this stitch, use the fabric strip that has not been turned under an extra 1/4 inch.)
To make each stitch, follow the directions in the "How to Hand Stitch" box.

Name _____

Date _____ Period _____

Activity 22-2: Choosing a Stitch

Fill in the chart below stating which stitch you would use for each of the situations given. Use the information provided earlier to help you complete this activity.

SITUATION	STITCH CHOICE	REASON FOR YOUR CHOICE
1. Fabric: Medium weight, may ravel slightly. Construction: Hem edge that has been turned under.		
2. Fabric: Sheer. Construction: Hem.		
3. Fabric: Heavy weight, will ravel. Construction: Finish seam edge.		
4. Fabric: Heavy weight, will not ravel. Construction: Hem.		
5. Fabric: Slippery. Construction: Seam.		
6. Fabric: Medium weight. Construction: Stitch around pocket		

Name _____

Date _____ Period _____

Activity 22-3: Evaluating Learning

The form below will be used to evaluate your hand stitches. The hand stitches will be rated using the following scale: E—Excellent, G—Good, F—Fair, P—Poor. The appropriate letters will be placed in the spaces provided below. Also, answer the question at the bottom of this page.

	Hemming Stitch	Slip Stitch	Basting Stitch	Catch Stitch
Stitches do not show on the outside of the sample.				
Stitches are evenly spaced.				
Knot at end of thread is hidden under the edge of hem.				
Fastening stitch is correctly and neatly done.				
Stitches are not too far apart or too close together.				
Sample looks very neat.				

What criteria do you use to determine which hand stitch to use in a given situation? List as many ideas as you can.

_____

_____

_____

_____

_____

_____

_____

_____

_____

Lesson 23 — Hemming Methods

Objectives

This lesson will help you to:
1. Identify the various hemming methods available.
2. Select the appropriate hemming method to use for various types of fabric.
3. Make four different types of hems.

Words to Know

double-stitched hem   machine hem   turned and
eased hem   serged hem   stitched hem
machine-blind hem   stitched and pinked hem

Gathering Information

An uneven, bulky hem can destroy the appearance of a garment. On the other hand, a properly constructed hem will give your garment a professional look. It will make you look your best when the garment is worn. To achieve that professional-looking hem, a number of choices must be made. This lesson will give you important information that will help you to make those choices.

HOW TO CHOOSE A HEM

When constructing a hem, many hemming methods are available from which to select. The method you select will depend upon the weight of your fabric and the degree that it ravels. You must choose a method because your pattern may not provide instructions to suit your specific needs. Do not be afraid to vary from the pattern instruction sheet when it comes to constructing the hem. Follow this guide:

1. Heavy or stiff fabrics and stable knits. Use a method that will provide the least bulk. Do not use a method that turns under the edge of the hem.

(Continued)

---

2. Fabrics that ravel. Use a method that will encase the edge of the hem to prevent raveling.

3. Stretch Knits. Use a method that will prevent the knit from raveling or curling.

HOW TO MAKE HEMS

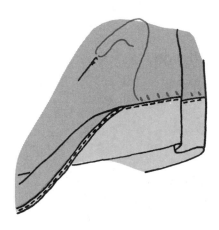

Turned and stitched hem. Use this hem on most light to medium weight fabrics. To make the hem, follow these steps:

1. Turn under the top edge of the hem 1/4 inch. Press in place.

2. Machine stitch close to the folded edge of the hem.

3. Turn the hem up and hand stitch to the garment. Use one of the methods in Lesson 22, ''Hand Stitching.'' Recommended hand stitch: slip stitch.

Eased hem. This is used when a hem has excess fullness, such as on a circular skirt. To make the hem, follow these steps:

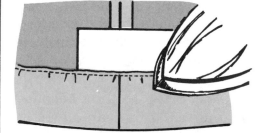

1. Using large stitches, machine stitch 1/4 inch from the edge of the hem.

2. Pull up the ease thread every few inches to fit in the extra fabric.

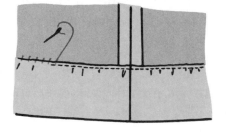

3. Turn the hem up. Press the eased portion of the hem using steam to shrink out some of the fullness. (Place brown paper between the hem and the garment as you press.)

4. Hand stitch the hem to the garment. Use one of the methods in Lesson 22, ''Hand Stitching.'' Recommended hand stitch: slip stitch.

(Continued)

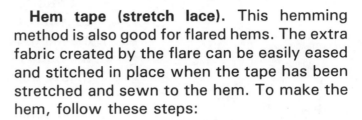

Hem tape (stretch lace). This hemming method is also good for flared hems. The extra fabric created by the flare can be easily eased and stitched in place when the tape has been stretched and sewn to the hem. To make the hem, follow these steps:

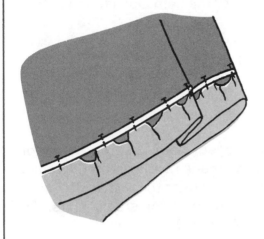

1. Fold the hem up to its finished position. Pin the stretch lace tape over the hem in the position it will be when the hem is finished. Do not stretch the tape. At this point, the hem will not lay flat against the garment. Only the tape will be the size of the finished hem.

2. Make sure the hem tape overlaps the edge of the hem when you pin it in place. You do not want to sew the tape too close to the edge of the hem or it will pull off easily.

3. Fold the hem down again and stitch the tape to the hem. Stretch the tape to fit the hem.

4. Turn the hem up into position again. Hand stitch the hem tape to the garment. Use one of the methods listed in Lesson 22, ''Hand Stitching.'' Recommended hand stitches: Hemming stitch, catch stitch, running stitch.

Hem tape (non-stretch). This method may be used for hems that have no flare, fabrics that are medium to heavy in weight, and fabrics that ravel. To make the hem, follow these steps:

1. Stitch the non-stretch tape to the edge of the hem. Be sure the tape overlaps the hem at least half the width of the tape. The stitching should be located close to the edge of the tape. If the tape and stitching are positioned too close to the edge of the hem, the tape will pull off easily.

2. Turn the hem up and hand stitch in place. Use one of the methods listed in Lesson 22, ''Hand Stitching.'' Recommended hand stitches: Catch stitch, hemming stitch, running stitch.

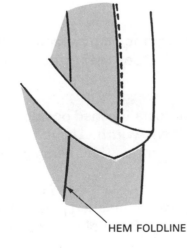

HEM FOLDLINE

(Continued)

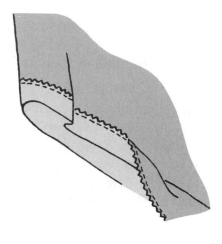

Stitched and pinked hem. This method is excellent for stable knits. Pinking the hem edge makes the hem less likely to show through to the outside of the garment. To make the hem, follow these steps:

1. Machine stitch 1/4 inch from the edge of the hem.

2. Pink the edge of the hem close to the stitching line.

3. Turn the hem up and hand stitch to the garment. Use one of the methods listed in Lesson 22, "Hand Stitching." Recommended hand stitch: Catch stitch.

Serged (zig-zagged) hem. Use on heavy or stiff fabrics. If the fabric ravels greatly, a taped hem is recommended over this method. This is also an optional method for stable knits. To make the hem, follow these steps:

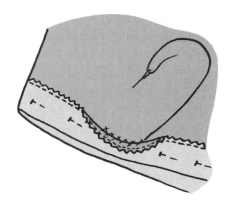

1. Zigzag or serge stitch close to the edge of the hem.

2. Turn the hem up and hand stitch to the garment. Use one of the methods listed in Lesson 22, "Hand Stitching." Recommended hand stitch: Catch stitch.

Double-stitched hem. Use this method for knit fabrics when the pattern instructions call for a wider hem. To make the hem, follow these steps:

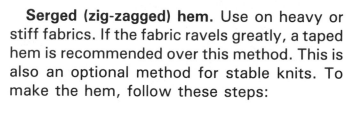

1. Prepare the edge of the hem as recommended for the fabric, possibly stitched and pinked.

2. Fold the hem up to its finished position. Roll back half the hem width. Using a catch stitch, stitch around the hem in this position.

3. Fold the hem up to its finished position and stitch around the hem again at the edge.

4. Press the finished hem.

HOW TO MAKE MACHINE HEMS

Your decision to use a machine stitched hem will depend on the design of the garment and the fabric you will be using. Machine hems are frequently used on knit fabrics. They are also common for jeans and some types of shirts. Your pattern may indicate whether this hem type is appropriate for your garment. The machine stitching will be seen on the outside of the garment so consider whether this is a look you want for your hem.

Narrow machine hem. To make this hem, follow these steps:

1. Decide how wide you want the finished hem to be. Normally, machine hems are kept narrow in width. Add 1/4 inch to the width of the finished hem.

2. Turn under the 1/4 inch and press.

3. Machine stitch close to the edge that you have turned under. You may also wish to stitch close to the lower edge of the hem.

Machine-blind hem. To make this hem, follow these steps:

1. Press the raw edge under 1/2 inch. Then fold the hem to the desired width.

2. Turn garment back, exposing 1/4 inch of the hem.

3. Adjust the machine for a blind hem stitch and stitch along the hem so that the machine stitching is on the hem.

4. Turn the hem flat and press.

Machine hem for knits. To make this hem, follow these steps:

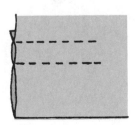

1. Trim the hem to 2 inches. Fold up and press.

2. Stitch through all layers 1 3/4 inch from the folded hem edge.

3. Stitch again through all layers 1/4 inch below the first row of stitching.

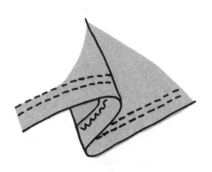

Twin-needle hem. To make this hem, follow these steps:

1. Turn the hem up to the desired width. Press.

2. Stitch through both layers from the right side, using a twin-needle and two thread spools. Follow the seam guide. Trim excess hem allowance after stitching.

Name _____

Date _____ Period _____

Activity 23-1: Choosing a Hem

Complete the activity below by indicating under each fabric sample which hemming method would be the most appropriate for that fabric. Also, indicate your reason for the choice you made. (For instance, the fabric is heavy, fabric ravels, etc.)

Hemming Methods

Hemming Method _____

Criteria _____

_____

Hemming Method _____

Criteria _____

_____

Heming Method _____

Criteria _____

_____

Hemming Method _____

Criteria _____

_____

Activity 23-2: Practicing

Supplies needed:

scraps of medium weight	needle
woven fabric	pins
scraps of heavy knit fabric	shears

From the medium weight fabric, cut one 3 by 4-inch square of fabric. Then cut one piece that is 6 inches long and 3 inches wide at the edges, but curved along one long edge. Also cut two 3 by 4-inch squares of knit fabric. Make the following four hems:

turned and stitched hem (Use the rectangle of medium weight fabric.)
eased hem (Use the fabric scrap with a curved edge.)
double-stitched hem (Use a rectangle of knit fabric.)
Machine hem for knits. (Use a rectangle of knit fabric.)

To make each stitch, follow the directions in the "How to Make Hems" and the "How to Make Machine Hems" boxes.

Name _____

Date _____ Period _____

Activity 23-3: Evaluating Learning

The hems that you have just finished will be evaluated below. They will be rated using the following scale: E—Excellent, G—Good, F—Fair, P—Poor. The appropriate letters will be placed in the spaces below. Also, compile a list of guidelines that would be helpful when selecting hemming methods for various types of fabrics.

	Turned and Stitched Hem	Eased Hem	Double-Stitched Hem	Machine Hem for Knits
Hem looks attractive from the right side of the sample.				
Stitches are spaced evenly.				
Stitches are not too far apart or too close together.				
Raw edges of hem are finished appropriately.				
Sample looks very neat.				

Guidelines for the Selection of a Hemming Method

1. _____

_____

2. _____

_____

3. _____

_____

4. _____

_____

5. _____

_____

Unit 4   Assessing Your Learning

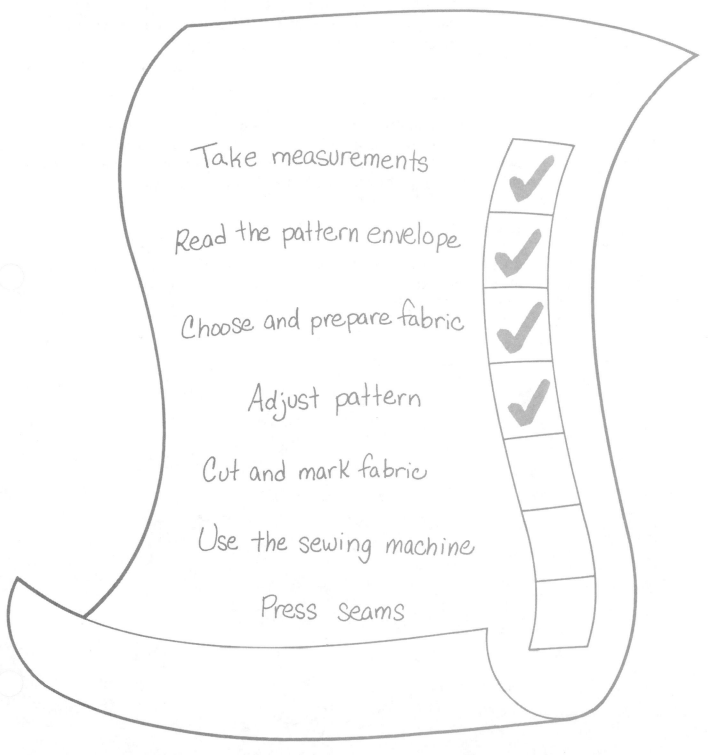

Take measurements ✓

Read the pattern envelope ✓

Choose and prepare fabric ✓

Adjust pattern ✓

Cut and mark fabric

Use the sewing machine

Press seams

Unit 4
Assessing Your Learning

This unit is designed to help you evaluate your learning before you begin your sewing project. It consists of two parts.

Basic Sewing Skills Posttest

This test reviews the most important concepts covered in Unit 3. It also includes questions on sergers, which are covered in Unit 7. If you have not used sergers in your classroom, your teacher may ask you to skip these questions. Taking this test will help you assess your understanding of the information in the various lessons.

Posttest Analysis

This form will help you and your teacher analyze the results of your posttest. You will be able to see areas in which you have gained sufficient knowledge. You will also be able to see areas you might want to review. You can use this information as you prepare to begin your sewing project.

Name _____

Posttest Score _____ Date _____ Period _____

BASIC SEWING SKILLS POSTTEST

This posttest will help you identify areas of clothing construction in which you have gained knowledge and skill. It will also help you identify areas you may want to review before beginning your sewing project. The questions in section A are a repeat of the pretest you took in Unit 2. Answering them will show you how much you have improved since taking the pretest. The questions in section B relate to lessons over which you were not previously tested. Your teacher may tell you to skip some of these questions depending on which lessons you completed.

Read each question carefully. Select the best answer and write the letter in the blank. When you have finished, your teacher will give you directions regarding how the test is to be corrected.

Section A

____ 1. When taking a back waist length measurement, the tape measure should be placed:
    a. From the top of the shoulder to the waist.
    b. From the waist to the desired finished garment length.
    c. From the prominent bone at the back of the neck to the waist.

____ 2. When taking a man's sleeve length measurement, the measuring tape is placed from the:
    a. Elbow to the wrist.
    b. Top of the spine to the wrist.
    c. Shoulder bone to the wrist.

____ 3. You are making a shirt for a friend with the following measurements: bust 32, waist 26 1/2, hips 36. Which pattern size would you select? (Refer to the chart below.)
    a. Size 10.
    b. Size 12.
    c. Size 14.

Size	10	12	14	16
Bust	32 1/2	34	36	38
Waist	25	26 1/2	28	30
Hips	34 1/2	36	38	40

(Continued)

Name _____

_____ 4. How much fabric would be required for View A in a size 12, if the fabric were 44/45" wide? (Refer to the Chart below.)
   a. 3 3/8 yards.
   b. 3 1/8 yards.
   c. 3 1/4 yards.

VIEW A	8	10	12	14
35" fabric	3 1/4	3 3/8	3 3/8	4 3/8
44/45" fabric	3	3 1/8	3 1/8	3 1/4
60" fabric	1 1/2	1 7/8	1 7/8	2
VIEW B				
35" fabric	3 1/2	3 1/2	4 3/8	4 3/8
44/45" fabric	3 1/4	3 1/4	3 1/4	3 1/2
60" fabric	2	2	2	2 1/8

_____ 5. The yardage requirement table for various views, sizes, and widths of fabric is found on the:
   a. Back of the pattern envelope.
   b. Front of the pattern envelope.
   c. Guide sheet.

_____ 6. Which of the following types of information would not be found on the pattern envelope?
   a. A description of the garment.
   b. Suggested fabric from which to construct the garment.
   c. A list of pattern pieces needed for the garment view being constructed.

_____ 7. The lengthwise grain of the fabric:
   a. Runs from cut edge to cut edge.
   b. Runs from selvage to selvage.
   c. Forms a 45 degree angle with the selvage edge.

_____ 8. The ends of woven fabric should be straightened by cutting along a pulled crosswise thread when the fabric has been:
   a. Cut from the bolt.
   b. Torn from the bolt.
   c. Either cut or torn from the bolt.

_____ 9. To determine whether or not a piece of fabric is on grain, the fabric should first be folded:
   a. Crosswise.
   b. On the bias.
   c. Lengthwise.

_____ 10. How can you determine whether or not the ends of the fabric are straight with the grain?
   a. Fold the fabric lengthwise to see if the raw, cut edges match.
   b. See if one crosswise thread ravels from selvage to selvage without being stopped by other crosswise threads.
   c. Pull on the true bias every few inches.

(Continued)

Name _____

In questions 11 through 16, match the pattern symbols with the letter that represents the symbol on the diagram. Use diagram A for questions 11 through 13. Use diagram B for questions 14 through 16.

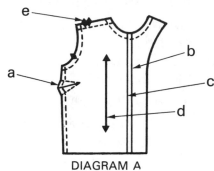

____ 11. Grain line.

____ 12. Center front line.

____ 13. Notch.

DIAGRAM A

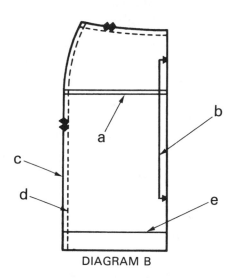

____ 14. Seamline.

____ 15. Place on the fold line.

____ 16. Length adjustment line.

DIAGRAM B

____ 17. To see if a pattern piece is placed on the fabric straight with the grain, measure the distance from:
   a. Both ends of the grainline arrow to the center front line.
   b. Both ends of the pattern piece to the selvage edge.
   c. Both ends of the grainline arrow to the selvage edge.

____ 18. When pinning the pattern to the fabric, pattern pieces should:
   a. All be placed on the fabric before pinning any of them in place.
   b. Be placed on the fabric and pinned one at a time.
   c. Be pinned and cut out one at a time.

____ 19. When cutting out a pattern piece, notches should be cut:
   a. In, toward the seam allowance.
   b. Straight across the notch.
   c. Out, away from the seam allowance.

____ 20. Which of the following is not a method for removing marks left by special fabric marking pens?
   a. Apply a cleaning compound made especially to remove the marks.
   b. Rub marks gently with a dampened cloth.
   c. Allow the marks to fade without doing anything.

(Continued)

Name _____

_____ 21. Marks made with a tracing paper and wheel:
   a. Should always be on the right side of the fabric.
   b. Should always be on the wrong side of the fabric.
   c. Are sometimes placed on the wrong side and sometimes on the right side.

_____ 22. The best method to use when transferring pattern symbols to a thick, fuzzy fabric would be:
   a. Tailor's tacks.
   b. Pins and chalk.
   c. Tracing paper and wheel.

_____ 23. The rule to follow when threading the sewing machine needle is to thread the needle from:
   a. The side of the last thread guide.
   b. Right to left.
   c. Left to right.

_____ 24. When the bobbin thread lies along the lower surface of the fabric, which statement below would be correct?
   a. The upper tension is too loose, so the tension regulator is turned to a smaller number.
   b. The upper tension is too tight, so the tension regulator is turned to a smaller number.
   c. The upper tension is too loose, so the tension regulator is turned to a larger number.

_____ 25. How should a sewing machine needle be placed in a machine?
   a. The short groove on the needle should be on the side of the last thread guide.
   b. The needle can be put in either way.
   c. The long groove on the needle should be on the side of the last thread guide.

_____ 26. The purpose of the sewing machine feed dog is to:
   a. Hold the thread in place.
   b. Move the fabric along.
   c. Control tightness of the thread and move the thread through the machine.

_____ 27. The correct direction for pressing horizontal darts is:
   a. Up, toward the armhole.
   b. Down, toward the hem.
   c. In either direction.

_____ 28. The general rule for pressing is to press:
   a. Each piece immediately after stitching.
   b. When the garment is finished.
   c. After several steps have been completed.

_____ 29. Which of the following garment areas should be pressed on the curved surface of a pressing ham?
   a. The darts.
   b. The hems.
   c. The cuff seams.

(Continued)

Name _____

_____ 30. Plain seams are usually pressed:
   a. To one side.
   b. On a curved surface.
   c. Open, using the point of the iron.

_____ 31. In general, vertical darts should be pressed to the:
   a. Right.
   b. Center of the garment.
   c. Left.

_____ 32. The purpose of staystitching is to prevent:
   a. Raveling while the garment is being made.
   b. Facings from showing on the right side of the garment.
   c. Stretching while the garment is being made.

_____ 33. When should staystitching be done?
   a. As the first stitching process on a garment piece.
   b. Just before the final pressing.
   c. At any point during the construction process.

_____ 34. The direction for staystitching should be:
   a. From the narrow to the wide part of the garment piece.
   b. Away from the center of the garment piece.
   c. With the grain of the fabric.

_____ 35. Where should staystitching be done?
   a. 1/4 inch from the cut edge of a garment piece.
   b. 1/2 inch from the cut edge of a garment piece.
   c. On the seam line of a garment piece.

_____ 36. A plain seam is stitched with:
   a. Right sides of the garment pieces together.
   b. Wrong sides of the garment pieces together.
   c. The right side of one garment piece against the wrong side of the other garment piece.

_____ 37. How far from the cut edge are most plain seams stitched?
   a. 3/8 inch.
   b. 1/2 inch.
   c. 5/8 inch.

_____ 38. If a very sturdy seam is desired, which of the following would be the best choice?
   a. Flat-felled seam.
   b. Plain seam.
   c. Double-stitched seam.

_____ 39. To conceal the seam allowance on a sheer fabric, which of the following would be the best seam choice?
   a. Plain seam.
   b. French seam.
   c. Flat-felled seam.

(Continued)

Name _____

_____ 40. Which of the seam allowances in a shirt is not trimmed?
  a. The facing seam allowance.
  b. The side seam allowance.
  c. The neckline seam allowance.

_____ 41. The purpose of trimming seam allowances is to:
  a. Relieve the strain on the seam allowance.
  b. Eliminate bulk.
  c. Allow the seam to spread and make a smooth curve.

_____ 42. Seam allowances that need trimming should be trimmed to
  a. 1/4 inch.
  b. 1/16 inch.
  c. 1/2 inch.

_____ 43. The term grading means to:
  a. Clip through the various layers of the seam allowance.
  b. Trim the seam allowance.
  c. Trim each layer of the seam allowance to a different width.

_____ 44. If the guide sheet tells you to clip a seam allowance, what should you do?
  a. Cut into the seam allowance several times at right angles to the seamline.
  b. Cut off part of the seam allowance parallel to the seamline.
  c. Cut into the seam allowance at center front.

_____ 45. When using heavy fabric that ravels, which of the following seam finishes would work best?
  a. Turned and stitched.
  b. Stitched and pinked.
  c. Zigzagged.

_____ 46. Which of the following is not a reason for finishing seam edges?
  a. To prevent the seam from raveling during laundering and wearing.
  b. To give the interior of the garment a finished look.
  c. To prevent the seam allowances from stretching.

_____ 47. When using very lightweight fabric that ravels, which of the following seam finishes would work best?
  a. Stitched and pinked.
  b. Turned and stitched.
  c. Zigzagged.

_____ 48. The selection of a seam finishing method to be used on a garment depends most on:
  a. The fabric weight.
  b. The garment design.
  c. The care requirements of the finished garment.

_____ 49. To clean finish the raw edge of a garment piece, you would turn the edge under:
  a. 1/8 inch.
  b. 1/2 inch.
  c. 1/4 inch.

(Continued)

Name _____

_____ 50. The purpose of clean finishing the raw edge of a garment piece is to:
a. Maintain the grainline.
b. Prevent raveling.
c. Prevent stretching.

_____ 51. Which of the following garment pieces should be clean finished?
a. Sleeve placket.
b. Neckline seam.
c. Facing.

_____ 52. The purpose of understitching is to:
a. Keep the facing turned to the underside.
b. Form a line on which to turn under the hem.
c. Keep the outside edge of the facing from raveling.

_____ 53. To understitch you would:
a. Stitch through the facing, seam allowance, and the outer layer of the garment.
b. Stitch 1/4 inch along the facing edge, turn under, press, and stitch again close to the facing edge.
c. Stitch the facing to the seam allowance close to the seamline.

_____ 54. Which of the following garment areas might be understitched?
a. Collar.
b. Waistline seam.
c. Placket opening.

_____ 55. Gathering requires the use of:
a. One row of stitching.
b. Two rows of stitching.
c. Three rows of stitching.

_____ 56. When the instruction sheet tells you to ease the shoulder seam, this means to:
a. Sew two lines of long stitches on the shoulder seam allowance.
b. Match notches and work in the extra fabric.
c. Match the garment pieces at the neckline and trim off the extra at the shoulder.

_____ 57. The size of stitches used for gathering as compared to those used for seams should be:
a. Longer.
b. Shorter.
c. The same size.

_____ 58. In which of the following areas of a garment is there no ease?
a. Waist seam.
b. Underarm portion of armhole seam.
c. Placket opening.

(Continued)

Name _____

Section B

____ 59. Which of the following statements is true?
   a. The only way to accurately determine the fiber content of a fabric is to read the label on the bolt end.
   b. The fiber content, in most cases, can be determined by feeling and looking at the fabric.
   c. The salesclerk will know the fiber content of the fabric.

____ 60. Which of the following characteristics is unique to natural fibers?
   a. Dry quickly.
   b. Build up static electricity.
   c. Absorb moisture and are comfortable to wear.

____ 61. Which of the following characteristics is unique to manufactured fibers?
   a. Tend to shrink.
   b. Are heat sensitive.
   c. Absorb moisture and are comfortable to wear.

____ 62. When selecting a fabric for a summer shirt, which of the following fibers would be the best choice?
   a. Acrylic and nylon blend.
   b. Cotton and polyester blend.
   c. 100 percent polyester.

____ 63. Which of the following characteristics would you expect from a fiber blend of 55 percent cotton and 35 percent rayon.
   a. Nonabsorbent.
   b. Shrinkage.
   c. Static electricity build up.

____ 64. Which of the following can be found on a pattern instruction sheet?
   a. Layout directions for each pattern view.
   b. Yardage requirements for each pattern view.
   c. Fabric recommendations for the garment.

____ 65. Select the statement that best describes the diagram.
   a. Pin wrong side of sleeveband to right side of sleeve, matching notches. Adjust gathers to fit. Stitch.
   b. Pin sleeveband to sleeve right sides together, matching notches and side edges. Adjust gathers to fit. Baste. Stitch.
   c. Pin sleeveband to sleeve right sides together, matching bottom edges and all notches. Baste along unnotched edge. Stitch.

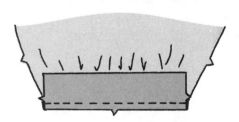

(Continued)

Name _____

_____ 66. Select the diagram that illustrates the following instructions: Turn lower edge of front facing to outside on foldline. Stitch 1 1/4 inch from lower edge.

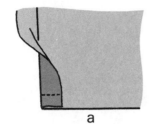
a

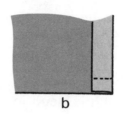
b

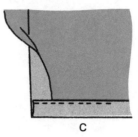
c

_____ 67. To find directions for sewing your garment together, read the instruction sheet starting at:
   a. The beginning of the written instructions.
   b. Any point that describes a garment detail for your view.
   c. The beginning of the written instructions for your view.

_____ 68. The term ease refers to the amount of:
   a. Extra fabric allowed in the garment to make it comfortable to wear.
   b. Fullness added to achieve a specific garment design.
   c. Extra fabric allowed to fit individuals with figure problems.

_____ 69. The amount of ease usually allowed in a waistline seam is:
   a. 2 inches.
   b. 1 inch.
   c. 1/2 inch.

_____ 70. To help you decide how a pattern design is going to fit, read the information given on the:
   a. Instruction sheet that explains how to alter the pattern.
   b. Envelope back that charts the body measurements.
   c. Envelope back that describes the garment features.

_____ 71. When increasing a pant waist seam by 1 inch, how much must the back pattern piece be increased at the side seam?
   a. 1 inch.
   b. 1/4 inch.
   c. 1/2 inch.

_____ 72. To prevent hand sewing thread from tangling, pull the thread over:
   a. An emery bag.
   b. Beeswax.
   c. A glue stick.

_____ 73. Which of the following items would be considered a notion?
   a. Pins.
   b. Seam Ripper.
   c. Zipper.

(Continued)

Name _____

____ 74. Ballpoint sewing machine needles are used to sew on:
   a. Knit fabrics.
   b. Dense fabrics such as denim.
   c. Sheer fabrics.

____ 75. Liquid seam finish may be used by applying it to:
   a. A cut accidently made on the outside of a garment.
   b. The whole length of a seam edge.
   c. The points of a collar.

____ 76. The main reason interfacing is used in a garment is to:
   a. Finish the raw edges of facing pieces.
   b. Provide body and shape to the garment.
   c. Provide a finished look to the inside of the garment.

____ 77. For best results, select interfacing that is:
   a. Slightly heavier than the fashion fabric.
   b. Slightly lighter than the fashion fabric.
   c. The same weight as the fashion fabric.

____ 78. Fusible interfacing may bubble on some fabrics when:
   a. Too much steam is used to apply the interfacing.
   b. The interfacing is too heavy for the fashion fabric.
   c. The iron is set at too high a temperature.

____ 79. Which of the following garment areas should usually be interfaced?
   a. Zipper fly.
   b. Skirt back.
   c. Collar.

____ 80. Which of the following is an example of topstitching?
   a. Turning under 1/4 inch on the facing edge and stitching on the right side of the facing close to the edge.
   b. Stitching on the right side of the facing through the facing and seam allowance.
   c. Stitching around the edge on the right side of the collar.

____ 81. To topstitch a waistband following the guidelines for directional stitching, you would stitch:
   a. From one end of the waistband all the way around.
   b. Each side of the waistband from the same direction.
   c. Each side of the waistband from opposite directions.

____ 82. The purpose of topstitching is to:
   a. Improve the appearance of the garment.
   b. Prevent the seams from rolling to the right side of the garment.
   c. Prevent the garment edges from stretching when it is worn.

____ 83. Topstitching would most likely add to the appearance of a:
   a. Sheer blouse.
   b. Satin evening dress.
   c. Jacket.

(Continued)

Name _____

_____ 84. A basting stitch would be used to:
    a. Temporarily stitch a hand worked buttonhole.
    b. Permanently hand stitch a seam together.
    c. Temporarily hold layers of fabric together.

_____ 85. To hand stitch a hem edge that has not been turned under, use a(n):
    a. Catch stitch.
    b. Overcast stitch.
    c. Slip stitch.

_____ 86. To hand stitch a hem edge that has been turned under, use a(n):
    a. Catch stitch.
    b. Overcast stitch.
    c. Slip stitch.

_____ 87. When hand stitching a pocket to the garment front, the best hand stitch to use would be a:
    a. Rolled-hem stitch.
    b. Catch stitch.
    c. Slip stitch.

_____ 88. Selection of a hemming method depends most on the:
    a. Texture of the fabric.
    b. Weight of the fabric and its tendency to ravel.
    c. Design of the garment being hemmed.

_____ 89. A taped hem would be best used on a garment made from:
    a. Stretch knit fabric.
    b. Fabric that ravels.
    c. Sheer fabric.

_____ 90. When making a shirttail hem, the best hem to use would be a:
    a. Narrow machine hem.
    b. Machine blind hem.
    c. Taped hem.

_____ 91. One function of the stitch finger on a serger is to:
    a. Determine the length of the stitch formed.
    b. Regulate the tension on the thread as the stitch is formed.
    c. Determine the width of the stitch formed.

_____ 92. A serger is generally threaded from:
    a. Right to left, the needle being threaded last.
    b. Left to right, the upper looper being threaded last.
    c. Left to right, the lower looper being threaded last.

_____ 93. Which of the following statements is true about a 3-thread overlock stitch?
    a. One needle and 2 loopers are used to form the stitch.
    b. A chain stitch is formed by the needle and lower looper.
    c. The stitch is not strong enough to sew seams.

(Continued)

Name _____

_____ 94. When the tension is balanced on a serge stitch, the:
   a. Looper threads will interlock at the edge of the fabric and the needle thread will be smooth.
   b. Needle thread and the upper looper thread will interlock at the stitching line.
   c. Looper threads will interlock at the stitching line and the needle thread will be smooth.

_____ 95. Which of the following is not a method for securing serged seam ends?
   a. Backstitching over the ends of the seam.
   b. Knotting the threads and securing them with seam sealant.
   c. Thread the excess chain through a large-eyed needle and run it back under six to eight stitches.

_____ 96. When the serger is not stitching correctly, the first thing to do is:
   a. Clean the lint from the knives and oil the machine.
   b. Check to see if the machine is properly threaded.
   c. Replace the needle.

_____ 97. When choosing a pattern to construct on the serger, select:
   a. A pattern having few seams and details.
   b. A loose, unfitted garment, or a garment where fit is achieved through the stretch of the fabric.
   c. Any pattern, as most are suitable for serging.

_____ 98. The term flat construction refers to a method of construction where:
   a. Edges are serged on flat items such as tableclothes, napkins, and scarves.
   b. Pockets, plackets, and other details are completed before side seams are sewn and sleeves are finally set in.
   c. Necklines, armseyes, sleeves, and hems are finished before underarm and side seams are sewn.

_____ 99. When pin basting garment pieces to be serged, place pins:
   a. Horizontally on the seamline.
   b. Parallel and to the right of the seamline.
   c. Parallel and to the left of the seamline.

_____ 100. When serging a tuck-in shirt hem, the best stitch to use is a:
   a. Finished-edge hem.
   b. Blind hem.
   c. Narrow rolled hem.

_____ 101. When constructing a lettuce-leaf hem on a serger, the ruffling effect may be increased by:
   a. Using stretchy fabric, shortening the stitch length, and gently pushing the fabric under the presser foot.
   b. Using stretchy fabric, shortening the stitch length, and gently stretching the fabric as it is stitched.
   c. Lengthening the stitch length and reducing pressure on the presser foot.

Name _____

Date _____ Period _____

POSTTEST ANALYSIS

Complete the chart below by referring to your corrected posttest. Circle the numbers in the first column of the chart that correspond with the test questions you answered correctly. The numbers in the second column tell how many questions should be answered correctly to demonstrate thorough understanding of the material in each lesson. If you have missed more than the specified number of questions for any lesson, place a check in the third column. This will indicate that you might want to review the lesson before beginning your sewing project.

Compare section A of the chart with section A on the Student Program Plan Sheet you completed in Unit 2. Notice areas in which you have improved. Also notice your areas of success in section B. Use this analysis as you work with your teacher to select and plan your sewing project.

SECTION A

Questions Answered Correctly (Circle)	Correct Number Needed	Lessons To Be Reviewed (✓)	Lessons
1 2 3	3		1—Taking Measurements & Selecting Size
4 5 6	3		2—The Pattern Envelope
7 8 9 10	3		4—Fabric Preparation
11 12 13 14 15 16	5		6—Pattern Symbols
17 18 19	3		8—Pattern Layout, Pinning, & Cutting
20 21 22	3		9—Transferring Pattern Symbols
23 24 25 26	4		11—Operating the Sewing Machine
27 28 29 30 31	4		12—Pressing as You Sew
32 33 34 35	3		13—Staystitching
36 37 38 39	4		14—Seams
40 41 42 43 44	4		15—Clipping, Notching, Trimming, & Grading
45 46 47 48	4		16—Seam Finishes
49 50 51	3		17—Clean Finishing
52 53 54	3		18—Understitching
55 56 57 58	3		19—Easing & Gathering

(Continued)

Name _____

SECTION B

Questions Answered Correctly (Circle)	Correct Number Needed	Lessons To Be Reviewed (✓)	Lessons
59 60 61 62 63	4		3—Making Fabric Choices
64 65 66 67	3		5—Reading the Instruction Sheet
68 69 70 71	4		7—Pattern Adjustments
72 73 74 75	4		10—Small Equipment & Notions
76 77 78 79	3		20—Interfacing
80 81 82 83	3		21—Topstitching
84 85 86 87	3		22—Hand Stitching
88 89 90	3		23—Hemming Methods
91 92 93 94 95 96	5		44—Operating the Serger Machine
97 98 99 100 101	5		45—Serger Construction Techniques

Unit 5 Project Selection and Planning

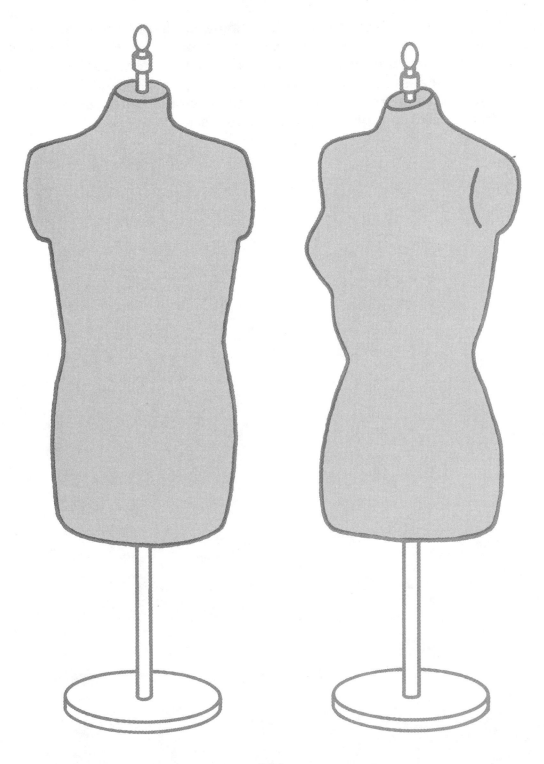

Unit 5
Project Selection and Planning

    This unit is designed to assist you in selecting and planning your sewing project. It is composed of worksheets that will help you choose a project suited to your skill level. Additional worksheets will help you analyze the cost and care requirements of your materials. A final set of worksheets lists steps you will need to follow in order to complete your sewing project. As you fill in these worksheets, you will be referring to lessons from Unit 3 and planning which lessons to complete in Unit 6.

Name _____

Date _____ Period _____

SKILL CHECKLIST

Below are four lists of sewing skills grouped by level of difficulty. Using the rating scale below, place the number in each box that indicates how well you perform that specific skill. Then total your score for each skill group in the space provided.

0 — Never attempted the skill before.
1 — Attempted the skill but did not do very well.
2 — Perform the skill moderately well.
3 — Perform the skill exceptionally well.

Skill Group A
1. Darts
2. Tucks
3. Plain seam
4. Zigzagged seam finish
5. Machine-worked buttonholes
6. Hooks and eyes or snaps
7. Patch pockets
8. Neck or armhole facing
9. Machine-stitched hem
10. Elastic casing
    Total score for Skill Group A

Skill Group B
1. Hand-sewn hem
2. Flat-felled seam
3. Pleats
4. Interfaced waistband
5. Waistline facing
6. Seam pocket
7. Two-lapped or centered zipper
8. One-lapped zipper
9. Fly front zipper
   Total score for Skill Group B

Skill Group C
1. Interfaced front bodice facing
2. Invisible zipper
3. Waistline seam stay
4. Flat collar
5. Rolled collar
6. Set-in sleeves
7. Raglan sleeves
8. Sleeve placket
9. Interfaced cuffs
10. Rolled cuffs
11. Interfaced collar band
12. Front opening placket
13. Bound seam
    Total score for Skill Group C

Skill Group D
1. Bound buttonholes
2. Lining or underlining
3. Shoulder pads
4. Interfaced lapels
5. Welt pockets
6. French seam
7. Bound hem
8. Rolled hem
   Total score for Skill Group D

Name _____

Date _____ Period _____

PROJECT SELECTION WORKSHEET

The type of project you choose should be related to your skill level. Refer to your total scores for each skill group on the Skill Checklist. Then use the chart below to determine the group from which you select your sewing project. If you plan to complete more than one sewing project, select future projects from a more advanced group. Record your project choice in the space provided.

PROJECT SELECTION CHART

To Select Your Project from Group	Your scores for these skill groups should be:		
	A	B	C
A	Less than 20	—	—
B	More than 20	Less than 18	—
C	More than 20	More than 18	Less than 26
D	More than 20	More than 18	More than 26

Group A	Group C
Jumper	Shirt with a collar and/or sleeves
Wraparound skirt	Dress with a collar and/or sleeves
Jumpsuit without sleeves or a collar	Jumpsuit with a collar and/or sleeves
Shirt without a collar or set-in sleeves	
Pants or a skirt with an elastic casing at the waist	
Group B	**Group D**
Pants with a waistband and a zipper	Blazer
Jeans	Jacket
Skirt with a waistband and a zipper	Coat
	Detailed dress

Project you have selected: _____

Name _____

Date _____ Period _____

PATTERN SELECTION WORKSHEET

You should consider your skill level when choosing a pattern. Try to select a pattern that is challenging but can be completed successfully. A pattern's level of difficulty is based partly on the number of pattern pieces required to make a garment. Patterns with a lot of pieces tend to be more difficult to construct than those with only a few pieces. The design of a pattern also affects its level of difficulty. For instance, a pattern with set-in sleeves would be more difficult than a pattern with armhole facings.

Remember that pattern companies have different classifications for different levels of difficulty. Use the information found in pattern catalogs to help you determine the pattern classification that is right for you. Then choose a pattern from this classification for the type of garment you selected on the previous page.

Fill in information about the pattern you choose in the box below. Then answer the questions that follow.

Pattern company:

_____

Pattern classification:

_____

Pattern number:

_____

Sketch a picture of your pattern in the space provided at the right. You may want to trace the picture on the pattern envelope. Your teacher will need this sketch for reference.

Complete the following statements.

1. My pattern is appropriate for my skill level because:

_____

_____

2. My pattern design is appropriate for my body structure because:

_____

_____

Name _____

Date _____ Period _____

FABRIC SELECTION WORKSHEET

The type of fabric you choose can add to the difficulty of your project. It can also affect the way your garment will look. Read the list of suggested fabrics on your pattern envelope. Then use this worksheet to help you choose one of those fabrics that is appropriate for your skill level. Record your fabric choice in the space provided and then answer the questions that follow.

REFER TO YOUR PROJECT SELECTION WORKSHEET.

If you selected your project from Group A on the Project Selection Worksheet, then select your fabric from Group 1 on this page.

> **Group 1**
>
> Tightly woven medium-weight fabrics
> Stable knits

If you selected your project from Group B, then select your fabric from Group 1 or 2 on this page.

> **Group 2**
>
> Light-, medium-, or heavy-weight fabrics
> Plaids, checks, or stripes
> One-way designs
> Napped fabrics such as corduroy

If you selected your project from Group C, then select your fabric from Group 1, 2, or 3 on this page.

> **Group 3**
>
> Stretch knits
> Loosely woven fabrics

If you selected your project from Group D, you may select your fabric from any group on this page. You may wish to select a fabric you have not used before as this will increase your learning.

> **Group 4**
>
> Slippery fabrics such as crepe de chine or satin
> Bulky fabrics
> Sheer or lace fabrics
> Pile fabrics such as velvet or velveteen
> Vinyls
> Synthetic leathers, suedes, or furs

Your fabric selection:_____

(Continued)

266

Name _____

Complete the following statements:

1. My fabric and pattern will look good together because:

   _____

   _____

2. My fabric is appropriate for my body structure because:

   _____

   _____

3. My fabric is appropriate for my skill level because:

   _____

   _____

Name _____

Date _____ Period _____

PROJECT COST WORKSHEET

Fill in the chart and then answer the questions below.

Cost of Project	
Total Yardage _____	
Price per Yard $_____	
Cost of Fashion Fabric	$_____
Cost of Lining	_____
Cost of Interfacing	_____
Cost of Notions Zipper $ _____	
Thread _____	
Pattern _____	
Trim _____	
Buttons _____	
Other _____	
_____	
_____	
Total Cost of Notions	_____
Total Cost of Project	$_____

1. Complete the following statements:

   a. I was willing to spend the amount shown for my materials because:

   _____

   _____

   b. I think making this project will be a worthwhile use of my time because:

   _____

   _____

2. Compare the cost and time involved in making your project with the cost and time involved in purchasing a comparable item.

   _____

   _____

   _____

Name _____

Date _____ Period _____

PLANNING YOUR PROJECT

Fill in the information required and attach swatches in the chart below. Then complete the exercises that follow. If necessary, refer to the lessons indicated.

FIBER CONTENT	CARE INSTRUCTIONS		SAMPLE SWATCH
Fashion Fabric:	Cleaning:		
	Pressing:		
Interfacing:	Cleaning:		
	Pressing:		
Linings and Underlinings:	Cleaning:		
	Pressing:		
Trims:	Cleaning:		
	Pressing:		

1. Explain whether all of the fabrics and trims you are using will be compatible in terms of care. (Refer to Lesson 3, ''Making Fabric Choices.'')

   _____

   _____

2. List any special finishes that have been applied to your fabric(s).

   _____

   _____

3. Based on the fiber content and special finishes, list the steps you will take to prepare your fabric(s) for construction. (Refer to Lesson 3, ''Making Fabric Choices.'')

   _____

   _____

   _____

4. Check all of the boxes that apply to your fashion fabric. Use your responses to help you answer the questions that follow.

   ☐ Lightweight   ☐ Tightly woven   ☐ Plaid

   ☐ Medium weight   ☐ Loosely woven   ☐ Stripe

   ☐ Heavy weight   ☐ Stable knit   ☐ One-way design

   ☐ Sheer   ☐ Stretch knit   ☐ Nap

   ☐ Bulky   ☐ Ravels

(Continued)

Name _____

5. Explain how you will fold your fabric and what techniques you will use when laying out your pattern pieces. (Refer to Lesson 8, "Pattern Layout, Pinning, and Cutting.")

_____

_____

6. Identify the method you will use to mark pattern symbols on your fabric and explain your choice. (Refer to Lesson 9, "Transferring Pattern Symbols to the Fabric.")

_____

_____

7. Check the pressing problems you may encounter for your fashion fabric. You may need to test a swatch of your fabric.

☐ Heat sensitivity ☐ Crushed nap ☐ Fusible inferfacing not compatible
☐ Shine from iron ☐ Iron marks
☐ Other _____ (Do a test swatch.)

Explain how you will avoid the problems you checked. (Refer to Lesson 12, "Pressing as You Sew.")

_____

_____

_____

8. Identify the type of seam you will use on your fabric and explain your choice. (Refer to Lesson 14, "Seams.")

_____

_____

9. Identify the type of seam finish you will use on your fabric and explain your choice. (Refer to Lesson 16, "Seam Finishes.")

_____

_____

10. Identify the type of interfacing you have chosen to use with your fashion fabric and explain your choice. (Refer to Lesson 20, "Interfacing.")

_____

_____

11. Identify the hemming method you will use on your fabric and explain your choice. (Refer to Lesson 23, "Hemming Methods.")

_____

_____

Name _____

Date _____ Period _____

BEGINNING YOUR PROJECT

Read through the following outline. In the last column, list the lessons that will help you complete each step.

Use this outline as a reference as you work on your project. Following the steps in order will help you construct your project with a minimum of difficulty. Be sure to complete each step before proceeding to the next step. Refer to the lessons you listed in the right-hand column as needed.

STEP	DESCRIPTION	LESSON REFERENCE
1	Prepare your fabric according to the decisions you made on your plan sheet. Straightening the grain and preshrinking the fabric may be steps you will need to complete.	
2	Select the pattern pieces for the view of the pattern that you are planning to make. Return all pieces that you will not be using to the pattern envelope. Write your name on the instruction sheet, the envelope, and on all pattern pieces.	
3	Prepare your pattern for layout and cutting by making any necessary alterations.	
4	Select and circle the layout diagram that you will be using. Keep in mind your pattern size and fabric width. Remember to use a ''with nap'' layout when appropriate. Lay out your pattern pieces according to the diagram you circled. Be sure to measure for grainline accuracy. Watch for fold lines and bias cut pieces. Match all plaids and stripes.	
5	Have your teacher check your layout before you begin to cut out the pattern pieces.	
6	Cut out the pattern pieces. Remember to keep fabric flat on the table while cutting. Cut with regular shears. Cut notches out away from seam allowances. Cut in the direction indicated on the pattern. Clean up scraps as you cut. Keep larger scraps until you have finished your project. Your teacher may have a scrap box for storing scraps you do not want.	
7	Mark pattern symbols according to the decision you made on your plan sheet. Remember, do not use pencil or pen to mark as it may not wash out.	
8	Staystitch curved areas such as necklines and waistlines. Be careful not to stretch your fabric.	
9	When using the sewing machine, always begin by looking at the dial settings. Check the tension by stitching on a fabric scrap. Adjust tension and settings if necessary.	
10	Read your direction sheet carefully to determine how you should proceed. Pattern construction steps will vary depending on the design of the garment. Remember to press as you sew.	

(Continued)

Name _____

STEP	DESCRIPTION	LESSON REFERENCE
11	Select the specific lessons for the construction details that you will be completing on your project. Read through the lessons that you need. Each lesson contains a statement of the objective, previously acquired skills, helps for success, and evaluation criteria. Read over the evaluation sheet before you begin constructing the detail. This will give you an idea of your construction goals. After you have completed the detail on your garment, fill out the evaluation form and take it to your teacher. Your teacher may also want to evaluate each step of your project.	
12	Turn in your garment. Be sure threads have been clipped and the garment has been pressed. Complete the final evaluation form. Turn it in with your project. Your teacher will also evaluate your project.	

Unit 6 Constructing the Project

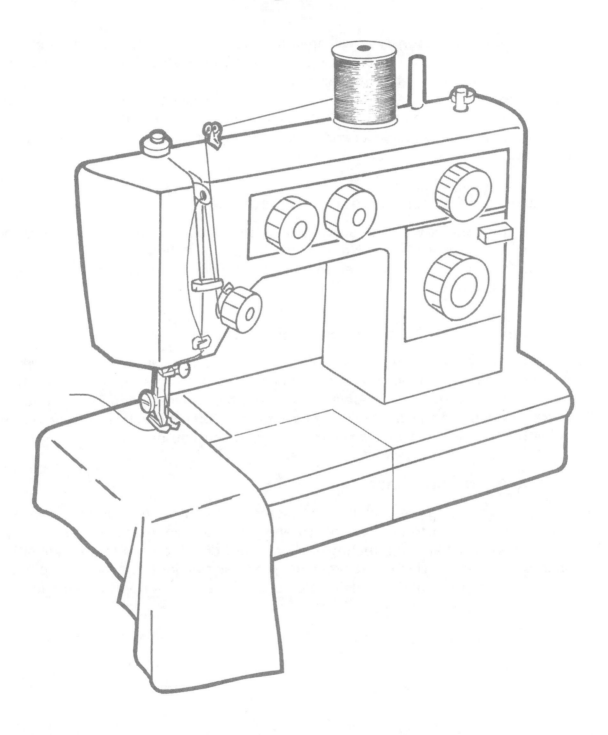

Unit 6
Constructing the Project

This unit consists of lessons you will need to study in order to construct your sewing project. You will need to be concerned only with those lessons that apply to your sewing project. You will not be using all of the lessons. Other students in your class may be using lessons different from the ones that you will be using. Read through each lesson before you begin constructing the detail discussed. If you do this, you will know what you must do to be successful and how to go about constructing each detail of your garment. The lessons include three sections.

The Objective and Previous Learnings Required

This part of the lesson will tell you what you are to learn. It will also tell you the previous learnings you will be applying. If you have any difficulties as you are constructing your project or feel you need to review the skills listed, return to the proper lesson in your textbook.

Helps for Successful Construction of Each Detail

For each garment detail, helps are given for construction. Study each help sheet carefully. Try to find information that may not be found on the pattern instruction sheet or that you do not already know. Always read your pattern instruction sheet and the help sheets before asking your teacher for assistance. You need to be informed before you talk with the teacher. However, ask for help when you need it.

An Evaluation Criteria Sheet

Be sure to read this page of each lesson before you begin constructing the garment detail. This will help you to identify the criteria for which you need to strive.

When you have finished constructing each garment detail, complete the evaluation sheet according to your teachers directions. Be prepared to take a few minutes to show your teacher what you have done and to discuss the evaluation with your teacher.

Lesson 24

Constructing Darts, Tucks, or Pleats

Objectives

This lesson will help you to construct darts, tucks, or pleats. You will apply the following, previously acquired skills:

Lesson 5:   Reading the Instruction Sheet
Lesson 6:   Pattern Symbols
Lesson 11: Operating the Sewing Machine
Lesson 12: Pressing as You Sew

Helps for Success

Darts, tucks, and pleats help give a garment the shape you want. They are generally constructed before garment seams are sewn. As you construct a dart, tuck, or pleat, these guidelines may be helpful.

CONSTRUCTING THE DART

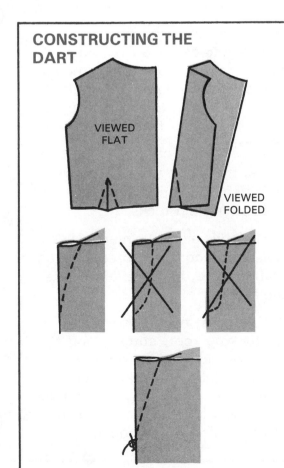

VIEWED FLAT

VIEWED FOLDED

The purpose of the dart is to shape flat fabric to fit curves of the body. To make good-fitting garments with darts, follow these steps:

1. Mark dart lines accurately.

2. Fold the dart (right sides together) along the solid center line and match the two outer broken lines. A pin may be pushed through both layers of fabric on the lines to match them exactly. Pin the dart for sewing.

3. Stitch along the broken lines. When stitching the dart, correct shaping is important for perfect fit. Strive for a dart stitching line that will curve slightly away from the body and have a finely tapered point.

   Begin stitching at the wide end of the dart. Be sure to backstitch. However, for the smoothest dart tip, do not backstitch at that end. Rather, hand tie the knot at the tapered point of the dart.

(Continued)

275

4. Press the finished dart toward center lines of the garment or downward, whichever is appropriate. Press the dart over a tailor's ham to maintain contour in the garment piece.

5. Check the dart for fit.

CONSTRUCTING TUCKS AND PLEATS

Tucks and pleats are used to provide fullness in desired areas of the garment. To make tucks and pleats, follow these steps:

1. You will usually have solid lines and broken lines. Mark both types of lines accurately.

2. Fold the solid line over to match the broken line. Insert a pin through both layers of fabric on the marked lines to check accuracy. Pin securely in place.

3. Double check before the final stitching to make sure that tucks or pleats are consistent in size and that they are turned in the correct direction.

CONSTRUCTING PIN TUCKS

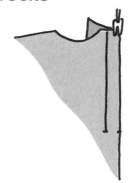

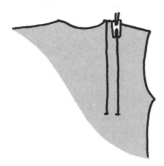

Pin tucks are used to create a decorative effect. Begin by marking the location of the pin tucks. Then stitch using one of the methods described below. When stitching pin tucks, always stitch in the same direction to avoid distorting the fabric.

Method 1. Fold the fabric along the marked line. Machine stitch 1/8 inch from the fold. Repeat with remaining pin tucks.

Method 2. Fold fabric along the marked lines. Using a serger and decorative thread, stitch close to the fabric edge, being careful blades do not cut the fabric.

Method 3. Using a twin needle and, if desired, a pin tucking foot; stitch along the marked lines. Do not fold the fabric. Increase the upper tension slightly to make the tuck more pronounced. Cording may be placed under the fabric and caught in the stitching to make the pin tucks more pronounced.

Name _____

Date _____ Period _____

Evaluation Criteria: Darts, Tucks, and Pleats

Before you begin construction, read through the criteria listed below. After constructing each detail, complete this form according to your teacher's directions. Turn this sheet in to your teacher and be prepared to discuss each item.

DARTS

	Did not follow procedure correctly.	Followed procedure but had some difficulty.	Nicely done but with more practice could do better	Exceptionally well done.
Darts are tapered to a fine point.				
Dart point is tied off.				
Darts are pressed down or toward center of garment.				
Darts fit curve of body.				
Threads are clipped.				

TUCKS AND PLEATS

Tucks and pleats are uniform in size.				
Tucks and pleats are pressed in the direction suggested by the pattern.				
Threads are clipped.				

notes

Lesson 25 Constructing Seams

Objectives

This lesson will help you to stitch seams and finish seam edges. You will apply the following, previously acquired skills:

Lesson 5:   Reading the Instruction Sheet
Lesson 11: Operating the Sewing Machine
Lesson 12: Pressing as You Sew
Lesson 14: Seams
Lesson 15: Clipping, Notching, Trimming, and Grading
Lesson 16: Seam Finishes

Helps for Success

Well constructed seams are the most basic part of any garment. For seam and seam finish variations, see Lessons 14 and 16. Other guidelines for sewing seams are given below.

PIN BASTING SEAMS

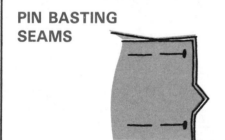

The seam should be pinned before stitching. Match the ends of the seam and all notches. Pin the layers together.

Place the pins at right angles to the seam so that they may be easily removed during stitching. Remove pins before sewing over them.

ADDING STRETCH TO SEAMS

Some seams will need to have more give. For instance, when sewing on knit fabric, seams should stretch with the fabric. Always test your stitching on a fabric scrap to see if it is strong enough to withstand any stress applied.

The following stitches may be used to add stretch to a seam: narrow zigzag stitch, multiple zigzag stitch, stretch stitch, and twin-needle stitch.

(Continued)

If you must use a straight stitch, some stretch may be added by gently pulling on the fabric in front of and behind the machine needle. Be sure you allow the fabric to feed under the machine foot as you pull gently. Test this method on your fabric because it may cause the seam to pucker.

DIRECTIONAL STITCHING

Seams should be stitched with the grain of the fabric. On an edge that has already been staystitched, seams may be sewn in any direction. This is because the area has already been stabilized. (For instance, the neck seam may be stitched in any direction.)

With napped or pile fabrics, stitch with the nap even if it is against the grain.

When you are unsure of the direction to stitch, a good rule is to stitch similar seams or seams that will be sewn together in the same direction. For instance, stitch all pant leg seams from the bottom to the top.

STABILIZING SEAMS

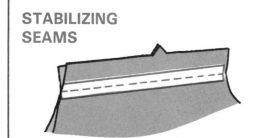

This procedure is especially useful on knit fabrics and in garment areas where greater stability is needed. Such areas include shoulder, armhole, neckline, crotch, and waistline seams.

To stabilize the seam, stitch narrow seam binding or twill tape into the seam.

MATCHING PLAIDS

Method 1: pin basting. To match plaids by pin basting, follow these steps:

1. Pin the layers of fabric together. Make sure each pin is positioned in a manner that will line up the plaid on the two layers of fabric.

2. Stitch up to each pin before removing it.

Method 2: hand basting. To match plaids by hand basting, follow these steps:

1. Press under a 5/8-inch seam allowance on the garment pieces that are to be sewn together.

2. With right sides of the garment pieces up, hand baste the seam together being sure to match the plaid.

3. Place right sides of garment pieces together again, and machine stitch the seam. Remove the hand basting stitches.

HELPFUL SEWING HINTS

Basting tape or a glue stick may be used to hold seams in place while stitching. They can be especially helpful when matching plaids for seams. To match plaids, begin by pressing a crease along one seamline. The crease will provide you with an accurate guide for placing the tape or glue. Next, apply basting tape or glue stick in the seam allowance along the crease line. Place the seam allowance of the second garment piece over the one with the tape or glue. Finger press the two layers of fabric together aligning the plaid as you go. Turn the pieces to the wrong side and machine stitch along the crease.

Name _____

Date _____ Period _____

Evaluation Criteria: Seams

Before you begin construction, read through the criteria listed below. After constructing each detail, complete this form according to your teacher's directions. Turn this sheet in to your teacher and be prepared to discuss each item.

	Did not follow procedure correctly.	Followed procedure but had some difficulty.	Nicely done but with more practice could do better.	Exceptionally well done.
Stitching is straight.				
Seam is even in width.				
Edge of seam is finished appropriately for fabric being used.				
Seam is backstitched at both ends.				
Appropriate stitch and stitch length is used.				
Appropriate method of constructing the seam is used.				
Seam is pressed.				
Threads are clipped.				

Lesson 26 Constructing Pockets

Objective

This lesson will help you to construct pockets. You will apply the following, previously acquired skills:

Lesson 5: Reading the Instruction Sheet
Lesson 6: Pattern Symbols
Lesson 9: Transferring Pattern Symbols to the Fabric
Lesson 11: Operating the Sewing Machine
Lesson 12: Pressing as You Sew
Lesson 15: Clipping, Notching, Trimming, and Grading
Lesson 16: Seam Finishes
Lesson 17: Clean Finishing
Lesson 20: Interfacing
Lesson 21: Topstitching

Helps for Success

Pockets are functional, but they should be attractive as well. Whether you construct a patch pocket or a seam pocket, the pocket should be durable, usable, and neat. The following tips will help.

PERFECTLY SHAPED PATCH POCKETS

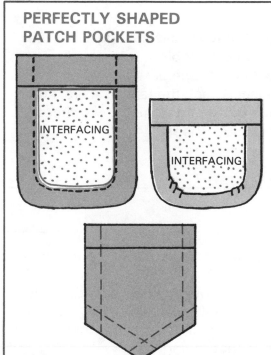

Two methods can be used to achieve perfectly shaped patch pockets.

Method 1. Cut fusible interfacing to the finished size of the pocket. Cut accurately. Position the interfacing inside the seamlines on the wrong side of the pocket and fuse in place.

Complete the pocket hem according to the pattern instruction sheet. On the remaining edges of the pocket, press the seam allowance up over the interfacing. The interfacing provides shaping for the pocket as well as a guideline for pressing over the seam allowance.

Method 2. Stitch along the pocket seamline. Be careful to stitch accurately. This will provide a guide for turning and pressing the pocket seam allowance.

ELIMINATING BULK

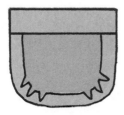

If the pocket has rounded corners, excess fabric must be removed from the seam allowance at the corners of the pocket. Cut small notches of fabric from the seam allowance on each curved area. This will allow the corner to lie smoothly when pressed over.

HEMMING

Finish the top edge of the pocket using a method that is appropriate for the fabric.

Light- to medium-weight fabrics. Turn under the edge 1/4 inch and stitch close to the folded edge.

Heavier fabrics. Zigzag or serge stitch the hem edge.

Stable knits and tightly woven fabrics. Stitch 1/4 inch from the edge and pink.

STAYS FOR BIAS CUT POCKET EDGES

Many pockets have a bias cut edge. The bias will stretch. You can stabilize this edge by stitching a piece of hem tape or twill tape over the seam allowance. Attach the tape as a first step. Then continue pocket construction as directed by your instruction sheet.

TOPSTITCHING

Topstitching often serves a functional purpose on pockets. It is used to prevent the pocket facing from rolling to the outside of the garment or to stitch the pocket to the garment. For ideas on maintaining even stitching, see Lesson 21, ''Topstitching.''

**POSITIONING
PATCH POCKET**

Do not feel that you must place pockets in the exact location indicated by the pattern. Place the pockets to enhance the appearance of the garment. A slight change in location may make the garment more attractive on you.

Take the following precautions to make sure the pockets are lined up correctly.

1. If you are positioning the pockets according to the pattern symbols, use a chalk pencil or pins to transfer the symbols to your fabric. Position the pockets; pin in place.

2. If you are lining up two pockets, one on each side of the garment, *measure* from the edge of the garment to the pockets. Then you will be sure they are the same on both sides of the garment.

3. Look to make sure the pockets are correctly located. Be sure to check and see how they look with the garment on the body.

VARIATIONS

Pockets can be made in many shapes and sizes. Try creating your own shape and stitching design.

SEAM POCKETS

Seam pockets are attached in the seam of a garment. They usually do not show on the outside when the garment is finished.

Use lining fabrics, if possible, for seam pockets. This will cut down on bulk and give a flatter look in the hipline and stomach areas. When using lining fabric for seam pockets, be sure the pocket will not show when the garment is worn.

Construct seam pockets according to the pattern instruction sheet.

Name _____

Date _____ Period _____

Evaluation Criteria: Pockets

Before you begin construction, read through the criteria listed below. After constructing each detail, complete this form according to your teacher's directions. Turn this sheet in to your teacher and be prepared to discuss each item.

	Did not follow procedure correctly.	Followed procedure but had some difficulty.	Nicely done but with more practice could do better.	Exceptionally well done.
An approved procedure was followed.				
Pockets are uniformly shaped.				
An appropriate method was used to finish the hem.				
Pockets are clipped and trimmed where necessary.				
Bias cut areas are stabilized with a stay.				
Lining fabric is used when possible to reduce bulk.				
Pockets are positioned evenly on the garment.				
Threads are clipped.				
Shows evidence of having been pressed as sewn.				
Topstitching is an even distance from edge.				
Pockets are cut out on the straight of grain.				

Lesson 27 Constructing Ties

Objective

This lesson will help you to construct ties. You will apply the following, previously acquired skills:

Lesson 5:   Reading the Instruction Sheet
Lesson 6:   Pattern Symbols
Lesson 11:   Operating and Sewing Machine
Lesson 12:   Pressing as You Sew
Lesson 14:   Seams
Lesson 15:   Clipping, Notching, Trimming, and Grading
Lesson 22:   Hand Stitching

Helps for Success

Ties made of fabric which coordinates with a garment are an attractive detail. Whether ties are wide or narrow, ties can be constructed easily with a few simple guidelines.

TURNING NARROW TIES

Follow these steps:

1. Prepare the tie for turning as directed by your pattern instruction sheet. *Do not* sew across either end of the tie.

2. Thread a needle with a very long double thread.

3. Attach the end of the thread to the tie as shown. Be sure the thread is securely attached. You do not want it to pull out as you are turning the tie.

4. Push the *blunt* end of the needle through the tie. Be sure not to pick up any of the fabric.

5. Once the thread and needle are through the tie, begin working the fabric through. Pull on the threaded needle with one hand and use the other hand to assist the fabric along.

**TURNING
WIDE TIES**

Follow these steps:

1. Prepare the tie for turning as directed by your pattern instruction sheet. Stitch across one end of the tie.

2. Begin at the stitched end of the tie. With a pencil or similar blunt object, push the end of the tie through the tube. A ruler works well for larger ties. Continue to work the fabric over the pencil until the tie has been turned right side out.

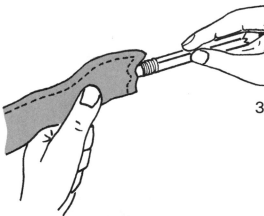

3. Once the tie has been turned, press the tie. To make sharp, well defined edges, roll the seam between the thumb and fingers. Press along the seam. Also, use a needle or pin to gently pull out the corners and make them square.

**MAKING CORDED
TUBING**

Follow these steps:

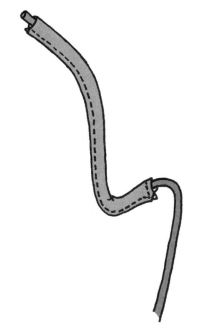

1. Determine the length of tubing you will need. Add several inches to the total called for by your pattern.

2. Cut out bias strips of fabric for the tubing. To get the required length of tubing, sew the strips together, if necessary.

3. Cut a piece of cording that is twice the length of the tubing strip.

4. Leave 1/2 inch of cord free at one end. Fold the fabric strip, wrong side out, around the cord. Pin the edges together. Leave half of the cord free at the other end.

5. Using a zipper foot, stitch across the end of the cording and tubing as shown. Pivot and stitch toward the cording.

(Continued)

6. Stitch the length of the tubing, close to the cording. Do not catch the cording in the seam. Stretch the strip slightly as you stitch. Remove pins before stitching over them. Backstitch at end of seam.

7. Trim seam allowance to 1/4 inch.

8. Turn the tubing by pulling on the loose 1/2 inch of cording with one hand. With the opposite hand assist the fabric along over the free half of the cord.

PULL

9. After the tubing has been turned, trim off the extra cording at both ends.

10. Push back the tubing at each end and trim off 1/4 inch of cord. Tuck the raw edges of the tubing inside and slip stitch each end closed.

Name _____

Date _____ Period _____

Evaluation Criteria: Ties

Before you begin construction, read through the criteria listed below. After constructing each detail, complete this form according to your teacher's directions. Turn this sheet in to your teacher and be prepared to discuss each item.

	Did not follow procedure correctly.	Followed procedure but had some difficulty.	Nicely done but with more practice could do better.	Exceptionally well done.
Ties are the same width throughout the full length.				
Ties are pressed on the seam edge.				
Threads are clipped.				
Ties are attached to the garment at the location indicated by pattern.				
Hand tacking shows as little as possible and knots are hidden.				

Lesson 28 Constructing Waistline Seams and Stays

Objective

This lesson will help you to construct a waistline seam and stay. You will apply the following, previously acquired skills:

Lesson 5: Reading the Instruction Sheet
Lesson 6: Pattern Symbols
Lesson 11: Operating the Sewing Machine
Lesson 12: Pressing as You Sew
Lesson 14: Seams
Lesson 16: Seam Finishes
Lesson 19: Easing and Gathering

Helps for Success

Waistline seams are fairly easy to construct. The guidelines below will help.

STITCHING THE WAISTLINE SEAM	Follow these steps:
	1. Adjust any tucks, gathers, or pleats that are indicated on the pattern.
	2. Baste the bodice and bottom units together. Be sure to keep a 5/8 inch seam allowance.
	3. Try on the garment and check the waist fit.
	4. Permanent stitch the seam and then finish the seam edge if needed. If you wish to use a stay, follow the directions below.

ATTACHING THE STAY	
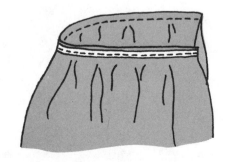	The stay provides greater stability in the waistline seam. It allows the seam to withstand the stress often given to this garment area. It also prevents this seam from stretching. The stay should be a non-stretch tape such as hem tape or twill tape.
	Cut the tape the same length as the waistline seam. Position the tape over the waistline seam and stitch in place.
	The finished seam is generally pressed toward the bodice.

Name _____

Date _____ Period _____

Evaluation Criteria: Waistline Seam and Stay

 . Before you begin construction, read through the criteria listed below. After constructing each detail, complete this form according to your teacher's directions. Turn this sheet in to your teacher and be prepared to discuss each item.

	Did not follow procedure correctly.	Followed procedure but had some difficulty.	Nicely done but with more practice could do better.	Exceptionally well done.
An approved procedure was followed.				
Seam is 5/8 inch in width.				
Seam is finished appropriately for fabric.				
Machine stitching is straight and appropriate length.				
Any tucks or gathers are evenly distributed.				
Bodice and lower part of garment joined according to pattern symbols.				
Shows evidence of pressing. Seam is pressed in recommended direction.				
Threads are clipped.				
Stay is a nonstretch material (twill tape or hem tape).				
Stay is stitched securely and centered over waistline seam.				
Waistline fits body.				

Lesson 29 Inserting Zippers

Objective

This lesson will help you to insert a zipper. You will apply the following, previously acquired skills:

Lesson 5: Reading the Instruction Sheet
Lesson 6: Pattern Symbols
Lesson 11: Operating the Sewing Machine
Lesson 12: Pressing as You Sew
Lesson 13: Staystitching
Lesson 14: Seams
Lesson 16: Seam Finishes
Lesson 21: Topstitching

Helps for Success

There are a number of methods for inserting zippers. For example, there are methods for inserting a zipper with one lap or two laps. Special methods can be used to insert zippers in stretch knit fabrics or to make an invisible zipper. Helps for a variety of methods can be found on these pages. Select the method that is most appropriate for your fabric and garment.

PREPARING THE SEAM	Finish the edge of the seam allowance where the zipper will be inserted according to the requirements of your fabric.
	In most cases, the seam below the zipper opening should be stitched closed. When inserting an invisible zipper, the seam is not stitched below the zipper until after the zipper is inserted.

BIAS CUT EDGES	
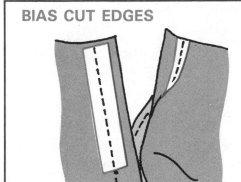	Sometimes a zipper must be inserted into a bias cut seam. This can create a problem because the bias will stretch. To prevent this problem, pin and stitch a piece of twill tape or non-stretch hem tape along the seamline of the bias edges. Stitch the tape to the wrong side of the fabric. Be sure not to stretch the fabric as you sew.

IF THE ZIPPER IS TOO LONG

Synthetic coil zippers are self-locking at any point along the zipper. Therefore, you may cut them off at either the bottom or top. However, never cut off the excess until you have sewn over the tape. You do not want the slider to zip off the zipper tape.

FOR EVEN TOPSTITCHING

There are many new, clear, plastic guides available that can be used to make topstitching easier. Begin by selecting the desired finished seam width on the guide. Then place the teeth on the underside of the guide along the seamline. With the zipper foot in place, stitch along the edge of the plastic guide.

If plastic guides are unavailable, try using 1/2-inch wide cellophane or masking tape as a topstitching guide. Place the tape along the folded edge for a one-lapped zipper. Center it over the seam for a two-lapped, or centered, zipper. Stitch along the edge of the tape.

Do not use this method on velvet or corduroy because it may damage the pile. Test your fabric if you are in doubt whether to use tape as a stitching guide.

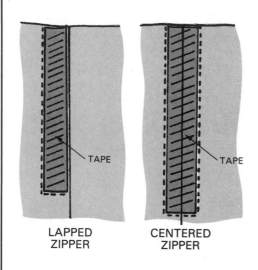

LAPPED ZIPPER   CENTERED ZIPPER

CENTERED ZIPPER

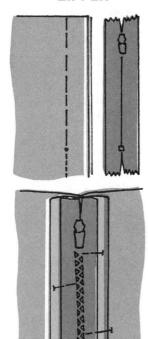

This type of zipper application is used for center back locations in dresses, jumpers, and skirts. It is also used for center front zippers on dresses, jumpers, and jumpsuits. To apply a centered zipper, follow these steps:

1. Mark the length of the zipper on the seam into which it will be inserted. Generally, the top edge of the zipper tape is placed even with the top of the seam.

2. Stitch the seam closed below the zipper marking.

3. Baste the seam closed above the zipper marking.

4. Press the seam open.

5. Center the zipper, face down, over the seam allowance. Make sure the coil is exactly over the seam. Pin in place. Baste or secure with basting tape.

(Continued)

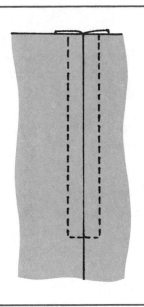

6. Select a method to ensure even topstitching. (See Lesson 21, "Topstitching.")

7. Attach the zipper foot to the sewing machine. On the outside of the garment, stitch along the sides and across the bottom of the zipper.

8. Remove the basting threads used to sew the seam together and to baste the zipper in place.

LAPPED ZIPPERS

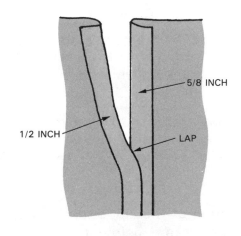

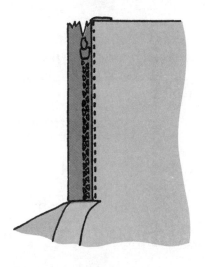

Use one-lapped zippers for skirt zippers, pant side seam or back zippers, and some back zippers on dresses or jumpers. To insert a lapped zipper in a side seam, follow these steps:

1. Mark the length of the zipper on the seam. Stitch the seam below the marking.

2. Press the front edge of the zipper opening to the wrong side along the seamline.

3. Press the back edge of the zipper opening to the wrong side. Press this side under 1/2 inch.

4. With the garment piece right side up, pin the zipper along the edge with a 1/2-inch allowance. The folded edge should be placed close to the zipper coil.

5. Attach the zipper foot to the sewing machine. Stitch close to the folded edge of the seam allowance. Stitch from the bottom of the zipper to the top.

(Continued)

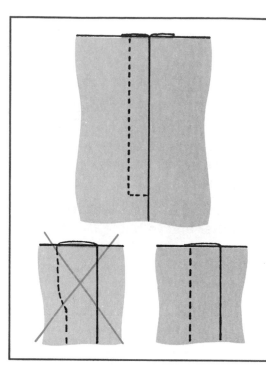

6. Lay the 5/8-inch seam allowance over the zipper. Place the folded edge so that it just covers the row of machine stitching made in the last step. Pin in place.

7. Select a procedure to help you topstitch evenly. (See Lesson 21, "Topstitching.")

8. Start at the bottom of the zipper. Stitch across the end. Pivot and stitch to within 1 inch of the top of the zipper. Leave the needle in the fabric. Lift the presser foot and zip the head of the zipper down. Lower the presser foot and continue stitching to the top of the zipper. This procedure will make sewing around the head of the zipper easier.

FLY FRONT ZIPPER

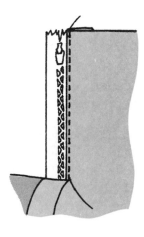

Fly front zippers are most often used for front openings on jeans and slacks. This type of zipper requires an extension on the garment where the zipper is to be placed. Many have a separate extension piece, or placket, which is sewn to the garment before the zipper is applied.

Methods of applying fly front zippers vary with different pattern instruction sheets. Use the following helps as they apply to your instructions:

1. Mark the location of the zipper and stitch the front crotch seam below the zipper marking.

2. Press under the right and left front seam allowances as shown on your pattern instruction sheet. Note that each side is pressed under different amounts.

3. Pin the zipper along the left front seam allowance.

4. Attach the zipper foot to the sewing machine. Stitch close to the folded edge of the seam allowance. This edge should be close to the zipper coil. Stitch from the bottom of the zipper to the top.

(Continued)

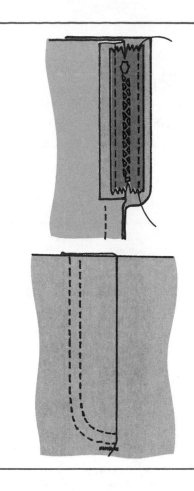

5. Place the garment pieces right sides together. (See diagram.) Make sure the zipper lies flat. Stitch from the bottom to the top of the zipper tape as shown.

6. Turn the garment right side up. Topstitch on the right side using as many rows of stitching as desired. Use a chalk pencil to sketch in stitching lines to ensure even topstitching.

7. For jeans, you may wish to add a bar tack at the bottom of the zipper. Do this by setting the machine on a small zigzag stitch. Practice on a scrap of fabric.

STRETCH KNIT ZIPPER INSERTION

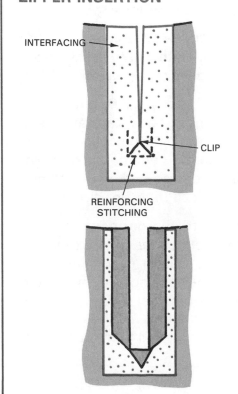

INTERFACING

CLIP

REINFORCING STITCHING

Use this method to insert a zipper into stretch knit garments. This method will prevent the zipper from rippling. Rippling is a major concern when working with this type of fabric.

This type of zipper insertion is one of a few where the zipper coil is visible on the outside of the garment. To insert a zipper with stretch knit fabric, follow these steps:

1. Fuse a piece of interfacing to the wrong side of the area into which the zipper will be inserted.

2. Reinforce stitch around the bottom of the zipper opening along the seamline.

3. Clip as shown.

4. Press under the seam allowance around the zipper opening.

(Continued)

5. Pin the zipper in the opening.
6. Attach the zipper foot to the sewing machine. Stitch close to the folded edges.

INVISIBLE ZIPPER INSERTION

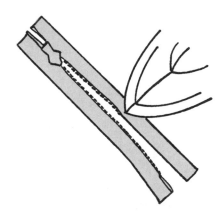

Use this method when you want the most zipper invisibility. It is most often used for center back or center front dress zippers. To insert an invisible zipper in the back of a garment, follow these steps:

1. Use the special sewing machine foot which is required to insert an invisible zipper. These may be purchased at most sewing centers. The foot must be assembled according to the sewing machine model being used. Follow the directions that come with the attachment.

2. Do *not* stitch the garment seam together in which the zipper will be inserted.

3. Open the zipper and lay it upside down on the ironing board. With the tip of the iron, press the inside edges of the zipper coil flat.

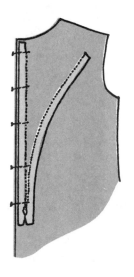

4. Place the open zipper face down on the right side of the right back garment piece (see diagram). The top of the coil should be 5/8 inch from the top edge of the garment piece. The zipper coil should be positioned along the seamline. Pin in position.

5. Stitch the zipper to the garment, making sure that the zipper coil feeds into the right hand groove of the zipper foot. Make sure the zipper coil remains in position along the seamline. Remove pins before sewing over them. Stitch until the foot reaches the stop at the end of the zipper and then backstitch.

(Continued)

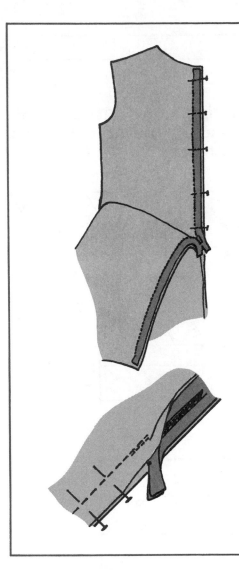

6. Place the remaining free side of the zipper on the right side of the left back garment piece (see diagram). Make sure the zipper is the same distance from the top of the garment piece as it was on the completed side. Position the coil along the seam allowance and pin in place. Stitch as before. This time make sure that the coil feeds into the left hand groove of the zipper foot. Begin stitching at the top of the zipper. Backstitch when you reach the zipper stop at the bottom.

7. Close the zipper. From the wrong side of the garment, pin the seams together. Lift the bottom, unstitched end of the zipper out of the way. Move the needle to the side of the zipper foot. Stitch, beginning as close as possible to where the zipper has been sewn to the garment. Stitch several inches. Change to a regular machine foot and stitch the rest of the seam.

Name _____

Date _____ Period _____

Evaluation Criteria: Zipper

Before you begin construction, read through the criteria listed below. After constructing each detail, complete this form according to your teacher's directions. Turn this sheet in to your teacher and be prepared to discuss each item.

	Did not follow procedure correctly.	Followed procedure but had some difficulty.	Nicely done but with more practice could do better.	Exceptionally well done.
Seam allowance is 5/8 inch.				
Seam is finished appropriately for fabric.				
The appropriate method is used for the type of zipper and garment.				
There is no gap at zipper top.				
Zipper does not ripple. If bias cut, a stay is used.				
Topstitching is an even distance from edge.				
Head of zipper does not show. Zipper does not show (except for knit method).				
Threads are clipped.				
Backstitching is not noticeable on right side of garment.				
Shows evidence of having been pressed as sewn.				

Lesson 30 Constructing Placket Openings

Objectives

This lesson will help you to construct a placket. You will apply the following, previously acquired skills:

Lesson 5:   Reading the Instruction Sheet
Lesson 6:   Pattern Symbols
Lesson 11: Operating the Sewing Machine
Lesson 12: Pressing as You Sew
Lesson 14: Seams
Lesson 15: Clipping, Notching, Trimming, and Grading
Lesson 20: Interfacing
Lesson 21: Topstitching
Lesson 22: Hand Stitching

Helps for Success

There are various types of plackets and methods of insertion. Follow your pattern instruction sheet and the helps given below.

INTERFACING THE PLACKET	Be sure to apply interfacing according to your pattern instruction sheet. This will provide the shaping needed in this area of your garment.

MATCHING SYMBOLS 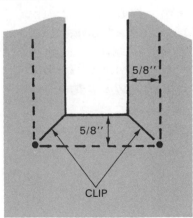	Matching symbols is a critical step in constructing the placket. To match symbols accurately, follow these steps: 1. Mark dots accurately. Dot placement is critical. 2. Place a row of reinforcement stitching 5/8 inch from the cut edge. This is important as you will be clipping to the corners later. 3. When your instructions tell you to clip, do so with great accuracy. Clip to the dots and no further. 4. When you attach the placket piece to the garment, match dots carefully.

FINISHING THE PLACKET END

Your pattern instructions will ask you to turn your garment to the wrong side and overlap the ends of the placket with the garment seam. You will then be asked to stitch across the end of the placket. You must be very accurate when you stitch this line. Be sure to stitch from corner (dot) to corner (dot). If you do not, you will find that the placket does not lie smoothly on the outside of your garment.

HELPFUL SEWING HINTS

When constructing plackets, an important step is to clip to the dots at the bottom of the placket opening. The clips must be made exactly to the dots or the placket will not lie flat on the outside of the garment. Clipping in this manner often weakens the seam at the point of the clip. This can result in fraying and eventual giving way of the seam. There is a solution to this problem.

Liquid seam finish may be applied at the point of the clip after the seam has been stitched. This is a liquid glue made to be used on fabric. It may be purchased at most fabric stores. The product is expensive and should be used in spot application only.

If this product is used on the outside of a garment, be sure to test it on the fabric first. The glue can darken and stiffen some fabrics. Once dry, the glue cannot be removed, so take care not to get it where you do not want it. If the glue has not dried, it may be removed by dabbing with alcohol. Use a cool iron when pressing areas where the liquid seam finish has been applied.

Liquid seam finish requires a 15-minute drying time. Be careful where you lay the garment piece when the glue is wet. If you want to speed drying time, use a hair dryer.

Name _____

Date _____ Period _____

Evaluation Criteria: Placket Openings

Before you begin construction, read through the criteria listed below. After constructing each detail, complete this form according to your teacher's directions. Turn this sheet in to your teacher and be prepared to discuss each item.

	Did not follow procedure correctly.	Followed procedure but had some difficulty.	Nicely done but with more practice could do better.	Exceptionally well done.
An approved procedure was followed.				
Sides of placket are even in width.				
Placket is interfaced to provide desired shaping.				
Placket laps neatly at bottom.				
Topstitching, if any, is an even distance from edge.				
Seams are trimmed to eliminate bulk.				
Hand stitching, if any, is uniform in size and shows as little as possible. Knots are hidden.				
Threads are clipped.				
Shows evidence of having been pressed as sewn.				
Placket piece is cut on the straight of grain.				

notes

Lesson 31   Constructing Facings

Objectives

This lesson will help you to construct a facing. You will apply the following, previously acquired skills:

Lesson 5:   Reading the Instruction Sheet
Lesson 6:   Pattern Symbols
Lesson 11: Operating the Sewing Machine
Lesson 12: Pressing as You Sew
Lesson 14: Seams
Lesson 15: Clipping, Notching, Trimming, and Grading
Lesson 16: Seam Finishes
Lesson 17: Clean Finishing
Lesson 18: Understitching
Lesson 20: Interfacing
Lesson 22: Hand Stitching

Helps for Success

Facings are needed to finish raw edges of a garment. There are many types of facings. Some examples are neck facings, sleeve facings, waistline facings, and front facings. In each case, the basic steps used to construct the facing will be the same.

PREPARING THE GARMENT AND FACING	Follow your instruction sheet carefully. When constructing facings, be sure not to leave out any of the steps given. Your instruction sheet may have you begin by doing any of the following: 1. Apply interfacing to the garment area. 2. Sew any necessary facing pieces together. 3. Clean finish the edge of the facing.

CLEAN FINISHING THE FACING EDGE

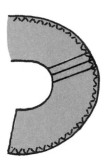

Clean finishing the edge of the facing will prevent it from raveling. Use one of the following methods.

Method 1: use with most fabrics. Follow these steps:

1. On the outside edge of the facing only, stitch 1/4 inch from the edge. Do not eliminate this step. It will help you to keep the edge of the facing smooth and rounded.

2. Press under 1/4 inch using the stitching line as a guide.

3. Stitch again along the edge of the facing that has been turned under.

Method 2: use with heavier fabrics. Zigzag or serge the facing edge. You can also stitch 1/4 inch from the facing edge and then pink the edge using pinking shears.

ATTACHING THE FACING TO THE GARMENT

FACING

After stitching the facing to the garment, grading and clipping are especially important. This is because facings are usually on a curved area of the garment.

Grade the seam by trimming the various layers to differing widths.

Clip the curved areas by cutting small "V's" out of the seam at 1/2 inch intervals. Press the seam toward the facing.

UNDERSTITCHING

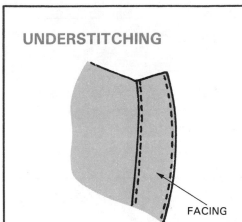

FACING

Understitching will prevent the facing from rolling to the outside of the garment. Be sure that the facing seam is pressed toward the facing and that it stays in that position while you are understitching.

Understitch by stitching around the facing, through the facing and seam allowance, as close to the neckline seam as possible.

TACKING THE FACING IN PLACE

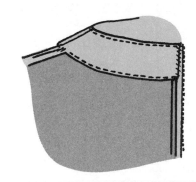

Tack the finished facing to the wrong side of the garment at seams. In some cases, you will tack along the top edge of the zipper. This will keep the facing in place. Use needle and thread. Make small, neat stitches that will not show through to the right side of the garment.

Name _____

Date _____ Period _____

Evaluation Criteria: Facings

Before you begin construction, read through the criteria listed below. After constructing each detail, complete this form according to your teacher's directions. Turn this sheet in to your teacher and be prepared to discuss each item.

	Did not follow procedure correctly.	Followed procedure but had some difficulty.	Nicely done but with more practice could do better.	Exceptionally well done.
An approved procedure was followed.				
Seams are trimmed, clipped, and graded where necessary.				
Facing is understitched.				
Facing edge is clean finished.				
Facing pieces are cut out on the straight of grain.				
Interfacing is used where necessary.				
Seam stitching curves smoothly.				
There are no tucks in the seams.				
Threads are clipped.				
Shows evidence of having been pressed as sewn.				
Facing hand tacked where needed.				
Hand stitching is uniform size and shows as little as possible. Knots do not show.				
Facings fit curve of body smoothly.				

Lesson 32 Constructing Yokes

Objectives

This lesson will help you to construct a yoke. You will apply the following, previously acquired skills:

Lesson 5:   Reading the Instruction Sheet
Lesson 6:   Pattern Symbols
Lesson 11: Operating the Sewing Machine
Lesson 12: Pressing as You Sew
Lesson 14: Seams
Lesson 15: Clipping, Notching, Trimming, and Grading
Lesson 16: Seam Finishes
Lesson 19: Easing and Gathering
Lesson 21: Topstitching

Helps for Success

Yokes are used in many garments. Often, the garment piece below the yoke is eased or gathered to add fullness. There are many types of yokes and methods of constructing them. Follow your pattern instruction sheet and the helps given below.

MARKING SYMBOLS	If your garment is designed with gathers or tucks, begin by marking the pattern symbols that will tell you where to place them.

GATHERING 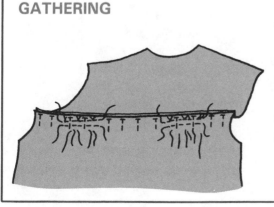	Follow the recommended procedure for gathering. Be sure to use two rows of basting. Place one row 1/2 inch from the fabric edge and another row 6/8 inch from the edge. Do not backstitch. Adjust gathers evenly by pulling on both top threads at one time. Pin and stitch the seam. Finish the seam edges if needed. Press seam toward the yoke.

TOPSTITCHING THE YOKE	You may choose to topstitch the yoke seam. See the helps for even topstitching (Lesson 21).

Name _____

Date _____ Period _____

Evaluation Criteria: Yoke

Before you begin construction, read through the criteria listed below. After constructing each detail, complete this form according to your teacher's directions. Turn this sheet in to your teacher and be prepared to discuss each item.

	Did not follow procedure correctly.	Followed procedure but had some difficulty.	Nicely done but with more practice could do better.	Exceptionally well done.
An approved procedure was followed.				
Pieces are cut on the straight of grain.				
Gathering or easing is evenly distributed.				
Seams are 5/8 inch.				
Corners, if any, are square.				
Topstitching, if any, is an even distance from edge.				
Seams are finished appropriately for the fabric.				
Threads are clipped.				
Shows evidence of having been pressed as sewn.				
Fits body properly.				

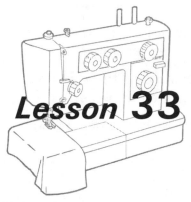

Lesson 33 Constructing Collars

Objective

This lesson will help you to construct a collar. You will apply the following, previously acquired skills:

Lesson 5:   Reading the Instruction Sheet
Lesson 6:   Pattern Symbols
Lesson 11: Operating the Sewing Machine
Lesson 12: Pressing as You Sew
Lesson 14: Seams
Lesson 15: Clipping, Notching, Trimming, and Grading
Lesson 16: Seam Finishes
Lesson 18: Understitching
Lesson 20: Interfacing
Lesson 21: Topstitching

Helps for Success

Constructing a collar requires several steps and careful attention to detail. But if care is taken, your garment will have a comfortable, attractive collar. There are many types of collars and methods of constructing them. Follow the pattern instruction sheet carefully. The guidelines below will also help.

| INTERFACING THE COLLAR | In most cases, the collar or neck band should be interfaced. The type and weight of interfacing will depend upon the fashion fabric. (See Lesson 20, "Interfacing.") |

| COLLAR STAYS 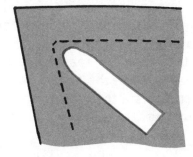 | Collar stays are optional. The purpose of collar stays is to retain the shape of the collar points. Stays may be purchased at most sewing centers. |

To apply the stay, follow these easy steps:

1. Position the stay in the point of the under collar piece at each end of the collar. Be sure the stay is not extended into the seam allowance.

(Continued)

2. Using fusible interfacing, cut out the interfacing piece for the under collar.

3. Position the interfacing over the stay on the under collar piece. Fuse in place.

4. Continue collar construction according to pattern directions.

STITCHING THE COLLAR POINT

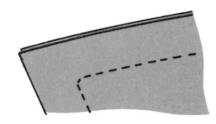

To achieve sharp points on the collar, sew one stitch across the point of the collar. This one stitch provides room for the excess fabric that will be in the point when the collar is turned.

TRIMMING, GRADING, AND CLIPPING

Eliminating bulk in seams is especially important for collars. Do not forget to perform the following steps:

1. Grade the seam (cut the seam layers at varying widths.)
2. Trim corners as shown.
3. Clip curved areas of the seam.

MATCHING SYMBOLS

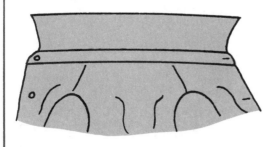

The most important steps in collar construction are marking and matching pattern symbols. Be very accurate as you complete these steps.

Throughout the construction process check to make sure that the collar and/or neck band are centered on the neckline seam. The neck band should extend beyond the collar the same distance at each end. Also, the ends of the neck band should line up exactly with the ends of the neckline seam.

EASING THE COLLAR TO THE NECK SEAM

Most collars or neck bands are made to be slightly larger than the neckline seam. This provides for the best fit when the collar is completed. This also means the collar must be eased to the neckline seam. To make the collar fit the neckline seam, you will need to clip the seam. Follow these steps:

1. Staystitch 1/2 inch from the edge of the neckline.

2. Pin the collar to the neckline *matching all symbols.*

3. Clip the neckline to the staystitching allowing it to "spread out" so that the collar will fit the neckline.

4. Stitch, being careful not to sew tucks in the seam. To prevent this problem, sew a few inches. Then check the underside of your work to see that it lies flat. Stitch a few inches more and then check again. Repeat until the seam is completely sewn.

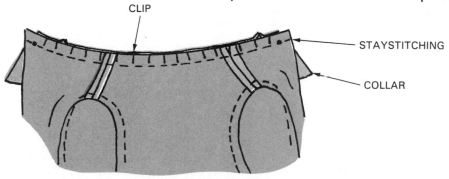

CLIP

STAYSTITCHING

COLLAR

Name _____

Date _____ Period _____

Evaluation Criteria: Collar

Before you begin construction, read through the criteria listed below. After constructing each detail, complete this form according to your teacher's directions. Turn this sheet in to your teacher and be prepared to discuss each item.

	Did not follow procedure correctly.	Followed procedure but had some difficulty.	Nicely done but with more practice could do better.	Exceptionally well done.
An approved procedure was followed.				
Pieces are cut on the straight of grain.				
Interfacing is used to give desired shaping.				
Collar is uniform in shape.				
Collar or band does not extend beyond edge of neck seam (centered on neck).				
Neck seam is graded and clipped so that it will lie flat.				
There are no tucks in neck seam.				
Topstitching, if any, is an even distance from edge.				
Band is even in width.				
Ends of band are smoothly curved or shaped according to design of pattern.				
Threads are clipped.				
Shows evidence of having been pressed as sewn.				

Lesson 34 Constructing Lapels

Objective

This lesson will help you to construct lapels. You will apply the following, previously acquired skills:

Helps for Success

Constructing lapels requires precise marking, pinning, and stitching. Care must be taken to produce a lapel that lies flat without bulges or puckers. Follow your pattern instruction sheet carefully. The following guidelines will also help.

SEWING THE LAPEL AND COLLAR SEAM

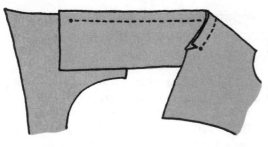

Sewing the lapel and collar seam can be one of the most difficult tasks you will encounter. However, following the procedure given below will make it much easier.

1. Mark the dots on the collar, undercollar, lapel facing, and lapel with precision.

2. Pin the collar to the lapel facing. Match the dots carefully.

3. Sew between the dots. This means that there will be 5/8 inch on each end of the collar that is not stitched down. Do the same with the undercollar and lapel.

4. Clip to the dots on the lapel and lapel facing.

(Continued)

315

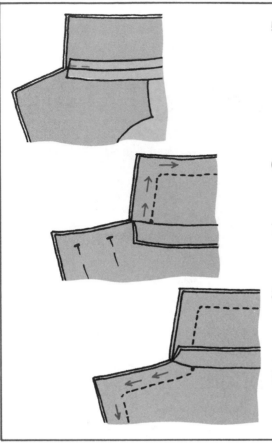

5. Pin the collar and lapel to the undercollar and lapel facing. Accuracy is very important. Place a pin close to the dot. Carefully line up the two seams. These two seams must be matched exactly. Do not remove this pin until after you have stitched the lapel and collar seam.

6. Fold down the neckline seam on both sides of your work. Begin stitching from the dot (be exact) and stitch in the direction shown.

7. Fold up the necklines seam on both sides of your work. Begin stitching from the dot (be exact) and stitch in the direction shown.

8. Check your accuracy by looking at the right side of your work. Make sure the lapel seams are lined up. (The lapels may not lie perfectly flat at this point.)

9. Grade and clip the lapel and collar seams. Turn the collar and lapels to right side and press.

TOPSTITCHING LAPELS

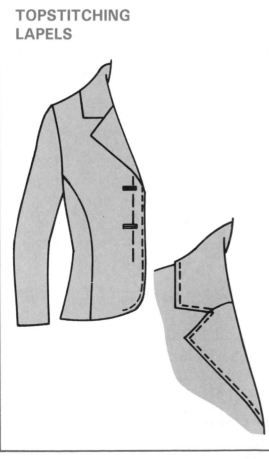

Lapels and collar edges may be topstitched if desired. Topstitching can help give the garment a more tailored appearance. When topstitching, remember that the exposed side of the garment changes because the collar and lapels are rolled. Follow these steps:

1. Begin topstitching from the bottom of the garment on the right side. Stitch to the roll line (see drawing). Remove the garment from the machine. Do not backstitch. To secure, pull the top thread through to the facing side, knot threads, and clip.

2. Resume topstitching from the facing side of the garment. Be careful to align with the first stitching.

3. At the notch where the lapel and collar meet, pivot and stitch as shown.

4. Continue to stitch along the collar and lapel to the other roll line. Change sides as before. However, pull the bottom thread through to the facing side to knot.

Name _____

Date _____ Period _____

Evaluation Criteria: Lapels

Before you begin construction, read through the criteria listed below. After construct-ing each detail, complete this form according to your teacher's directions. Turn this sheet in to your teacher and be prepared to discuss each item.

	Did not follow procedure correctly.	Followed procedure but had some difficulty.	Nicely done but with more practice could do better.	Exceptionally well done.
An approved procedure was followed.				
Pieces are cut on the straight of grain.				
Lapel seam is matched accurately.				
Lapel is uniform in shape and rolls smoothly.				
Seams are graded and clipped where necessary.				
Interfacing is used to achieve appropriate shaping.				
Threads are clipped.				
Shows evidence of having been pressed as sewn.				
Edge of facing is finished appropriately for fabric.				
Topstitching, if any, is an even distance from edge and neat.				

notes

Lesson 35 Constructing Sleeves

Objective

This lesson will help you to construct a sleeve. You will apply the following, previously acquired skills:

Lesson 5:   Reading the Instruction Sheet
Lesson 6:   Pattern Symbols
Lesson 11: Operating the Sewing Machine
Lesson 12: Pressing as You Sew
Lesson 14: Seams
Lesson 15: Clipping, Notching, Trimming, and Grading
Lesson 16: Seam Finishes
Lesson 19: Easing and Gathering
Lesson 24: Constructing Darts, Tucks, and Pleats

Helps for Success

There are various types of sleeves and methods of construction. Read your pattern instruction sheet carefully to find out how you should proceed. The following guidelines will also help.

GATHERING

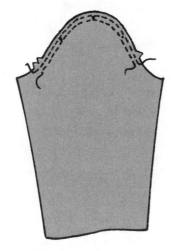

Your instruction sheet may tell you to use one row of gathering stitches around the sleeve cap. But you will have less difficulty getting the sleeve to fit the armseye smoothly if you use two rows.

Place one row of gathering stitches at 1/2 inch from the edge. Place another row of gathering stitches at 6/8 inch. Stitch only from the double notch around the sleeve cap to the single notch. (Or stitch as otherwise indicated on the pattern instruction sheet.)

Adjust the gathering stitches so that fullness is placed evenly around the cap of the sleeve.

SETTING THE SLEEVE IN THE ARMSEYE

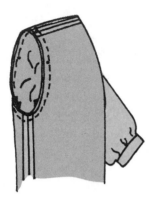

Sleeve and armseye symbols must be matched when setting the sleeve into the armseye. Sleeves are not interchangeable from one armseye to the other. They must be inserted into the correct armseye.

The large dot at the sleeve top should be matched with the shoulder seam. (There is sometimes an exception to this rule. For instance, other rules apply if you have a dropped shoulder seam. Read your instruction sheet carefully.)

Match the double notches on the sleeve with those on the armseye. The double notches will always be to the back of the garment. Then match the front single notches. Finally, match the small dots on both the front and back of the sleeve and armseye.

When you permanently stitch the sleeve seam, you will be stitching between the two rows of gathering stitches. The two rows of stitching will hold the fullness in place while you permanent stitch. You will need to remove the gathering threads after you have stitched the sleeve into the armseye.

Name _____

Date _____ Period _____

Evaluation Criteria: Sleeves

   Before you begin construction, read through the criteria listed below. After constructing each detail, complete this form according to your teacher's directions. Turn this sheet in to your teacher and be prepared to discuss each item.

	Did not follow procedure correctly.	Followed procedure but had some difficulty.	Nicely done but with more practice could do better.	Exceptionally well done.
An approved procedure was followed.				
Pieces are cut on the straight of grain.				
Tucks, if any, are uniform in size and evenly spaced.				
Darts, if any, are tapered to a fine point.				
Gathering or easing is evenly distributed with no large tucks.				
Seam edges and seam width are appropriate for garment and fabric.				
Sleeves are set in with notches and dots correctly matched.				
Hem, if any, is appropriately finished for fabric and garment design.				
Handstitching, if any, is uniform in size and shows as little as possible. Knots are hidden.				
Threads are clipped.				
Shows evidence of having been pressed as sewn.				
Fitting is good—appropriate length, grainlines hang straight, fits armseye correctly.				

notes

Lesson 36 Constructing Sleeve Openings

Objective

This lesson will help you to construct a sleeve placket. You will apply the following, previously acquired skills:

Lesson 5:   Reading the Instruction Sheet
Lesson 6:   Pattern Symbols
Lesson 11: Operating the Sewing Machine
Lesson 12: Pressing as You Sew

Helps for Success

Openings are needed on cuffed sleeves to make getting the sleeve over the hand possible. A number of methods can be used to finish openings. With some methods, a placket, or separate fabric extension, is used. Your pattern instruction sheet will give directions for your type of placket. The guidelines below will also help.

TYPES OF OPENINGS

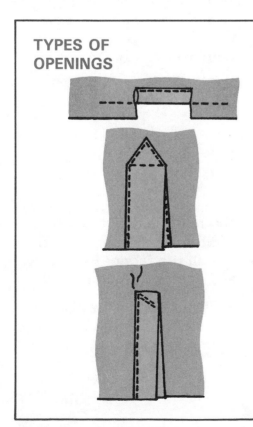

There are three basic types of sleeve openings:

1. Hemmed opening. This is the easiest sleeve opening to construct. If you use this type, be sure to use staystitching. This will reinforce clipping.

2. Shirt placket. This is the most difficult to construct. Follow your pattern instruction sheet exactly. Use caution to be sure that you have lapped the sides correctly.

3. Continuous lap placket. This is the most common finish for sleeve openings. Directions are given in the next box for this method.

CONSTRUCTING CONTINUOUS LAP PLACKETS

To construct a continuous lap placket, follow these steps:

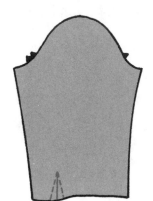

1. Stitch along the "V" shaped marking. Use a small machine stitch for greater reinforcement. Make sure that you have marked and stitched the "V" in the correct location on the sleeve. If you have made a mistake, the placket may appear on the front of the sleeve rather than the back.

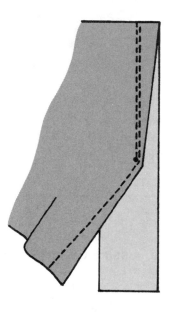

2. Slash up the center of the "V" to the exact point. Do not cut your reinforcement stitching.

3. Cut placket strips according to pattern instructions.

4. Lay the wrong side of the sleeve on top of the right side of the placket strip. Edges will be together at the edge of the sleeve. The tip of the "V" will be 1/4 inch from the edge of the placket strip. Do not try to pin down the other side of the "V".

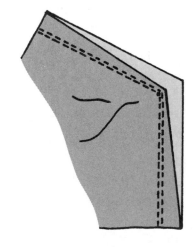

5. Stitch along the reinforcement line that you can see. Stitch to the point. Stop. Leave the needle in the fabric. Raise the presser foot and pivot the fabric.

6. Line up the remaining side of the placket as shown. Continue stitching along the reinforcement line.

(Continued)

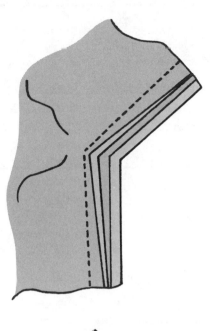

7. Press the seam toward the placket strip. Also, press under 1/4 inch along the edge of the placket piece.
8. Fold the placket strip over again, folding only to the stitching line. Stitch as shown. Again, pivot at the point of the "V".

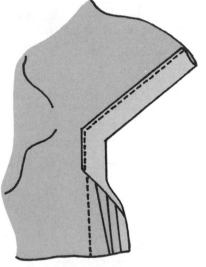

9. On the inside of the garment, backstitch across the placket point as shown.

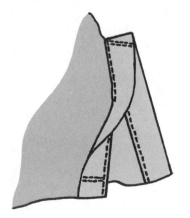

10. Turn the front edge of the placket to the inside of the sleeve and backstitch in place as shown.

Name _____

Date _____ Period _____

Evaluation Criteria: Sleeve Placket

Before you begin construction, read through the criteria listed below. After constructing each detail, complete this form according to your teacher's directions. Turn this sheet in to your teacher and be prepared to discuss each item.

	Did not follow procedure correctly.	Followed procedure but had some difficulty.	Nicely done but with more practice could do better.	Exceptionally well done.
An approved procedure was followed.				
Stitching is used to reinforce stress points.				
There are no puckers.				
Placket is the same width the whole length.				
Placket is securely stitched.				
Threads are clipped.				
Shows evidence of having been pressed as sewn.				
Placket laps in the correct direction.				
Placket point and lap are tacked in place.				

Lesson 37 Constructing Cuffs

Objective

This lesson will help you to construct a cuff. You will apply the following, previously acquired skills:

Lesson 5:   Reading the Instruction Sheet
Lesson 6:   Pattern Symbols
Lesson 11: Operating the Sewing Machine
Lesson 12: Pressing as You Sew
Lesson 14: Seams
Lesson 15: Clipping, Notching, Trimming, and Grading
Lesson 16: Seam Finishes
Lesson 19: Easing and Gathering
Lesson 20: Interfacing
Lesson 21: Topstitching
Lesson 22: Hand Stitching
Lesson 24: Constructing Darts, Tucks, and Pleats

Helps for Success

There are a great variety of cuff designs and methods of application. Follow your pattern instruction sheet. Also read the helps below.

INTERFACING THE CUFF

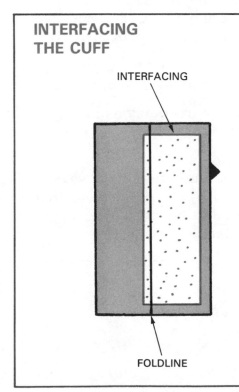

In most instances, you will need to interface the cuff. This provides the needed shaping and body. To apply the interfacing, follow your pattern instructions. If you need to, review Lesson 20, Interfacing.

If the cuff piece is turned in half to achieve the finished cuff, follow the steps below:

1. Cut interfacing to half the width of the cuff pattern plus 1/4 inch.

2. Trim excess from the seam allowances of the interfacing on three sides.

3. Extend the interfacing 1/4 inch over the cuff foldline. The 1/4 inch of the interfacing will give a soft, professional look to the cuff.

4. Fuse in place. (See Lesson 20, Interfacing, for directions on applying non-fusible interfacing.)

CUFF LAP

Be sure the cuff laps toward the back when the sleeve is positioned on the body. The buttonhole will be placed on the front cuff edge. It will lap over the back edge of the cuff. A very noticeable error will result if the cuff lapping is reversed. As you proceed, make sure you have not made this mistake.

TOPSTITCHING

Topstitching on cuffs is sometimes functional. Other times, it may be optional. Experiment to see what topstitching techniques will look best on your fabric and garment. See Lesson 21, Topstitching, for ideas and methods to maintain even topstitching.

ROLLED CUFFS

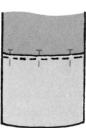

Rolled cuffs do not always need a hand sewn hem. To save time constructing rolled cuffs, follow these steps:

1. Pin the hem in place. Try on the garment to check hem length.

2. Finish hem edge depending on fabric weight and stability of weave. (See Lesson 23, Hemming Methods.) Generally, the hem edge may be turned under 1/4 inch.

3. Machine stitch the hem to the garment. Stitch close to the turned edge of the hem.

4. Turn up the cuff on the outside of the garment. The cuff will cover the row of machine stitching.

5. You may wish to tack the cuff in several locations to keep it in place. Be careful that your tacking stitches are not visible on the outside of the garment.

Name _____

Date _____ Period _____

Evaluation Criteria: Cuffs

Before you begin construction, read through the criteria listed below. After constructing each detail, complete this form according to your teacher's directions. Turn this sheet in to your teacher and be prepared to discuss each item.

	Did not follow procedure correctly.	Followed procedure but had some difficulty.	Nicely done but with more practice could do better.	Exceptionally well done.
An approved procedure was followed.				
Pieces are cut on the straight of grain.				
Interfacing is used to provide the desired shaping.				
Cuff is correctly positioned on the sleeve according to pattern symbols.				
Topstitching is an even distance from edge.				
Cuff is uniform width, and all corners are square and sharp.				
Handstitching is uniform in size and shows as little as possible. Knots do not show.				
Seams are graded to eliminate bulk.				
Thread are clipped.				
Shows evidence of having been pressed as sewn.				

notes

Lesson 38 Constructing Shoulder Pads

Objective

This lesson will help you to construct shoulder pads. You will apply the following, previously acquired skills:

Lesson 5:   Reading the Instruction Sheet
Lesson 11: Operating the Sewing Machine
Lesson 12: Pressing as You Sew
Lesson 20: Interfacing
Lesson 22: Hand Stitching

Helps for Success

The importance of shoulder pads changes with the season and with current fashion trends. They may be used to achieve a more pronounced shoulder line. They may also be used to make the garment fit correctly.

To improve garment fit, shoulder pads may be used to conceal uneven or sloping shoulders. To decide whether shoulder pads should be used, try on the garment and check for the desired fit through the shoulder and sleeve area.

Shoulder pads may be purchased in varying sizes and shapes at most sewing centers. Making your own is also quite easy.

HOW TO MAKE YOUR OWN SHOULDER PADS

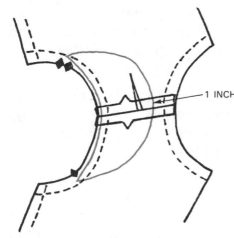

1 INCH

To make your own shoulder pads, follow these steps:

1. Begin by making a shoulder pad pattern. Take the front and back pattern pieces of your garment and pin in any darts or tucks located in the shoulder area. Then overlap the shoulder seams and pin the two pattern pieces together.

2. Trace a curved line on the pattern from the armhole notches to within 1 inch of the neckline seam.

3. Transfer this shape to tracing paper. Mark the front and back on your new pattern. Also, mark the location of the shoulder seam.

(Continued)

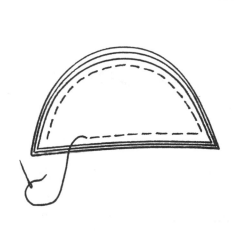

4. Cut two or three layers of polyester fleece for each shoulder pad, depending on desired thickness. Grade each layer along the curved edge. Sew the layers together by hand.

5. Make a cover by cutting two fabric pieces for each shoulder pad. You may want to use your lining fabric or fashion fabric. Add 5/8 inch all the way around each of these pieces for a seam allowance. Stitch, leaving an opening to turn inside out. Turn and place pad inside. Hand stitch opening closed.

ATTACHING PERMANENT SHOULDER PADS

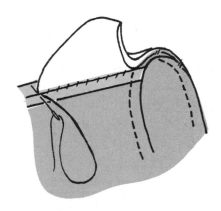

For many types of garments, you will want to permanently hand stitch the shoulder pads in place. Lined garments fall into this category. Attach the shoulder pads before inserting the lining. Follow these steps:

1. Position the shoulder pad over the shoulder seam so that it falls about 2/3 toward the back. The straight side should extend 1/2 inch beyond the armhole seam.

2. Pin in place. Try on the garment to be sure the fit is as desired.

3. Loosely hand stitch the pad in place along the shoulder seam and armhole seam.

ATTACHING REMOVABLE SHOULDER PADS

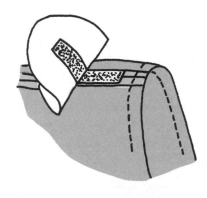

For some garments, you may prefer to make the shoulder pads removable. Hook and loop tape is excellent for this purpose. Follow these steps:

1. Hand stitch the hook side of the tape to the top side of the shoulder pad. Position the tape toward the end of the pad that will be closest to the neck.

2. Try on the garment and position the shoulder pad as desired. Pin in place. Remove the garment. Mark the position of the loop side of the tape. Stitch in place on the garment shoulder seam.

Name _____

Date _____ Period _____

Evaluation Criteria: Shoulder Pads

Before you begin construction, read through the criteria listed below. After constructing each detail, complete this form according to your teacher's directions. Turn this sheet in to your teacher and be prepared to discuss each item.

	Did not follow procedure correctly.	Followed procedure but had some difficulty.	Nicely done but with more practice could do better.	Exceptionally well done.
Pads are appropriately shaped.				
Layers of fleece are graded.				
Pads are securely tacked to the garment.				
Pads are positioned according to the instruction sheet and for the best fit.				
Hand stitching is uniform in size and shows as little as possible. Knots are hidden.				
Pads improve fit and appearance of garment.				

notes

Lesson 39 Constructing Waistbands

Objective

This lesson will help you to construct a waistband. You will apply the following, previously acquired skills:

Lesson 5: Reading the Instruction Sheet
Lesson 6: Pattern Symbols
Lesson 11: Operating the Sewing Machine
Lesson 12: Pressing as You Sew
Lesson 14: Seams
Lesson 15: Clipping, Notching, Trimming, and Grading
Lesson 16: Seam Finishes
Lesson 20: Interfacing
Lesson 21: Topstitching
Lesson 22: Hand Stitching

Helps for Success

There are various methods for applying a waistband. Follow your pattern instruction sheet carefully. As you learn the various application methods, you will find that you have a preference for a certain method. You may then begin to adjust your pattern instructions to use the method you prefer.

FITTING	Try on your garment before applying the waistband. Attaching the waistband to the garment will not greatly change the fit of the waist. Make any needed fitting adjustments before applying the waistband.
	After you have prepared the waistband, baste it to the garment. Try on the garment again to make sure the fit is correct.

INTERFACING

Interfacing is a must inside the waistband. Best results will be achieved if a stiff interfacing is used. This will prevent rolling during wearing. An easy way to get the results you want is to use one of the precut, fusible interfacings made especially for areas such as waistbands. Follow the package directions for applying.

For non-fusible interfacings follow these steps:

1. Press the waistband in half lengthwise. You now have a crease down the center in the waistband.

2. Cut out the interfacing making it 1/4 inch wider than half the width of the waistband.

3. Pin and machine baste the interfacing to the wrong side of the waistband along the notched side and both ends.

4. Using a catch stitch, hand sew the interfacing just above the fold crease. (Stitches may be as large as 1/2 inch.)

5. Trim the interfacing close to the machine stitching.

6. Attach the waistband to the garment according to the pattern instruction sheet.

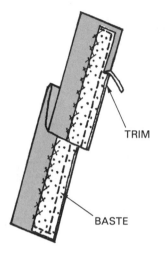

TRIM

BASTE

WAISTBAND LAP

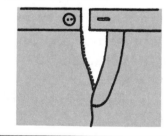

The waistband must extend beyond the garment to provide a lap for button and buttonhole placement. (This may vary some with the garment design.) Check your pattern instruction sheet to find out which way your waistband should lap. Find out which notches and/or dots will need to be matched.

TUCKS AND GATHERS

Make sure any gathers or tucks on the garment are evenly distributed before applying the waistband.

Name _____

Date _____ Period _____

Evaluation Criteria: Waistbands

Before you begin construction, read through the criteria listed below. After constructing each detail, complete this form according to your teacher's directions. Turn this sheet in to your teacher and be prepared to discuss each item.

	Did not follow procedure correctly.	Followed procedure but had some difficulty.	Nicely done but with more practice could do better.	Exceptionally well done.
An approved procedure was followed.				
Waistband is cut on the straight-of-grain.				
Band lies flat without wrinkling or buckling.				
Band is the same width the whole length.				
Corners are square and sharp.				
Seams are graded to eliminate bulk.				
Band ends overlap to allow for placement of fasteners.				
Band is interfaced to prevent rolling.				
Topstitching, if any, is an even distance from edge.				
Belt loops, if any, are evenly spaced.				
Band shows evidence of having been pressed as sewn.				
Threads are clipped.				
Hand stitching, if any, is uniform size and shows as little as possible. Knots do not show.				
Band fits waist.				

notes

Lesson 40 Constructing Elastic Casings

Objective

This lesson will help you to construct an elastic casing. You will apply the following, previously acquired skills:

Lesson 5: Reading the Instruction Sheet
Lesson 6: Pattern Symbols
Lesson 11: Operating the Sewing Machine
Lesson 12: Pressing as You Sew
Lesson 14: Seams
Lesson 16: Seam Finishes

Helps for Success

There are many types of casings and methods of construction. The method you select will depend upon the garment design. Follow your pattern instruction sheet and use the helps below.

WIDTH OF CASING	The width of the casing should be slightly larger than the size of the elastic or drawstring. If the casing is too large the elastic will roll and twist. If it is too small, you will not be able to insert the elastic in the casing. Check the pattern for the amount to turn under for the casing. Purchase the recommended width of elastic for your garment. Measure and press the casing into place before doing any stitching.

FINISHING THE CASING EDGE 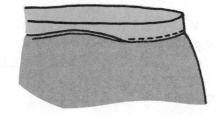	Finish the edge of the casing according to the weight of your fabric. Follow this guide: **Light to medium weight fabric.** Turn under the edge (see pattern for amount) and press. Turn over the casing width required by the pattern. Pin and stitch close to the folded under edge.

(Continued)

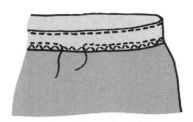

Heavy to stiff fabrics. Serge stitch or zigzag the edge. Turn under width of casing required by the pattern. Stitch close to edge.

For both types of fabric, your pattern instructions may recommend stitching on the top edge of the casing as well.

Leave an opening in the bottom row of stitching so that the elastic may be inserted. After inserting the elastic, stitch the opening closed.

DETERMINING LENGTH OF ELASTIC

Fit the elastic around the part of the body for which the casing is being made. Stretch the elastic slightly until it feels comfortable. Be careful not to make the elastic too tight. Add 1 inch to overlap ends of elastic later.

SEWING ENDS OF ELASTIC TOGETHER

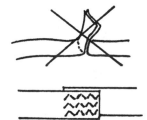

Insert the elastic in the casing. A safety pin works well for this task. Attach the pin to the end of the elastic and then push the pin through the casing.

After the elastic is through the casing, overlap the ends as shown.

Zigzag or straight stitch several times across the ends of the elastic. Make sure the stitching is secure and will not pull out later.

BUTTONHOLES FOR DRAWSTRING CASINGS

Two buttonholes must be made to provide openings for drawstrings.

Your pattern will show the correct position of these buttonholes. Mark the location accurately.

Fuse or baste two small pieces of interfacing to the wrong side of the fabric where the buttonholes will be located. Do this before making the buttonholes to provide greater stability for the buttonhole.

CASINGS FOR KNIT FABRICS

An effective method of constructing a casing on knit fabric is to stitch the elastic to the garment. This will prevent the elastic from rolling and twisting during wearing. Follow these steps:

1. Measure the elastic to the correct length. Overlap ends and stitch securely.

2. Fold the elastic in half. Place a pin at each end.

3. Fold the elastic in half again by placing the first two pins together. Place a pin at each end. You have now divided the elastic into four sections.

4. Place the elastic on the wrong side of the garment with upper edges together. Match the pins with the center front, center back, and side seams.

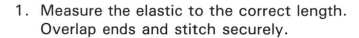

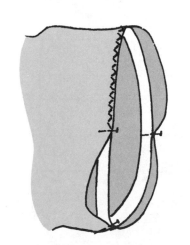

5. Zigzag the elastic to the garment casing edge. Stretch the elastic to fit the garment as you sew.

6. Turn the elastic and casing to the inside. Stitch around the elastic again, stretching as you sew. You will be sewing through the casing edge, elastic, and garment.

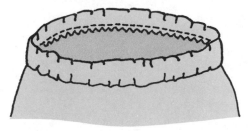

Name _____

Date _____ Period _____

Evaluation Criteria: Elastic Casings

Before you begin construction, read through the criteria listed below. After constructing each detail, complete this form according to your teacher's directions. Turn this sheet in to your teacher and be prepared to discuss each item.

	Did not follow procedure correctly.	Followed procedure but had some difficulty.	Nicely done but with more practice could do better.	Exceptionally well done.
An approved procedure was followed.				
Casing is even in width.				
Elastic is not twisted inside casing.				
Stitching is straight and even.				
Elastic is correct length to fit body.				
Width of elastic is suitable for the design and purpose.				
Threads are clipped.				
Shows evidence of having been pressed as sewn.				
Edge of casing is finished appropriately for fabric.				

Lesson 41 Constructing Linings

Objective

This lesson will help you to construct a lining. You will apply the following, previously acquired skills.

Helps for Success

Linings are usually included in more advanced sewing projects. Suit jackets, coats, and some skirts and dresses may be lined.

Linings help give a garment an attractively finished interior. But they also prevent pulling and sagging in the fashion fabric. Partial linings can be used in stress areas to prevent sagging. Skirt backs and pant knees are two places that may be partially lined for this reason.

Before you construct a lining, read your pattern instruction sheet and the helps below.

STITCHING LINING PIECES TOGETHER

Stitch the lining together according to the pattern instruction sheet. Generally, the steps in sewing the lining pieces together will be similar to those followed to sew the body of the garment together.

The lining back will usually be larger than the garment back. A pleat is formed with the excess fabric in the lining back to provide ease for shoulder movement.

FITTING THE LINING

A body form is handy for fitting the lining into the garment. The garment can be placed wrong side out on the form. Then the lining can be pinned in place.

If a form is not available, lay the garment flat on a table and fit the lining into the garment. Match up any seams, darts, etc. and pin these together. Smooth the lining with your hands. Make sure the lining is not too small for the garment. Pin in place, turning under the seam and hem allowances around the lining.

Slip on the garment to make sure the lining fits correctly. This is an important step.

Hand stitch around the lining, except the hem, using a stitch that will not be visible.

HEMMING THE LINING

Skirt, coat, and dress linings should not be attached to the garment at the hem. Hem these linings separately as you would hem any fabric of this weight. Also, always make the lining a little shorter than the garment. This way, the lining will not show when the garment is being worn.

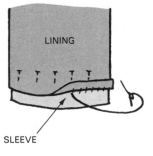

LINING

SLEEVE

Sleeve and jacket linings are attached to the garment at the hem. When constructing these hems, ease must be provided for body movement. To add ease, a tuck is sewn into the lining at the hem.

To form the tuck, pin the lining in place above the hemline. The edge of the hem should be 1/2 inch above the garment hem edge. Fold back the lining about 1/2 inch and stitch the lining to the garment. Be sure not to catch the top layer of lining. Turn the lining down again after stitching.

Name _____

Date _____ Period _____

Evaluation Criteria: Lining

Before you begin construction, read through the criteria listed below. After constructing each detail, complete this form according to your teacher's directions. Turn this sheet in to your teacher and be prepared to discuss each item.

	Did not follow procedure correctly.	Followed procedure but had some difficulty.	Nicely done but with more practice could do better.	Exceptionally well done.
An approved procedure was followed.				
Lining fits the garment.				
Handstitching is a uniform size and shows as little as possible. Knots are hidden.				
Bar tack, if any, is neatly sewn.				
Hem allows for body movement.				
Seams of lining are 5/8 inch.				
Lining seams are finished appropriately for fabric.				
Threads are clipped.				
Shows evidence of having been pressed as sewn.				
Lining is cut on the straight of grain.				

notes

Lesson 42 Constructing Hems

Objective

This lesson will help you to construct a hem. You will apply the following, previously acquired skills:

Lesson 5:   Reading the Instruction Sheet
Lesson 11: Operating the Sewing Machine
Lesson 12: Pressing as You Sew
Lesson 15: Clipping, Notching, Trimming, and Grading
Lesson 22: Hand Stitching
Lesson 23: Hemming Methods

Helps for Success

Several hemming methods were explained in Lesson 23. This lesson will help you mark and prepare a hem on a garment. It will also show you how to do three less frequently used hemming methods.

MARKING THE HEM	Try on the garment. Have another person pin the hem up to the desired length. For dresses and skirts, a yard stick is still the best method of getting an even hem all around. Place one end of the yard stick on the floor and measure to determine the length of the hem.

PREPARING THE HEM	Follow these steps:

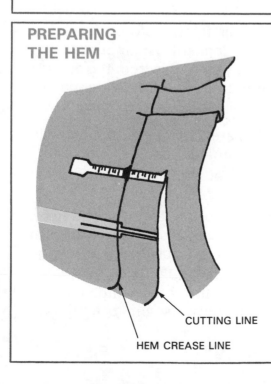

CUTTING LINE

HEM CREASE LINE

Follow these steps:

1. Press in a light crease where the hem has been pinned to the desired length.

2. Decide how wide the hem should be. Generally, your pattern will indicate the width of hem to use.

3. Trim the hem to the desired width. Use a seam gauge to measure as you cut. Be accurate and careful.

4. To avoid a bulge at seams, trim away the seam allowances that will be inside the hem. Do not trim the seam to less than 1/4 inch.

5. Prepare the edge of the hem using a method that is appropriate for your fabric and garment design.

RIPPLED OR LETTUCE HEM

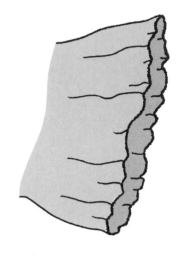

Use this hem on soft, stretch knit fabrics when a ruffled effect is desired. This method may not be suitable for all knits. If the knit runs, try another method. To make the hem, follow these steps:

1. Mark the hem as suggested in the general instructions. There will be no hem allowance. Trim the hem to the desired finished length or add 3/8 inch depending on the hemming method.

2. Adjust the sewing machine zigzag stitch. Make the stitch suitable for the fabric you will be using. Practice on a scrap of fabric before hemming the garment.

3. Make a row of zigzag stitches along the edge of the fabric, stretching gently to make the hem curl. (Greater stretch will produce more ripples.)

4. If you are working with fabric that will ravel, press under 3/8 inch along the hem edge. Then straight stitch (or zigzag) along the edge stretching gently.

5. When finished, the fabric will spring back from being stretched. It will have a ruffled appearance.

FUSED HEM

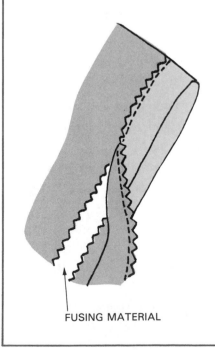

FUSING MATERIAL

Do not use this hem on rough textured fabrics, heavy fabrics, or those that ravel. Use with caution on all fabrics.

Always test your fabric before applying a fused hem to the garment. An imprint of the fusing material may be visible from the outside of the garment with some types of fabric. To make the hem, follow these steps:

1. Mark and prepare the hem as suggested in the general instructions.

2. Pink the edge of the hem for the most invisibility.

3. Cut a fusible strip the length of the hem. Pinking the edges of the strip may help to prevent fusing lines from showing through to the outside of the garment.

4. Position and fuse the strip according to the package instructions on the fusing materials.

BOUND HEM

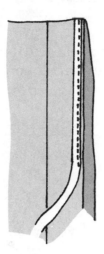

Use this hem method when you want to enclose the hem edge and obtain an attractive, finely finished edge. To make the hem, follow these steps:

1. Mark and prepare the hem as suggested in the general instructions.

2. Cut a piece of bias tape the length of the hem.

3. Press both folded edges of the bias tape flat.

4. With right sides together, place the edge of the bias tape along the edge of the hem. Stitch 1/4 inch from the edge of the hem.

5. Press the bias tape up and over the hem edge.

6. Stitch in the ditch (into the fold of the seamline) on the top side of the hem.

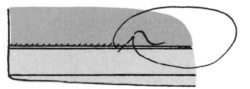

7. Hand stitch the hem edge to the garment. The blind stitch is recommended. (See Lesson 22, Hand Stitching.)

Name _____

Date _____ Period _____

Evaluation Criteria: Hem

Before you begin construction, read through the criteria listed below. After constructing each detail, complete this form according to your teacher's directions. Turn this sheet in to your teacher and be prepared to discuss each item.

	Did not follow procedure correctly.	Followed procedure but had some difficulty.	Nicely done but with more practice could do better.	Exceptionally well done.
The hemming method is appropriate for the type of fabric and garment design.				
No puckers are in the hem.				
Width of hem is appropriate for garment (neither too wide nor too narrow).				
Hand stitching is uniform in size and shows as little as possible. Knots do not show.				
Machine stitching is even.				
Shows evidence of having been pressed as sewn.				
Hem is same width the whole length.				
Hem hangs straight when garment is worn.				
Hem is correct length.				

Lesson 43   Attaching Fasteners

Objective

This lesson will help you to attach fasteners. You will apply the following, previously acquired skills:

Lesson 5:   Reading the Instruction Sheet
Lesson 6:   Pattern Symbols
Lesson 9:   Transferring Pattern Symbols to the Fabric
Lesson 11: Operating the Sewing Machine
Lesson 20: Interfacing
Lesson 22: Hand Stitching

Helps for Success

Attaching fasteners is often the final step of constructing a garment. These guidelines will help you attach them securely and in the proper location.

MARKING BUTTONHOLE LOCATION	Transfer buttonhole markings from the pattern to the garment. A chalk pencil works well for this process.
	Mark on the outside of the garment piece. For front openings, buttonholes will usually be on the left front for men's clothing. They will be on the right front for women's clothing.
	Check accuracy by measuring between the buttonhole markings.

MAKING THE BUTTONHOLE	Always practice making a buttonhole on a scrap of the fabric that you are using. Work on a sample that is exactly like the garment— generally two layers of fabric with a layer of interfacing between.
	Follow the directions for making a buttonhole that come with the sewing machine model that you will be using. (See Lesson 11, "Operating the Sewing Machine.")

MARKING BUTTON LOCATION

Mark the location of one button at a time, starting at the top or bottom button on the garment. Stitch the button in place. Then close the button and mark the location of the next button. If buttons are randomly stitched onto the garment, excess garment fabric between the buttons may result. This will mean taking off all the buttons and stitching them in place again.

SEWING ON THE BUTTON

Follow these steps:

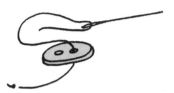

1. Use a threaded needle that has been knotted at one end. Make a small stitch in the fabric where the button will be located. Insert the needle through one of the holes on the underside of the button. Pull the thread through the button.

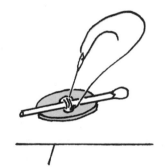

2. Hold a match, toothpick, or other similar object on top of the button between the holes. Push the needle down through the second hole and on through the fabric. Repeat four or five times.

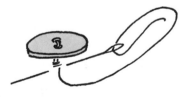

3. Remove the match or toothpick and pull the button up. Wrap the thread around the loose threads under the button. Do this four or five times. This creates a shank for the button to allow easy buttoning.

4. End the stitching by bringing the needle through to the back of the fabric. Take several small stitches running the needle through the thread loop and pulling tight.

5. Some buttons are made with shanks. Simply sew these on to the garment beginning and ending as described above.

Note—buttons may be reinforcing by stitching a small button on the underside of the fabric. Or, a small piece of hem tape may be used under the button between the facing and fashion fabric.

SEWING ON HOOKS AND EYES

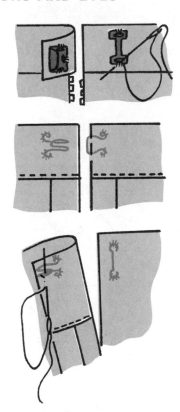

There are a number of types of hooks and eyes. Select the type that is best for your purpose.

A larger hook works best for waistband closures. Sew the hook close to the edge of the top lap of the waistband. Close the opening and position the eye so that the opening will lie flat when completed.

Neckline hooks are smaller than those used on waistbands. They come with two types of eyes: round or straight. The rounded eye should be used when the edges of the garment meet but do not overlap. When using this type of eye, extend the eye over the edge of the garment slightly. The straight eye should be used when the garment edges overlap. When using this type of eye, sew the hook on first. Then position the eye for a flat closing.

Position the hook on the wrong side of the overlapping part of the garment about 1/8 inch from the edge. Sew with small stitches, catching only the inside layer of the fabric. Also, sew the end of the hook to the fabric.

HOOK AND LOOP TAPE

Hook and loop tape comes as either iron-on or sew-on. It may be purchased by the inch or in packages of precut pieces. Follow the manufacturer's directions for attaching the iron-on variety. For best results, use on medium to heavy fabrics. Do not use on heat-sensitive fabrics. Test fuse on a fabric scrap to be sure adhesive does not bleed through or fabric does not scorch.

To apply the sew-on variety, pin in desired location and machine stitch or hand stitch around edges of tape.

SEWING ON SNAPS

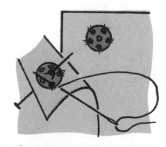

Place the half of the snap with a prong or ball in its center onto the wrong side of the overlapping part of the garment. It should be positioned about 1/8 inch from the edge of the garment. With small stitches, catching only the inside layer of fabric, sew in place.

Position the socket half of the snap in place. Be sure that the garment will lie smoothly when snapped. Stitch as before.

Name _____

Date _____ Period _____

Evaluation Criteria: Fasteners

Before you begin construction, read through the criteria listed below. After constructing each detail, complete this form according to your teacher's directions. Turn this sheet in to your teacher and be prepared to discuss each item.

	Did not follow procedure correctly.	Followed procedure but had some difficulty.	Nicely done but with more practice could do better.	Exceptionally well done.
Fasteners are located so that garment openings lie flat.				
Handstitching is uniform in size and shows as little as possible. Knots do not show.				
Fasteners are securely attached.				
Buttonholes fit size of button.				
Machine buttonholes are neatly done.				
There is interfacing under buttons and buttonholes.				
Buttonholes are evenly spaced and appropriate distance from edge of garment.				
Threads are clipped.				

Unit 7 Learning to Sew with Sergers

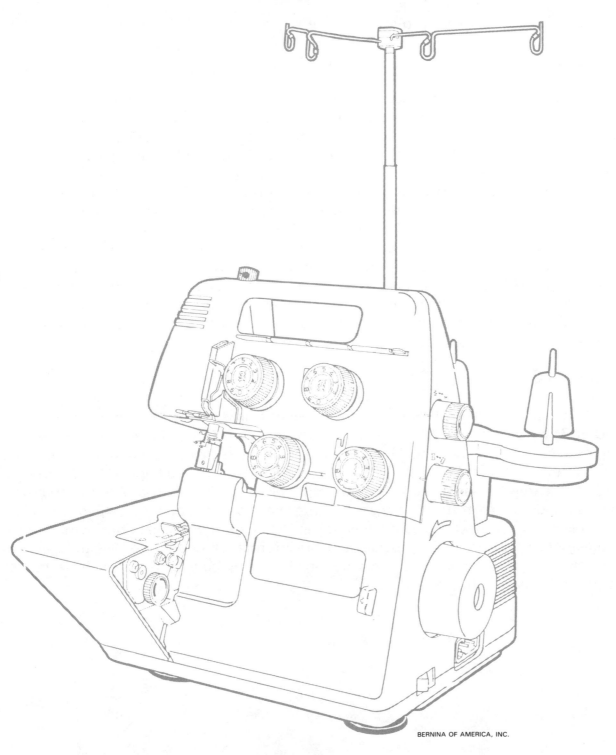

BERNINA OF AMERICA, INC.

Unit 7
Learning to Sew with Sergers

This unit introduces you to sewing with sergers. It consists of three lessons.

Lessons 44 and 45

You will begin learning about sergers by studying Lesson 44, ''Operating the Serger Machine.'' Once you have mastered using the serger, Lesson 45, ''Serger Construction Techniques,'' will provide you with information on specific construction techniques. These techniques are very different from those you learned when using a conventional sewing machine.

These lessons are organized like the lessons in Unit 3. Each lesson includes a list of objectives that you should be able to demonstrate after completing the lesson. A list of basic sewing terms is included. You will find that some words in these lessons were defined earlier in this textbook. You may want to refer back to the appropriate lessons, if you have any questions. You will also find the three types of learning processes with which you have become familiar: gathering information, practicing learning, and evaluating learning. As before, your teacher will give you directions on how the lessons are to be completed. Your teacher may work through the lessons with you, or ask you to complete the lessons on your own.

Lesson 46

The format of this lesson will also look familiar. This is the same format you followed in Unit 6, when you constructed a project using a conventional machine. This lesson begins with a list of previously acquired skills needed to successfully complete the lesson. As you study this lesson, you will discover that you must apply the knowledge and skills learned in earlier lessons in this textbook. If you have any problems constructing a serged project, return to the appropriate lessons and review the necessary skills.

In this lesson, you will also find the familiar Helps for Success sections. Study these suggestions carefully. They provide valuable information on how to construct details of serged projects. Your pattern instruction sheet may be another valuable source of helpful information for serging.

Lesson 44 Operating the Serger Machine

Objectives

This lesson will help you to:
1. Explain how sergers make sewing fast and easy and how they differ from conventional sewing machines.
2. Locate and explain the functions of various serger machine parts.
3. Identify the different types of serger stitches.
4. Explain the considerations to be made when selecting thread.
5. Thread a serger.
6. Operate and maintain a serger.

Words to Know

chaining off	knives	stitch finger
cone adapters	loopers	stitch length regulator
cones	needle clamp screws	stitch width regulator
cross-wound thread	power and light switch	tension regulators
differential feed regulator	presser foot	thread guides
easy threading method	pressure regulator	3-thread overlock stitch
feed dogs	seam sealant	3/4-thread overlock stitch
flatlocking	serger or overlocker	throat plate
5-thread stitch	spool cap	2-thread chain stitch
4-thread stitch	spool pins	2-thread overedge stitch
hand wheel		

Gathering Information

This lesson will provide you with information and activities that will teach you how to use a serger, sometimes called an overlocker. You will learn how sergers differ from conventional sewing machines and how to operate them correctly. This will give you a chance to experience fast, fun, and creative sewing using a serger!

<table>
<tr><td>

**HOW SERGERS MAKE
SEWING FAST AND EASY**

</td><td>

Sergers have been used by the ready-to-wear industry since the early 1900s. Today, a wide variety of models are available to the home sewer. Sergers can save you time, and help you create professional-looking projects. Sergers can stitch, trim, and finish seams all in one sim-

</td></tr>
</table>

ple step. The inside of unlined garments can be finished to look terrific. Outer edges can also be finished, eliminating the need for facings, ribbings, and bands. Narrow or rolled hems can be constructed quickly on anything from single-layer ruffles to flared skirts to tablecloths.

Sergers can sew on a wide variety of fabrics. Slippery fabrics are easier to keep in place with a serger than with a conventional machine. Lace and elastic can be applied faster than ever before. Stretch fabrics can be stitched in a snap, allowing you to make swim wear, aerobic wear, and knit items look like ready-to-wear garments. Sergers can also be used to create decorative stitching using lightweight yarns, metallic threads, and even thin ribbons.

HOW SERGERS DIFFER FROM CONVENTIONAL MACHINES

Although you will find endless ways to use a serger, you still need to use a conventional machine. Sergers can't do everything. For instance, buttonholes and topstitching cannot be stitched by a serger, and you may not want to use sergers to insert zippers. Here are a few other ways sergers differ from conventional machines:

- Sergers are fast! They can stitch from 1300 to 1700 stitches per minute. Conventional machines stitch only 900 to 1000 stitches per minute.

- Sergers have a longer presser foot and feed dogs that hold fabric firmly in place. Fabric won't shift as you sew. Lightweight fabric won't pucker or slip. You usually don't need to pin or baste seams.

- Sergers won't jam when sewing without fabric.

- Sergers use two to five spools of thread, one for each needle and looper.

- Sergers do not have bobbins. Instead they have loopers, usually upper and lower.

(Continued)

- Sergers have upper and lower knives that trim the seam allowance before the seam is finished.

- Sergers use a knitting process to form stitches. The needle threads intertwine with the looper threads as they are wrapped over the stitch finger.

SERGER MACHINE PARTS

Although there are a variety of types and models of sergers, they have many similarities. Following is a list of the names and functions of the basic parts found on most sergers. As you read about each part, locate it on the machine diagrams in this lesson.

Thread guides (1). Guide the threads from the spools to the needles and loopers.

Spool pins (2). Hold spools, cones, or tubes of thread.

Stitch length regulator (3). Adjusts the number of stitches per inch. Adjustments may be made by loosening a screw, moving a lever, or turning a dial.

Differential feed regulator (4). Adjusts the front and back feed dogs to operate at different speeds. Not all sergers have this control.

Hand wheel (5). Turns to raise or lower the needles.

Power and light switch (6). Turns on the serger and light.

Tension regulators (7). Apply tension to the threads so they feed at a constant rate.

Stitch width regulator (8). Adjusts the position of the knives and stitch finger. Not all sergers have this control.

Throat plate (9). Covers the area below the needle.

Stitch finger (10). A metal prong around which stitches are formed. The width of the stitch finger determines the stitch width. The stitch finger may be located on the throat plate or the presser foot.

Pressure regulator (11). Adjusts the amount of

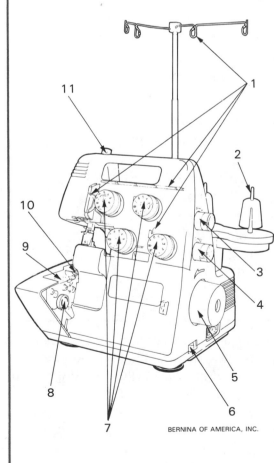

BERNINA OF AMERICA, INC.

(Continued)

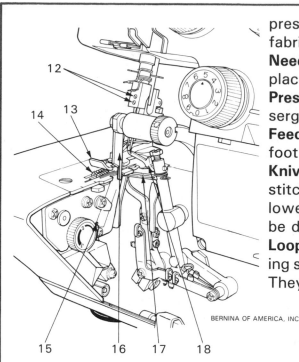

BERNINA OF AMERICA, INC.

pressure applied to the presser foot and the fabric.

Needle clamp screws (12). Hold needles in place.

Presser foot (13). Holds fabric in place as the serger stitches.

Feed dogs (14). Move fabric under the presser foot.

Knives (15 and 16). Trim seam allowances as stitches are formed. Sergers have upper and lower knives. On some sergers, the knives can be disengaged when trimming is not desired.

Loopers (17 and 18). Are necessary in forming stitches. Sergers have one to three loopers. They are referred to as upper and lower.

CHANGING THE SERGER NEEDLE(S)

You will occasionally need to replace the serger needle(s). In fact, you will find that needles wear out faster on sergers than on conventional machines. A blunted or burred needle can cause stitching problems. Always check the needle(s) before you begin serging.

When changing needle(s), refer to the machine manual for the correct type and size. Some sergers use conventional needles, while others use industrial needles. Both types are available in a variety of sizes for serging on different weight fabrics. Ballpoint needles are available. To insert the needle(s) correctly, always place the grooved side to the front and the flat side to the back.

CHANGING THE KNIVES

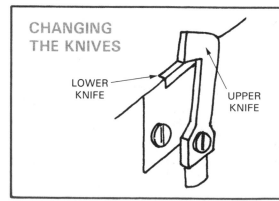

LOWER KNIFE

UPPER KNIFE

As you serge, the excess seam allowance is trimmed away by the knives. These knives will eventually become dull. Generally, one knife is made from a hard alloy material. This knife will not dull as fast and will not need to be replaced as often as the other, less durable knife. Sewing with thick or synthetic fabric can cause the knives to dull faster. To change the knives, follow the directions in the machine manual.

SELECTING THREAD

Although regular sewing thread may be used with sergers, thread designed especially for sergers offers many advantages. Following are tips for selecting the right thread:

Size and strength. Serger threads are finer in size and have an extra smooth finish for high-speed sewing. Always use a good quality thread to prevent excess breaking and lint accumulation. For normal, nondecorative stitching, use the same type of thread for the needles and loopers to reduce tension adjustments.

Color. When selecting serger thread to match your fabric, you may not find a wide choice of colors. Try selecting a color that blends rather than matches. A shade slightly darker than the fabric will blend best. You may wish to match the needle thread more closely than the other threads, since it is more likely to be seen.

Spool types. Because sergers use more thread, buying larger spools will be more economical. Serger thread may be purchased in tubes or cones. These vary in size. Serger threads are generally cross-wound on the spool. This allows the thread to peel off the top evenly and easily during high-speed sewing.

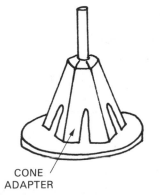

CONE
ADAPTER

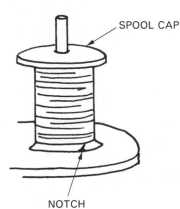

SPOOL CAP

NOTCH

Thread cones and conventional spools require special adapters before they can be used. Cone adapters and spool caps usually come with sergers. They help thread pull off the spools evenly. How they are used will vary with each serger. Generally, the cone adapter is placed on the spool pin and the thread cone is slipped over it. Conventional spools are placed on the spool pin with the notched end of the spool down. The spool cap is then placed over the spool.

Decorative threads. Many specialty threads are available for decorative seaming and edging. Buttonhole twist, pearl cotton, lightweight baby yarn, soft sport yarn, and thin ribbon are examples. Metallic thread, texturized nylon thread, crochet thread, embroidery thread, and tatting thread can also be used for decorative serging. In fact, you can use any thread or yarn that will fit though the eye of the looper.

THREADING THE SERGER

Threading sergers may seem complicated at first. However, with practice, you will soon be able to do it quickly and easily. Following the threading chart located in the machine manual or printed on the serger is helpful. Thread guides are often color or symbol coded to make threading easier.

Thread sergers in the order suggested by the manufacturer. Most sergers thread right to left, with the needles being threaded last. Loopers and needles must be threaded in the correct order. Otherwise, threads may break, or stitches may not form correctly. The lower looper will be the most difficult to thread. Use long handled tweezers to make this task easier. Also, make sure the threads are properly positioned in the tension regulators. Tug on each thread. If the thread pulls with some resistance, it is generally positioned correctly.

Keep in mind that loopers use more thread than needles in forming stitches. Rotate thread spools occasionally to use the thread up evenly.

REMOVING STITCHES FROM THE STITCH FINGER

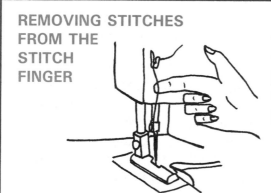

Occasionally, stitches must be removed from the stitch finger. To do this, raise the presser foot and needle. Gently pull the needle thread just above the last thread guide. This will provide a little slack in the thread. Then carefully pull the thread chain off the stitch finger.

EASY THREADING METHOD

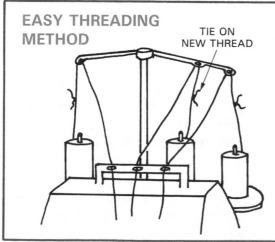

TIE ON NEW THREAD

There is no need to thread the serger each time you change thread. Instead, you can follow these easy steps:

1. Clip threads below the thread guides located above the spools. Replace the spools and tie the threads from the new spools to the old threads using square knots. Tug on the knots to make sure they are secure. (You do not want the knots to pull out halfway through the serger.) Trim thread ends.

(Continued)

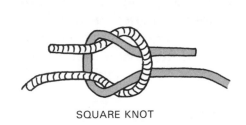

SQUARE KNOT

2. Lift the presser foot and raise the needle. Some sergers may require the tension to be loosened. Remove the threads from the stitch finger and pull each one through the serger. First pull the lower looper thread through, then pull the upper looper thread through. Pull the needle thread(s) through last. Do not try to pull the knots through the eye(s) of the needle(s). Instead, cut the knot from the thread and rethread the needle. Some sergers can be run slowly to draw the thread(s) through them.

TYPES OF SERGER STITCHES

Sergers are classified by the number of threads they use. They perform differently depending upon the number of threads, needles, and loopers they have. Sergers can have two to five threads, one to two needles, and one to three loopers. Presently, there are seven basic serger stitches. Many sergers can make more than one stitch by varying the number of needles and loopers used. However, no one serger can make all the stitches. Read your machine manual to learn what your serger is capable of doing. Following is a list of the basic serger stitches.

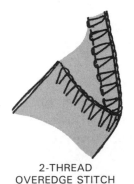

2-THREAD OVEREDGE STITCH

2-thread overedge stitch. *(1 needle and 1 looper)* The threads do not connect or lock at the seamline. This stitch is not strong enough to sew seams. However, it is excellent for finishing edges and flatlocking. (Flatlocking is joining two layers of fabric together by serging a seam and then pulling the seam apart until it lies flat.) Some 3- and 4-thread sergers can convert to 2-threads.

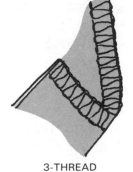

3-THREAD OVERLOCK STITCH

3-thread overlock stitch. *(1 needle and 2 loopers)* The threads connect or lock at the seamline. The stitch can be used to sew seams or finish edges. Flatlocking is possible with tension adjustments. The stitch is stretchy and good for constructing swim wear, aerobic wear, and knit garments. The stitch is also strong enough to use on woven fabrics.

3/4-thread overlock stitch. *(2 needles and 2 loopers)* This is a 3-thread stitch with a fourth

(Continued)

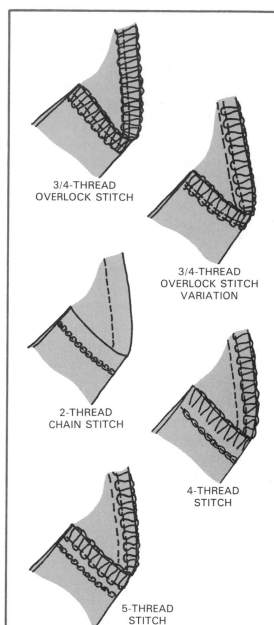

3/4-THREAD OVERLOCK STITCH

3/4-THREAD OVERLOCK STITCH VARIATION

2-THREAD CHAIN STITCH

4-THREAD STITCH

5-THREAD STITCH

stitch running down the middle, adding durability. Seams constructed with this stitch stretch almost as much as a 3-thread stitch. The stitch is good on all fabric weights. It is especially good for constructing active wear. For a wide 3-thread stitch, drop the inside needle. For a narrow 3-thread stitch, drop the outside needle.

3/4-thread overlock stitch variation. *(2 needles and 2 loopers)* This stitch is a variation of the 3/4-thread overlock stitch above. This stitch looks slightly different. The right needle thread cannot be dropped. The left needle thread may be dropped for a narrow stitch.

2-thread chain stitch. *(1 needle and 1 looper)* This stitch is formed by the left needle and the lower looper on the 4- and 5-thread machines.

4-thread stitch. *(2 needles and 2 loopers)* This stitch combines a 2-thread chain stitch and a 2-thread overedge stitch. The chain stitch makes a secure seam. The overedge stitch finishes seam edges. The 4-thread stitch is excellent for woven fabrics. It is not as good for stretch knits, because it has less stretch than a 3-thread stitch.

5-thread stitch. *(2 needles and 3 loopers)* This stitch consists of a 2-thread chain stitch and a 3-thread overlock stitch. Each stitch can be used alone.

MACHINE STITCHING

You will find stitching with a serger quite different from stitching with a conventional machine. To serge, follow these steps:

1. Begin without fabric under the presser foot. With the presser foot in a lowered position, hold the thread chain or tails lightly behind it. Step on the foot control and form a few inches of chain. This is called "chaining off."

2. Place fabric in front of the presser foot, aligning it to the proper seam width. Usually, there is no need to lift the presser foot,

(Continued)

as the longer feed dogs will pull the fabric under it. For some slippery or heavy fabrics, you may have to lift the presser foot.

3. Step on the foot control and guide the fabric under the presser foot, controlling the seam width as you serge. Be sure not to push or pull the fabric.

4. After serging the seam, chain off about 5 inches. Then use the serger to cut the chain. This is done by bringing the fabric to the front of the serger. Place the chain over the presser foot and into the knives. As you run the serger, the knives will cut the chain. For some sergers, the chain must be placed under the presser foot. Be sure to leave at least 2 inches of chain attached to the fabric.

WHEN THREADS BREAK

Occasionally, you will run out of thread, or a thread will break as you are serging. When this happens, lift the presser foot. Raise the needle out of the fabric and remove the fabric from the serger. Gently pull the chain off the stitch finger. Rethread the machine and chain off 3 inches. Place the fabric back under the presser foot. Line it up so that the previous stitching will overlap 1/2 inch and the seam edge rests against the knife. Then, place the needle in the fabric. Lower the presser foot and stitch, being careful not to cut the original stitches.

SEAM GUIDELINES

Some sergers have seam guidelines marked on the machine front. They may be located in different places, depending on the serger. If your serger does not have seam guidelines, make your own with masking tape. You may also mark the seamline on the fabric using a water soluble or air erasable marking pen. When serging, the seamline is where the needle enters the fabric. As you serge, learn to watch the knives, rather than the needles as in conventional sewing. This will correctly guide fabric through the serger.

ADJUSTING THE TENSION

Learning to regulate the tension on a serger is very important. The tension must be adjusted with any change in fabric, thread, or stitch pattern. A serger may have from two to five tension regulators—one for each thread. Therefore, learning to adjust the tension may seem confusing at first. However, with practice, you will soon be able to do it quickly and easily.

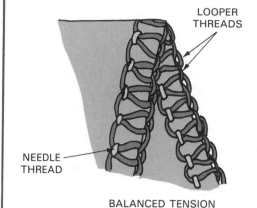

LOOPER THREADS

NEEDLE THREAD

BALANCED TENSION

For a strong seam that will not pull apart, use a balanced tension. When the tension is balanced, the needle threads should be smooth with no loops. The looper threads should interlock at the edge of the fabric. Loops should not pull to either side. Fabric in the seam should not curl or pucker. The tension can be balanced by tightening or loosening the needle and looper tensions. Check your machine manual for correct tension settings and how to make adjustments. Always serge a test seam on scraps from the fabric you will be using.

ADJUSTING THE STITCH LENGTH

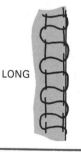

LONG

SHORT

Stitch length can be varied using the stitch length regulator. The number of settings available depends on the machine brand. Use a longer stitch length for heavy fabrics and a shorter stitch length for lightweight fabrics. You will need to adjust the stitch length when finishing edges and constructing narrow rolled or unrolled hems.

ADJUSTING THE STITCH WIDTH

WIDE

NARROW

Stitch width refers to the bite of, or the amount taken by, the overlock stitch. Stitch width can be varied by removing a needle, or adjusting the knife position and size of the stitch finger. Some sergers have a dial that changes stitch width by adjusting the position of the knives and stitch finger for you. Generally, a wider stitch width is used for heavy fabrics and a narrower stitch width is used for lightweight fabrics. Tension adjustments may also be necessary when changing from one stitch width to another.

ADJUSTING THE DIFFERENTIAL FEED REGULATOR

Some sergers have a differential feed regulator. This control adjusts the speed at which the feed dogs move the fabric under the presser foot. This feature makes it possible to serge stretchy, heavy, or slippery fabrics without causing stretching or puckering.

Read the machine manual to determine the normal setting. By moving the differential feed regulator to a higher number, the front feed dog will move at a faster rate. This causes more fabric to feed under the front of the presser foot, than is released from the back. Use this setting for heavy or stretchy fabrics. Moving the regulator to a lower number will cause the front feed dog to move at a slower rate than the rear feed dog. Use this setting for slippery or lightweight fabrics. Always do a test on a fabric scrap before serging on your project.

ADJUSTING THE PRESSURE REGULATOR

The pressure regulator is located on top of the serger. To increase pressure on the presser foot, turn the regulator to the right. To decrease pressure, turn it to the left. Increase pressure for heavy fabrics and decrease pressure for lightweight fabrics. However, if you are using extremely heavy fabric, such as fake fur, you may need to decrease the pressure.

SECURING SEAM ENDS

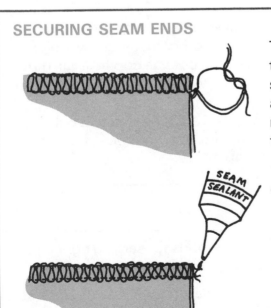

Backstitching is not possible on a serger. Therefore, other means must be used to secure the serging at the beginning and end of the seams. When a serged seam is crossed by another seam, securing the ends may not be necessary. When seam ends must be secured, try any of the following methods:

Method 1. Knot the chain close to the fabric edge.

Method 2. Use seam sealant on the thread chain near the fabric edge at the end of the seam. Seam sealant, a liquid glue, is best used in small areas where it will not show, because it can stiffen and darken the fabric. After the sealant dries, cut off the excess chain. If

(Continued)

desired, the chain may be knotted before seam sealant is applied.

Method 3. Secure the chain tails in the seam. At the beginning of the seam, make one stitch on the fabric. Lift the presser foot and swing the chain to the serger front. Then, place the chain on the seam allowance, lower the presser foot, and serge over the chain.

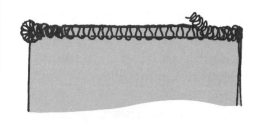

At the end of the seam, stop serging when the needle is one stitch off the fabric. Pull a little slack in the thread above the needle. Lift the presser foot, and raise the needle. Slip the chain off the stitch finger. Flip the fabric over and to the front of the serger. Lower the presser foot and serge over the last few stitches and off the edge of the fabric. Be careful not to cut the stitches already sewn.

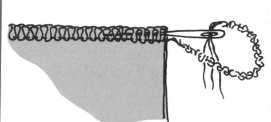

Method 4. Thread the excess chain through a large-eyed needle. Run the needle under six to eight stitches. Cut off the excess chain.

SERGING CURVES

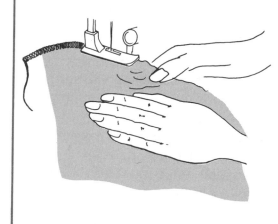

Serging curved areas can be tricky. Serge slowly, feeding the fabric with your hands at the front of the presser foot. Do not try to guide the fabric from the side or behind the presser foot. If seams are very curved, lift the presser foot every few inches and turn fabric under it.

You will not always be able to serge outside curves using a serger. For instance, when constructing a collar, the outside curved edge must be clipped. This allows the collar to lie flat when turned. Clipping would cause the serged stitching to be cut, and the seam would not hold. Use a conventional machine for seams with outside curves.

TURNING OUTSIDE CORNERS

There are two methods for serging right angle outside corners. Follow the procedures below:

Method 1. This method will be the easiest, but not the most attractive. Serge one side,

(Continued)

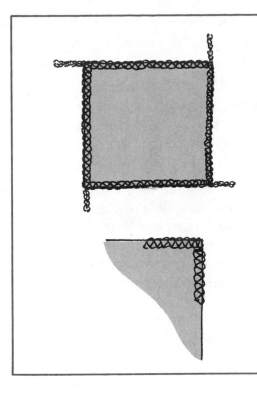

leaving a chain at both ends. Serge the remaining sides in the same manner. As you serge remaining sides, you will cross previous stitching, cutting off the chain ends. When finished, secure seam ends.

Method 2. This method will be more attractive, but requires experience. Serge slowly to the corner. When the needle is one stitch off the fabric, stop. Lift the needle and presser foot. Pull a small amount of slack in the thread above the needle. Be careful, because too much slack will result in a loop in the stitching. Gently pull the chain off the stitch finger. Turn the fabric, so the next edge is touching the knife blade. Lower the presser foot and continue serging.

TURNING INSIDE CORNERS

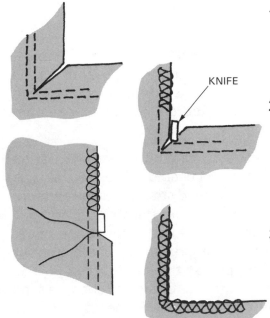

KNIFE

Serging right angle inside corners can be difficult. Follow these steps:

1. Mark stitching and cutting lines for 1 inch on each side of the corner. Clip to the corner.

2. Serge the seam until the knife comes to the cutting line on the next edge. Lift the presser foot and straighten the corner. Fold the fabric away from the knives. A pleat will form to the left.

3. Serge the remaining edge. The fabric should lie flat after serging. Do not clip the stitching at the corner.

SERGING IN A CIRCLE

Serging in a circle refers to serging that begins and ends in the same place. Serging seen around the edges of some place mats and

(Continued)

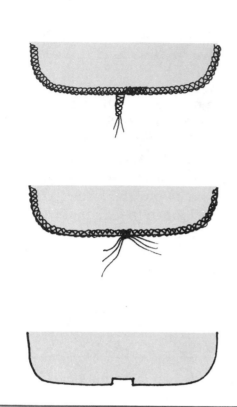

along the hems of some garments are examples. There are two ways to serge in a circle. Follow the methods below:

Method 1. When the edge will not show on the finished item, simply serge all the way around, overlapping stitching. Then, serge off the fabric edge and trim the chain.

Method 2. When you want an attractive edge on necklines, hems, or place mats, try this method. Pull unchained threads from the stitch finger. Hold the thread tails to the back of the serger. Beginning in an inconspicuous place, serge around the edge. Overlap only a few stitches at the end. Then, lift the presser foot and needle and pull unchained threads from the serger. Tie knots in the threads. Trim the threads and secure with seam sealant.

This technique can also be used when trimming off a seam allowance. Cut away the seam allowance 1 inch at the place you plan to begin serging.

RIPPING OUT SERGING

It is best to avoid making mistakes when using a serger. Ripping out serged seams can be time-consuming. Also, since sergers trim seam allowances as they stitch, some mistakes are difficult to correct.

However, seams can be ripped out when needed. The method used depends on the type of stitch. For a 2-thread stitch, slide a seam ripper down the fabric under the stitches and pull out the threads. For 3- and 4-thread stitches, snip the needle threads every three or four stitches. Then, pull on the looper threads. The stitching will unravel. Chain stitches can be removed by pulling on the looper thread.

CARE OF THE SERGER

Proper care of the serger will result in fewer machine problems. Follow care and maintenance recommendations in your machine

(Continued)

manual. Oil the serger regularly. Because the serger trims fabric as it stitches, special attention must be given to keeping it clean. Use a soft brush to remove lint from the knife area. Cans of compressed air are also available for this task.

MACHINE PROBLEMS

As with any conventional machine, your serger may not always work properly. If you have problems, run through this checklist:

- Check to see if the serger is properly threaded. If necessary, pull all the threads from the serger. Rethread the serger in the order recommended by the manufacturer.

- Check to see if the knife area is clean and free from lint.

- Check the tension. Refer to your machine manual for how to make adjustments.

- Check to see if the needles are inserted correctly. If they are not, replace them according to the machine manual.

Name _____

Date _____ Period _____

Activity 44-1: Identifying Serger Machine Parts

At the bottom of this page is a list of basic serger machine parts. Notice the headings. They will help you learn the functions of the various parts.

Your teacher will give you a diagram of the serger you will be using. Attach the diagram in the space provided below. On the diagram, locate each of the parts listed at the bottom of the page. To help you do this, refer to the "Serger Machine Parts" box.

Note: Some sergers may not have all of the following parts.

THREADING
thread guides
tension regulators (2-5)
loopers (1-3)
spool pins (2-5)

NEEDLE
needles (1-2)
needle clamp screws
throat plate

PRESSURE
pressure regulator
presser foot
presser foot lever

KNIVES
movable knife
stationary knife

FEEDING
feed dogs
differential feed regulator

MISCELLANEOUS
power and light switch
hand wheel

STITCH CONTROL
stitch length regulator
stitch width regulator
stitch finger

In addition to the parts listed above, your teacher may help you locate the following:

needle/knife guard
sewing light

seam guidelines
thread guide pole

thread stand
threading chart

Name _____

Date _____ Period _____

Activity 44-2: Practicing Using the Serger

Supplies needed:

serger	scissors
conventional machine	machine needles
serger machine manual	serger attachments
cones and spools of thread	screwdriver (if required)
fabric swatches	

The left-hand column of the following chart lists various tasks required in using the serger. Demonstrate your ability to perform each task. Then complete the right-hand column by providing the sign of task performance requested. This may require that you make a sample or answer a question. You may need to obtain the signature of someone who observed you perform the task. In this case, your teacher will tell you who is to observe your task performance.

TASK	SIGN OF TASK PERFORMANCE
HOW SERGERS DIFFER FROM CONVENTIONAL MACHINES Using previously learned knowledge of conventional machines and sergers, analyze how they are different.	What machine parts does the serger have that the conventional machine does not have?_____ _____
CHANGING THE SERGER NEEDLE(S) Remove the needle(s). Inspect for blunt or burred ends. Replace the needle(s) correctly following the machine manual.	Signature of observer: _____
LOCATING THE KNIVES Locate the upper and lower knives on the serger. Read the machine manual to learn how the knives are removed. Do not attempt to remove them.	Signature of observer: _____
SELECTING THREAD Prepare your serger for both spools and cones of thread. Use the cone adapter and spool cap for your serger. Follow the directions in the ''Selecting Thread'' box.	Signature of observer: _____
THREADING THE SERGER Thread the serger, using the threading diagram provided on the machine or in the manual. For easy viewing, use a different color thread for each spool. Be sure to use the correct spool adapters. Use the same type of thread throughout for easy tension control.	Signature of observer: _____
EASY THREADING METHOD To shorten threading time, thread the serger by using the easy threading method. Follow the directions given in the ''Easy Threading Method'' box. Continue to use different color thread.	Signature of observer: _____

(Continued)

Name _____

TASK	SIGN OF TASK PERFORMANCE
TYPES OF STITCHES Read the machine manual to identify which types of stitches your serger can make.	Signature of observer: _____
MACHINE STITCHING Practice machine stitching. Follow the procedure described in the ''Machine Stitching'' box. Use the serger to cut the chain at the end of stitching.	Did you end stitching by cutting the chain using the serger knives? Yes_____ No_____ What type of stitch does the serger make? See the ''Types of Serger Stitches'' box. _____ Are any other stitches possible? Can either needle thread be dropped? Can the serger chain stitch? _____ _____ Show samples of the various stitches that can be made.
WHEN THREADS BREAK Serge a seam, stopping in the middle of the seam. Remove the fabric from the serger. Resume serging, following the procedure described in the ''When Threads Break'' box.	Show sample.
SEAM GUIDELINES Find the seam guidelines on the machine front. Align raw edges of the fabric to a 5/8-inch seam width. Serge, allowing the serger to trim away the seam allowance.	Where are the seam guidelines located? _____ How wide is the finished seam? _____ How much did the serger trim away? _____
ADJUSTING THE TENSION Serge a long sample seam, stopping and making tension adjustments at various points along the seam. Adjust one tension dial at a time. Turn the dial tighter, then looser. Serge after each adjustment. Check to see how the adjustments affect the stitch. Return the serger to a normal balanced tension.	Show sample of various tension adjustments ending with a balanced tension.
ADJUSTING THE STITCH LENGTH Serge a long sample, making stitch length adjustments at various points along the sample.	Show sample of various stitch lengths.
ADJUSTING THE STITCH WIDTH Serge a long sample. Make stitch width adjustments at various points along the sample.	Show sample of various stitch widths.

(Continued)

Name _____

TASK	SIGN OF TASK PERFORMANCE
ADJUSTING THE DIFFERENTIAL FEED REGULATOR Locate the differential feed regulator on the serger. Serge on various weights of fabric, experimenting with the differential feed regulator.	What effect did the differential feed adjustments have on the various types of fabrics?_____ _____ _____
LOCATING THE PRESSURE REGULATOR Locate the pressure regulator on the serger.	Signature of observer: _____
SECURING SEAM ENDS Secure seam ends by knotting threads and using seam sealant on the thread chain near the fabric edge. Secure seam ends at the beginning and the end by serging the chain in the seam. Thread the excess chain through a large-eyed needle. Run the needle under the stitching.	Show sample. Show sample. Show sample.
SERGING CURVES Cut two pieces of fabric, one an inside curve and the other an outside curve. Edge stitch each sample using a serger. Serge the same samples again, but this time serge on the 5/8-inch guideline. You will be cutting off the first line of stitching.	Show samples. Where did you place your hands in order to control the fabric as you serged the curves? _____ _____ When will you not be able to serge outside curves? _____
TURNING OUTSIDE CORNERS Serge outside corners using both methods described in the ''Turning Outside Corners'' box. To complete this task, you will also need to refer to the ''Removing Stitches from the Stitch Finger'' box.	Show sample of Method 1. Show sample of Method 2.
TURNING INSIDE CORNERS Cut an inside right angle corner on a piece of fabric. Serge the corner. Follow the directions in the ''Turning Inside Corners'' box.	Show sample of a serged inside corner.
SERGING IN A CIRCLE Serge a circle, following the procedure for Method 2 described in the ''Serging in a Circle'' box.	Show sample of Method 2. When would you use Method 1? _____
RIPPING OUT STITCHING Serge a seam. Using a seam ripper, remove the stitching.	What is the easiest way to remote stitching for the serger you are using? _____ _____
CARE OF THE SERGER Brush away the lint that has collected around the knives of the serger.	Signature of observer: _____
MACHINE PROBLEMS List the points you would check if you were having trouble with your serger. Try to list them in the order you would check them. See the ''Machine Problems'' box for assistance, if necessary.	Serger Machine Problem Checklist 1. 2. 3. 4.

Name _____

Date _____ Period _____

Activity 44-3: Evaluating Learning

Evaluate your learning by filling in the information requested on this page. Complete the final section to evaluate your skill mastery.

1. Briefly explain how sergers make sewing fast and easy.

2. List four ways sergers differ from conventional machines.

    a.

    b.

    c.

    d.

3. In your own words, explain the function of the following serger machine parts:

PART	FUNCTION
Loopers	
Stitch finger	
Knives	
Differential feed regulator	

4. Match the following serger stitches with their names.

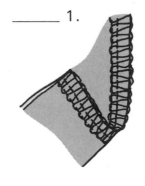 _____ 1.

 _____ 3.

a. 2-thread overedge stitch.

b. 5-thread stitch.

c. 3/4-thread overlock stitch.

d. 4-thread stitch.

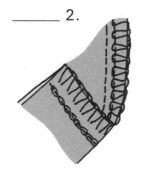 _____ 2.

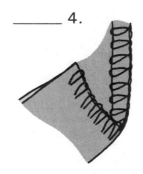 _____ 4.

(Continued)

Name _____

5. List three factors to consider when selecting thread.

   a. _____

   b. _____

   c. _____

6. List three steps you would take if your serger was not forming stitches correctly.

   a. _____

   b. _____

   c. _____

7. Answer the following questions by circling yes or no.

   a. Do you feel you know how to thread the serger?   Yes   No
   b. Do you feel you know how to thread the serger using
      the easy threading method?   Yes   No
   c. Do you know how to replace serger needle(s)?   Yes   No
   d. Do you know how to adjust the tension regulators?   Yes   No
   e. Do you know what to do when the serger stitches
      incorrectly?   Yes   No
   f. Do you know how to clean and care for the serger?   Yes   No
   g. Do you feel comfortable performing most of the
      techniques presented in this lesson?   Yes   No

   If the answer is no, circle those you feel uncomfortable doing.

   Machine stitching   Securing seam ends
   Resuming stitching when threads break   Serging curves
   Following seam guidelines   Turning inside corners
   Adjusting the stitch length   Turning outside corners
   Adjusting the stitch width   Serging in a circle
   Adjusting the differential feed regulator Ripping out stitching

notes

Lesson 45 Serger Construction Techniques

Objectives

This lesson will help you to:
1. Explain how using sergers affects pattern choice and fabric selection.
2. Identify areas on a sewing project where serging would be appropriate.
3. Determine construction order of a serged project.
4. Explain how using sergers changes conventional construction techniques.
5. Demonstrate serger construction techniques, such as seaming, gathering, hemming, and decorative stitching.

Words to Know

decorative lapped seam
decorative serging
finished-edge hem
flat construction
flatlocked hem
flatlocked seam

lettuce-leaf hem
mock band hem
mock flat-felled seam
mock French seam
narrow double-stitched seam
narrow rolled hem

narrow turned-under hem
narrow unrolled hem
ribbon-finished hem
serged/topstitch seam
single-layer construction
stabilize

Gathering Information

This lesson presents important information and sewing techniques that will help you construct a project using a serger. As you read through the information, you will discover that sewing with a serger is very different from using a conventional machine. Don't worry! You will soon master the skills required to construct a project using a serger.

SELECTING A PATTERN	Any pattern can be sewn faster and more professionally with a serger. However, because sergers trim seam allowances as they stitch, they are best used to construct projects that do not require precise fitting. Select patterns for loose, unfitted garments, or garments where fit is achieved through the stretch of the fabric. Seams do not need to lie flat, and fitting adjustments are generally not as important for these types of garments.

MAKING FABRIC CHOICES

Most fabric is suitable for serging. In fact, fabrics that would create stitching problems on conventional machines can be easily stitched on sergers. These include slippery, lightweight, and stretchy fabrics. Knits and stretch wovens are especially suitable for serging, because sergers form stitches that stretch with the fabric.

When you select fabric, consider its weight. Quite often serged projects are constructed using single-layer construction. This means interfacings, facings, and undercollars are eliminated. Therefore, the fabric selected must have enough body to maintain its shape with a single layer of fabric. Also, be sure to consider both sides of the fabric. In single-layer construction, cuffs, collars, and lapels may be turned back so that both sides of the fabric are seen.

DECIDING WHERE TO SERGE

DECORATIVE FINISHING

DECORATIVE SEAMS

SERGED SEAMS

SERGED BELT LOOPS

SINGLE-LAYER CONSTRUCTION

SERGED HEM

After selecting your pattern and fabric, you must decide where to serge on your project. The pattern instruction sheet may help you make this decision. All major pattern companies offer patterns featuring special instructions for sergers. However, you will have to make the final decision about where to serge. As you become more familiar with what sergers can do, you will find it easier to make these judgments.

Look through your pattern instruction sheet. Decide where the serger can be used to save you time. However, be sure you can still achieve the look you want. Here are some questions to ask yourself:

- Can seams be serged, or only edge finished?
- Can decorative serging be used?
- Can collar, cuff, or lapel facings be eliminated and single-layer construction used?
- Can linings be eliminated by serging seams and edges?
- Can bands, ribbing, elastic, and lace be attached using a serger?
- Can pockets, ties, straps, belt loops, ruffles, and hems be constructed using a serger?

DETERMINING CONSTRUCTION ORDER

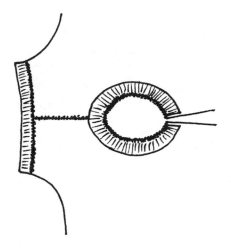

Your decisions about where to serge on your project can affect the construction order. The pattern instruction sheet may give you suggestions for construction order. However, you will have to make the final decision based upon the look you want to achieve.

A sewing method, called flat construction, is often used to assemble garments. It is more efficient when serging, and decorative stitching can be ended more attractively. Flat construction means that necklines, armseyes, sleeves, and hems are finished before the underarm and side seams are serged. Generally, one shoulder seam is serged first, and then the neckline is finished. Following, the other shoulder seam is serged, and then the sleeve cuffs or hems are finished. The underarm and side seams are serged next. Finally, the garment is hemmed.

Careful consideration must also be given to the construction order of pants. Flat construction can be used to some extent. For instance, you may decide to finish the seam allowance edges. This will be your first step. Then you construct tucks or darts, insert the zipper, and attach the pockets. Complete these details before sewing the side seams, inseams, and crotch seams using a conventional machine. After the seams have been stitched, construct the waistband and attach it to the pants. Finally, edge finish and hem the pants. If you decide to serge the pant seams and attach an elastic waistband, your construction steps will vary. Refer to your pattern instruction sheet to help you make important decisions about construction order.

PATTERN ADJUSTMENTS

Make sure garments fit before you serge. Seams are difficult to rip out because sergers trim the seam allowances as they stitch. If you plan to serge a fitted garment, pin seams together first and try the garment on. Make any adjustments necessary to make it fit right. Then serge the garment pieces together.

TRANSFERRING PATTERN SYMBOLS TO THE FABRIC

Notches and clips are generally used to align fabric layers. In most cases, you will still be able to follow these guides. However, if you are finishing seam edges using a serger, the notches and clips will be trimmed away. In this case, mark notches and clips in the seam allowance using an air erasable or water soluble marking pen, tailor's tacks, or chalk.

PRESSING AS YOU SERGE

You have already learned how very important pressing is in achieving a professional-looking garment. Pressing is just as important when using a serger. Press seams open or to one side to relax threads and achieve a flat, finished look.

STAYSTITCHING

When constructing a serged project, you may still need to staystitch curved and bias cut edges using a conventional machine. This prevents stretching. To conceal the staystitching, use decorative serging. See Lesson 13, "Staystitching," for correct staystitching procedures.

BASTING

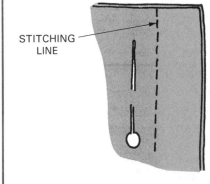

STITCHING LINE

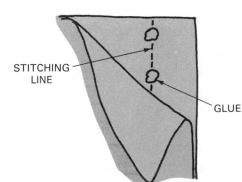

STITCHING LINE

GLUE

When serging, there is little need to baste fabric layers together. The longer presser foot and feed dogs hold the fabric securely and feed it evenly. Simply match the fabric ends together before beginning to serge.

Occasionally pin basting will be necessary. Use caution! Serging over pins will damage the knives. Remove all pins before serging over them. There is less chance of serging over pins if they are placed to the left of the seam, parallel to the seamline. Use pins with large heads to avoid losing them in the fabric.

Several other methods of basting may be useful. Small dots of water soluble glue may be placed two to three inches apart along the seamline of one layer of fabric. Press the second layer to the first and serge. Glue dots may be placed closer together on slippery fabric. Hand basting can also be used to hold layers of very slippery fabrics together.

FINISHING SEAM ALLOWANCES AND EDGES

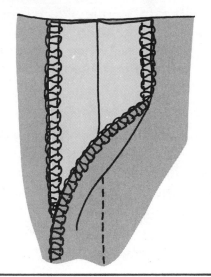

Sometimes you will want to use a serger to finish the edges of facings and hems. Perhaps you want to keep the traditional 5/8-inch seam allowance and then serge the seam edges. To finish edges and seam allowances, use a medium to long stitch length and a medium to wide stitch width. Serge along the fabric edge, being careful not to cut the fabric. There is no need to finish edges that will later be encased, such as necklines and waistlines.

SERGING SEAMS

Sergers make seam construction fast and easy. Sergers stitch seams, trim off seam allowances, and finish edges all in one simple step. They can be used to simplify making traditional seams by neatly finishing edges. You can also make your own creative seams by using decorative threads. The type of seam you choose will depend on the project design, fabric characteristics, and durability desired. You may want to refer back to Lesson 14, "Seams," to compare serged seams with their conventional counterparts. The pattern instruction sheet may give you suggestions for the type of seam to use. You will need to make decisions based on your own fabric and needs.

Most seams are serged along the standard 5/8-inch seamline unless otherwise specified. Here are a few types of serged seams:

Narrow double-stitched seam. Using a conventional machine, straight stitch the seam at 5/8 inch with right sides together. Using the serger, serge with the needle in the seam allowance 1/8 inch from first line of stitching. Use this seam with knits where moderate stretch is desired and light to medium weight wovens. Use this seam where reinforcement is needed, such as crotch seams and the underarm area of set-in sleeves.

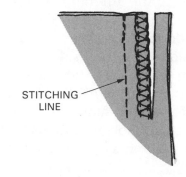

STITCHING LINE

(Continued)

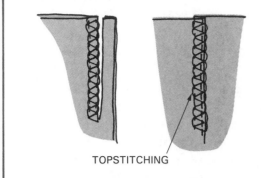

Serged/topstitch seam. With wrong sides of fabric together, serge the seam. If desired, decorative thread may be used. Open the fabric out and press the seam to one side. Using a conventional machine, topstitch the seam to the fabric. Use this seam when decorative stitching is desired on light to medium weight fabrics.

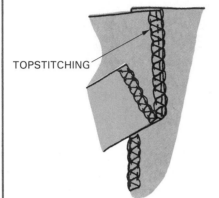

Decorative lapped seam. Decide which edge of the seam you wish to appear on the outside of the project. With decorative thread, serge the overlap edge along the stitching line, trimming away the seam allowance. Finish the underlap edge using regular serger thread. Trim the seam allowances only slightly.

To construct the seam, lap the decorative seam edge over the top of the regular seam edge, matching the 5/8-inch stitching lines. Using a conventional machine, topstitch the seam in place. Fusible web may be used to hold the seam in place while stitching. Use this seam when decorative stitching is desired on medium to heavy weight fabrics.

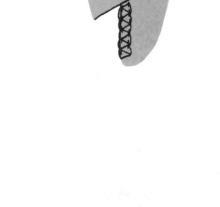
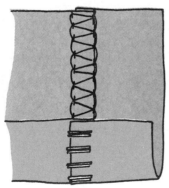

Flatlocked seam. To make this seam, begin by adjusting the serger for flatlocking. For a 2-thread stitch, slightly loosen the needle and looper tensions. For a 3-thread stitch, almost completely loosen the needle tension and tighten the lower looper tension. Refer to the machine manual for specific directions.

Serge two layers of fabric together. Pull the two layers of fabric apart so the seam allowance lies flat inside the stitching. The appearance of the stitch on the outside of the project will differ. This depends on whether you serge with the right sides or wrong sides of the fabric together. Some sergers may not flatlock. Use this seam when decorative stitching is desired. It is good for many fabric weights. However, it may not be suitable for fabrics that ravel. Test stitch on a fabric swatch to check for desired effect.

(Continued)

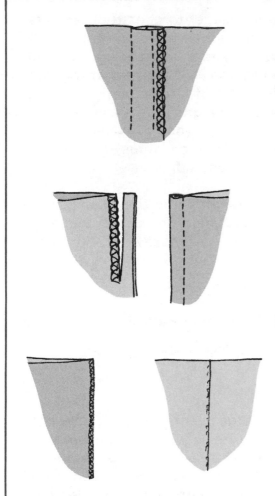

Mock flat-felled seam. Decide which direction you want the seam allowance to lie. Serge the edge that will end up being the longest. Stitch the seam using a conventional machine. Trim the unserged seam allowance to 1/4 inch. Lay the long serged edge over the unserged edge and topstitch from the right side using a conventional machine. Use this seam on medium to heavy fabrics.

French seam. With fabric pieces wrong sides together, serge a 1/4-inch seam, leaving a 1/8-inch seam allowance. Turn the fabric right sides together, encasing the seam and press. Using a conventional machine, straight stitch 1/4 inch from the edge. Use this seam on sheer and lightweight fabrics.

Mock French seam. Serge this seam using a narrow rolled hem. Use this seam when serging on sheer fabric.

GATHERING WITH THE SERGER

Sergers can be used to gather fabric when you need to work in fullness. Here are two methods for gathering with sergers:

Method 1. Using a 3-thread serger, serge along the gathering line. Gently pull on the needle thread to form gathers. Adjust gathers as desired. Secure gathers according to the pattern instruction sheet.

Method 2. Gathering may also be done by serging over a thin cord. Place the cord under the presser foot and hold it against the knife. Serge over the cord, being careful not to cut the cord or catch it in the stitching. Some sergers have a special cording foot that feeds the cord automatically. To form gathers, secure one end of the cord with a pin and pull on the other end. Adjust gathers as desired. If gathers are secured by stitching, remove the cord.

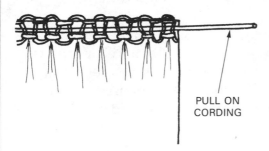

PULL ON CORDING

STABILIZING SEAMS AND EDGES

When using a serger to construct projects, there will be occasions when seams and edges need stabilizing. Areas such as pant crotch seams, shoulder and neckline seams, and front edges receive a lot of stress during wearing. They need extra strength. This is especially important when using loosely woven or very stretchy fabrics. Here are three methods for stabilizing seams and edges:

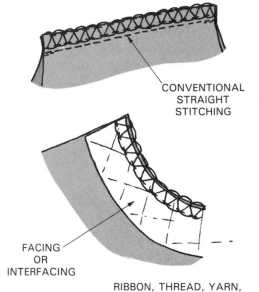

CONVENTIONAL STRAIGHT STITCHING

FACING OR INTERFACING

RIBBON, THREAD, YARN, TWILL TAPE, SEAM BINDING, OR BUTTONHOLE TWIST

Method 1. Straight stitch the seam using a conventional machine. Then serge the seam, stitching close to the first row of stitching.

Method 2. Serge interfacing or a facing to the project.

Method 3. Serge over trims, such as ribbon, seam binding, 1/4-inch twill tape, thread, yarn, or buttonhole twist. Be careful not to cut the fabric and trims you are serging over. When serging over thread, yarn, or buttonhole twist, lay it through and over, rather than under the presser foot. This may prevent it from getting cut. Using a cording foot or a tape sewing foot can be helpful.

CONSTRUCTING HEMS

There are many ways to construct hems using a serger. The method you select will depend on the project design and fabric weight. Here are some types of serged hems:

Finished-edge hem. Serge the fabric edge using a medium stitch width and length. Use this when a very flat hem is desired. It is excellent for hemming tuck-in blouses. A decorative thread may be used to add detail to the hem edge.

Narrow turned-under hem. Serge the fabric edge as for a finished-edge hem. Then turn the

(Continued)

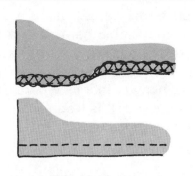

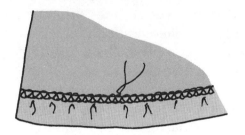

hem up 1/4 inch and edge stitch or topstitch in place, using a conventional machine. Use this hem when a flat, narrow hem is desired.

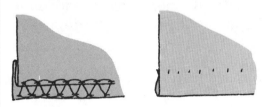

Eased hem. Loosen the needle thread tension and serge the hem edge. Pull on the needle thread to ease in fabric fullness. Following the directions for preparing an eased hem in Lesson 23, "Hemming Methods," turn, press, and hand stitch the hem. This hem is appropriate for wider, turned hems on A-line skirts.

Blind hem. Fold the hem up and back as you would for a conventional blind hem. Serge, barely catching the fold in the stitching. Stitching may show on the outside of the project. A blind hem foot will make serging this hem easier. Use this hem when you want a quick machine stitched hem. Practice on a fabric swatch before serging on your project.

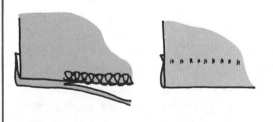

Flatlocked hem. Fold the hem up and back as when making a blind hem. Flatlock with the needle running just on top of the fold. Be careful not to cut the fold. When finished, turn down the hem to flatten the stitches and press. The smaller the needle bite, the less the stitches will show. Use this hem when decorative stitching is desired. It works best when a straight or moderately curved hem is desired.

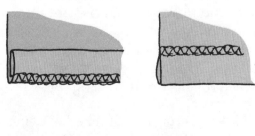

The reverse side of the stitches can appear on the right side of the fabric. Fold up the hem twice to the wrong side and press lightly. From the right side, flatlock along the second fold. Be careful not to cut the fold. Turn the hem down and flatten the stitches. Press.

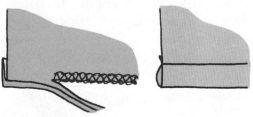

Mock band hem. Fold the hem up and back. Serge, barely cutting off the fold. Use this hem when a decorative band effect is desired. It can also be used to form casings for elastic.

(Continued)

Narrow unrolled hem. Serge, using a 2- or 3-thread stitch to make this hem. Use a narrow to medium stitch width and a short stitch length. Decorative thread may be used. This hem is excellent for heavier fabrics where a less bulky, flat edge is desired. It is frequently used to finish the edges on place mats, tablecloths, ruffles, and scarves.

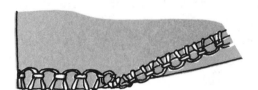

Narrow rolled hem. This hem is made using an unbalanced stitch. As stitches are formed, the fabric edge is rolled under. Tension adjustments are necessary to make a rolled hem. Check the machine manual to see if your serger will make this stitch and for specific settings. Some sergers also require a special foot or throat plate with a narrow stitch finger.

A very short stitch length will produce a satin stitch edge. A little longer stitch produces a picot or scalloped edge. Be sure to do a test sample.

The narrow rolled hem is a very versatile and durable hem. It is often found on ruffles, scarves, circular hems, tablecloths, and napkins. This hemming method is especially useful on delicate, sheer fabrics. It may not be appropriate for loosely woven fabrics, because it may pull out.

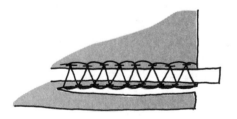

Ribbon-finished hem. To make this hem, use 1/16- to 1/4-inch satin or grosgrain ribbon. Place the ribbon on the right side of the fabric next to the hem fold line. Adjust the stitch width slightly wider than ribbon. Adjust the stitch length so the ribbon will show between stitches. Serge over the ribbon, cutting off the hem allowance. Be careful not to cut the ribbon. Use this hem when a decorative effect is desired. It is especially good for lingerie.

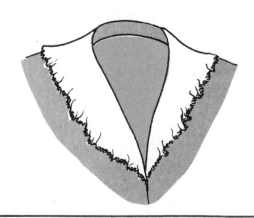

Lettuce-leaf hem. Serge the fabric edge using a rolled or unrolled satin stitch edge. The more stretch the fabric has and the shorter the stitch length, the more the fabric will ruffle. Increasing the pressure on the presser foot will also cause the fabric to ruffle more. You may also gently stretch the fabric as it is being

(Continued)

stitched to increase ruffling. This method can be used to hem dresses, skirts, scarves, ruffles, collars, sleeves, belts, or other project areas where ruffling is desired.

DECORATIVE SERGING

Many decorative stitches can be created using the serger. Here are a few tips for decorative serging:

- Try mixing thread colors and textures to find the combinations you like best. See Lesson 44, "Operating the Serger Machine," for the types of thread that can be used for decorative serging. Stitching is more visible when you use contrasting, shiny, or unusual threads with a shortened stitch length.

- Determine if both sides of the stitch will be visible. Then decide in which needles and loopers the decorative thread should be placed. Use decorative threads in the loopers as often as possible for easier threading. Decorative threads can be used in combination with regular threads.

- Adjust the width, length, tension, and pressure of the stitch. Even small adjustments can make big changes in the look of a finished product. When serging with thicker decorative threads, you will almost always need to use a longer stitch length and loosen the tension. Yarn and ribbon may work better when not threaded through the tension regulators at all. Always do a test sample.

- Hand wind decorative yarn or ribbon onto a spool or arrange it at the back of the serger, so it will not tangle.

- Use sharp, new needles.

- Place the fabric under the presser foot. Hold the thread tail lightly when starting to serge. Serge slowly.

- Use flat construction as much as possible, so the ends of stitching will be attractive.

Name _____

Date _____ Period _____

Activity 45-1: Practicing Serger Construction Techniques

This activity will help you practice the serging techniques you have just studied. Complete the exercises below as best you can. Then practice serger construction techniques following the directions. Refer to the information in this lesson as necessary.

1. In the space provided below, briefly explain how using a serger affects the following:

Pattern Selection	
Fabric Selection	
Pattern Adjustment	
Transferring Pattern Symbols	
Pressing	
Staystitching	
Basting	

2. List three methods for stabilizing seams and edges when serging.

   a. _____

   b. _____

   c. _____

3. For the following garments, indicate the construction order for each detail of the garment. Number the details 1 to 8 in the left-hand column for the knit shirt, and 1 to 10 for the pants. In the right-hand column, indicate the type of machine you would use to construct each detail. Mark S (serger) or C (conventional machine) in the spaces provided.

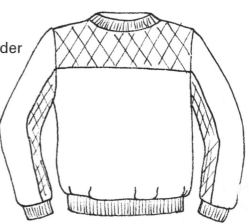

Order S/C Knit Shirt with Ribbing

a. ____ ____ Stitch underarm and side seams.

b. ____ ____ Stitch front and back together at shoulder seams.

c. ____ ____ Attach ribbing to bottom of shirt.

d. ____ ____ Stitch pattern blocks together on front and back.

e. ____ ____ Stitch upper and under sleeve pattern blocks together.

f. ____ ____ Stitch sleeves to bodice.

g. ____ ____ Attach neck ribbing.

h. ____ ____ Attach cuff ribbing.

(Continued)

Name _____

Order S/C Pants

a. ____ ____ Finish pant hem edges.
b. ____ ____ Insert zipper.
c. ____ ____ Construct tucks.
d. ____ ____ Attach waistband to garment.
e. ____ ____ Finish the seam allowance edges.
f. ____ ____ Stitch pockets to pants.
g. ____ ____ Topstitch waistband.
h. ____ ____ Stitch inseams, side seams, and around the pockets.
i. ____ ____ Stitch crotch seam.
j. ____ ____ Hem pants.

Practicing Serging

Practice seaming, gathering, and hemming using the serger. Your teacher will give you additional instructions regarding which seams and hems you are to make. He or she will also tell you how to go about doing them.

Supplies needed:

serger	pins
conventional machine	fabric scraps
thread	decorative thread
shears	water soluble glue

PRACTICING SEAMING For each seam, cut two 6 by 2 inch fabric samples. Place them together to form the seam. If using pins, be careful not to serge over them. Also, try using water soluble glue to hold the fabric layers together. Use decorative threads where appropriate.	Choose from these seams: conventional seam with serged finish narrow double-stitched seam serged/topstitched seam decorative lapped seam flatlocked seam mock flat-felled seam French seam mock French seam
PRACTICING GATHERING Check the machine manual to see how to gather with the serger you are using.	Follow the directions in this lesson for gathering over cording.
PRACTICING HEMMING For each hem, cut one 6 by 4-inch fabric sample. Use decorative thread when appropriate.	Choose from these hems: finished-edge hem narrow turned-under hem eased hem blind hem flatlocked hem mock band hem narrow unrolled hem narrow rolled hem ribbon-finished hem lettuce-leaf hem

Name _____

Date _____ Period _____

Activity 45-2: Evaluating Learning

Evaluate the samples you prepared in Activity 45-1. In the spaces provided on the form, fill in the seams and hems you constructed. Rate your samples from 1 to 5, 1 being poorly done and 5 being very well done. After rating your samples, complete the exercises below. Turn in the samples and evaluation form to your teacher. Be prepared to discuss the results of your evaluation.

	Seam or Hem Types										
Correct procedure followed.											
Correct tension for type of stitch.											
Serging free from puckers and skipped or broken stitches.											
Correct stitch length and width for type of stitch.											
Decorative thread used for appropriate seams or hems.											
Sample looks attractive on both sides.											
Correct seam or hem allowance trimmed away.											
Conventional machine stitching is straight, at an even distance from edge.											

In your own words, explain the following terms:

Flat construction _____

Single-layer construction _____

Mark T (True) or F (False) in the spaces provided below:

_____ 1. Serged seams are best for fitted garments.

_____ 2. Lightweight fabrics are best for single-layer construction.

_____ 3. Make sure a garment fits before serging the seams.

_____ 4. Fabric must be selected carefully for a serged garment, as most is not suitable for this sewing method.

_____ 5. Knits are especially suitable for serging.

_____ 6. When serging seam allowances, it is necessary to mark notches using clips.

_____ 7. Pressing is not as important when serging and can often be skipped.

_____ 8. Curves and bias cut edges of garments need to be staystitched when using a serger.

_____ 9. Pins should be placed parallel and to the left of the seam allowance when serging.

Name _____

Date _____ Period _____

Activity 45-3: Planning a Serged Project

To help you plan a serged project, complete the exercises below. Then answer the following questions. Your teacher may ask you to complete other project planning worksheets included in Unit 5.

Briefly evaluate your pattern in terms of its suitability for serger construction.

_____

_____

_____

_____

Sketch your project below. In the correct order, list the steps you will follow to construct your garment. Indicate the type of machine you would use for each step. Mark S (serger) or C (conventional machine) in the left-hand column.

Sketch

S/C   Construction Steps

a. ____ _____

b. ____ _____

c. ____ _____

d. ____ _____

e. ____ _____

f. ____ _____

g. ____ _____

h. ____ _____

i. ____ _____

j. ____ _____

1. What type of serged seams will you use on your project? Where will they be used?

_____

_____

_____

_____

2. Do you need to stabilize the serged edges on your project? Which method will you use?

_____

_____

_____

_____

(Continued)

Name _____

3. Do you plan to use the serger for edge finishing? What areas of the project do you plan to edge finish?

_____

_____

_____

_____

_____

_____

_____

_____

_____

4. Do you plan to use decorative stitching? Where do you plan to do so?

_____

_____

_____

_____

_____

_____

_____

_____

_____

_____

5. Which hemming methods do you plan to use?

_____

_____

_____

_____

_____

_____

_____

_____

_____

Lesson 46 Constructing a Serged Project

Objectives

This lesson will help you construct a project using a serger. You will apply the following, previously acquired skills:

Unit 3: Learning the Basic (Lessons 1-23)
Unit 6: Constructing the Project (Lessons 24-43)
Lesson 44: Operating the Serger Machine
Lesson 45: Serger Construction Techniques

Helps for Success

Construction methods using a serger are quite different than those used when sewing on a conventional machine. The suggestions given in this lesson will help you construct your project. Read them carefully. Also read the pattern instruction sheet as it may offer additional ideas for serging your project.

In Unit 8, you will find two evaluation forms for the serged project. Read these over before beginning your project. This will help you identify the criteria you should strive to meet. Complete the forms after you finish your project.

CONTINUOUS STITCHING	To save time serging, try serging several seams without stopping in between. Do not stop to cut the chain or lift the presser foot. Simply serge one seam, chain off 4 inches, and serge another. Serge as many seams as you need. After you have finished, cut the chains between seams and secure the ends if necessary.

CONSTRUCTING DARTS 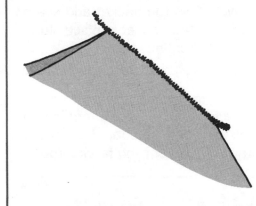	Darts may be constructed using the serger. Mark and shape the darts according to the directions given in Lesson 24, ''Constructing Darts, Tucks, and Pleats.'' Pinning is not necessary. If desired, hand baste or use water soluble glue instead. Serge the dart, from the wide end to the narrow end. The serger knives will trim the dart as you serge. To form the point of the dart, serge off the fabric edge, tapering to a point. Secure stitching at the dart point. Press.

CONSTRUCTING DECORATIVE TUCKS

Sergers can be used to make fast and easy decorative tucks. Decorative tucks can sometimes be constructed on fabric before pattern pieces are cut out. To make tucks, begin by pressing the tucks in the fabric. Adjust the stitch width for the desired tuck size. Then serge along each fold, being careful not to cut it. Knives may be disengaged if desired. Serge all tucks in the same direction, so stitching will appear the same. If desired, use decorative thread in the looper that will be most visible. After the tucks are made, lay pattern pieces over the tucked fabric and cut out as directed.

CONSTRUCTING PATCH POCKETS

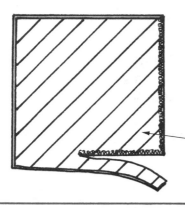

INTERFACING

Begin by fusing interfacing to the wrong side of the pocket for reinforcement. Serge along the facing line and seamline, trimming away the seam allowance and facing. Neatly secure the ends. Align the pocket with the placement markings on the garment. Use a conventional machine to straight stitch the pocket in place.

CONSTRUCTING SEAM POCKETS

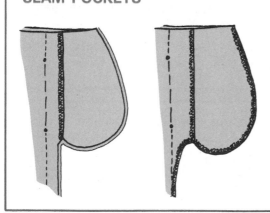

Follow the pattern instruction sheet for basic pocket construction information. Begin by serging the pocket pieces to the garment. Using a conventional machine, straight stitch from the waistline to the first dot. Machine baste to the lower dot. Using a regular stitch length, continue straight stitching several inches below the second dot. Serge the side seam from the lower edge of the garment up to the straight stitching and around the pocket as shown. Fold the pocket and seam toward the front. Serge the pocket in place along the waistline. Remove basting.

CONSTRUCTING TIES AND STRAPS

Without any fabric under the presser foot, stitch a chain 6 inches longer than the strap. Do not cut the chain. Fold the right side of the fabric around

(Continued)

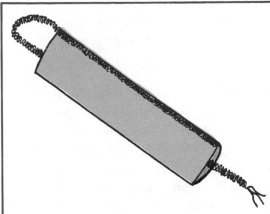

the chain, matching edges. Serge edges together, being sure not to catch the chain in the stitching. The chain should be encased in the fabric. To turn the strap or tie, pull on the chain.

When making spaghetti straps, cut woven fabrics on the bias and knits with the stretch of the fabric. This will provide greater stretch, making them easier to turn and more comfortable to wear. Use a narrow rolled hem for narrow straps. The stitch will act as stuffing for the strap.

CONSTRUCTING BELT LOOPS

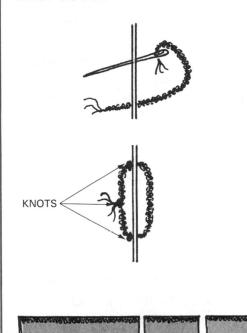

KNOTS

Quick and easy belt loops can be made with the serger. Here are two methods:

Method 1. To make thread belt loops, make a thread chain using the serger. Use topstitching thread in the needles and loopers for added strength. Adjust the machine for a short stitch length and a narrow stitch width. After chaining off enough for all your belt loops, cut the chain into the lengths needed. Then sew the chains into the side seams of your garment. You can also thread the chains in a large-eye or self-threading needle and hand stitch them to the garment. To do this, push the needle through the garment at the desired location from inside to outside to back inside again. Knot as shown.

Method 2. To make fabric belt loops, use heavy single-layered fabrics. If working with lightweight fabric, use a double layer of fabric. Experiment to determine the best belt loop size and stitch width. Serge fabric edges. Then cut the strip into desired lengths. The narrower the belt loop, the narrower the stitching should be.

CONSTRUCTING CENTER-GATHERED RUFFLES

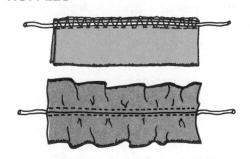

Here is an easy way to make center-gathered ruffles using the serger. Hem the ruffle edges using a narrow rolled hem. Fold the ruffle in half, right sides together. Place cording along the folded edge. Serge over the cording being sure not to cut the cord or fabric. Pull on the cording to gather and adjust the ruffle. Using a conventional machine, stitch the ruffle to the garment using a straight stitch or narrow zigzag stitch.

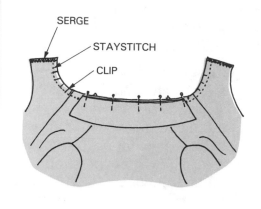

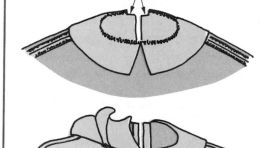

There are numerous ways to attach collars to garments. Directions for attaching two types of collars are given below:

Convertible collar. Prepare the collar following the pattern instruction sheet. Staystitch the neck edge and clip to stitching. Then serge the facing ends. Correctly position the collar on the garment neck edge, matching pattern symbols. Ease the collar to fit the neck edge and pin in place. Fold the facing ends back over the collar and pin.

Serge the neckline seam, removing pins before serging over them. Turn the facing right side out and press. If corners are too bulky, they may be reinforced with conventional straight stitching, and then trimmed and graded. To keep the neckline seam in place, it may be stitched to the bodice from shoulder seam to shoulder seam using a conventional machine. The collar will cover this row of stitching when the garment is worn.

Peter Pan collar. Prepare the collar and finish the neck edge opening according to the pattern instruction sheet. Then pin the right side of the collar to the wrong side of the neck edge, matching pattern symbols. Serge the collar to the garment. Flip the collar over to the right side of the garment. The serged seam will be under the collar.

ATTACHING RIBBING

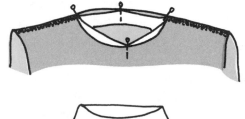

Serge the garment shoulder or sleeve seams together. Then serge the ribbing ends together. Pin the ribbing to the garment neck or sleeve edge. Place the garment under the presser foot, ribbing side up. Serge, stretching the ribbing as needed to fit the garment opening.

For a decorative effect, place the right sides of the ribbing and garment together and flatlock. The stitching will appear on the right side of the garment.

(Continued)

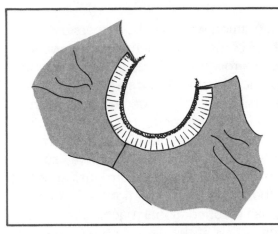

Ribbing can also be attached to garments using flat construction. Serge one shoulder or sleeve seam together. Attach the ribbing. Then serge the other shoulder or sleeve seam, stitching through the ribbing as well.

CONSTRUCTING SLEEVE OPENINGS

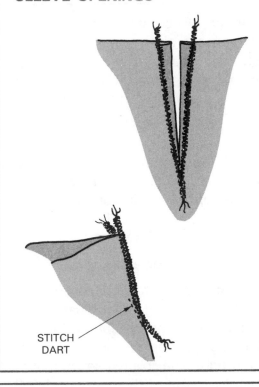

STITCH DART

Mark the location of the sleeve placket on your fabric. Make sure you have done so correctly. If you make a mistake, the opening may appear on the front of the sleeve rather than the back.

Slash the center of the "V" to the point. Carefully serge the opening edge, without trimming. When the knife reaches the corner, lower the needle into the fabric and lift the presser foot. Straighten out the fabric. A pleat will form to the left. Continue serging, being careful not to stitch a tuck in the corner. Practice this technique before serging on your garment. Also review "Turning Inside Corners" in Lesson 44.

Finally, place the right sides of the sleeve placket together and straight stitch a small dart at the end of the placket, using a conventional machine. This is done to keep the placket turned to the underside of the garment. Press as shown.

ATTACHING CUFFS

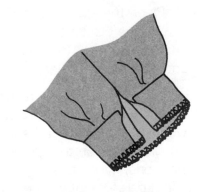

Construct the cuff according to the pattern instruction sheet. The cuff may also be constructed by placing the pieces together and serging along the ends and bottom. When wrong sides are placed together, the stitching will appear on the outside of the cuff as decorative stitching. If you choose to have stitching on the inside of the cuff, place fabric right sides together, serge, turn, and press. Pin the cuff to the sleeve, matching pattern symbols. Be sure the cuff is centered correctly. Fold 1/4 to 3/8 inch of the placket opening back over the cuff. Serge through all thicknesses and secure seam ends. Turn and press.

CONSTRUCTING WAISTBANDS

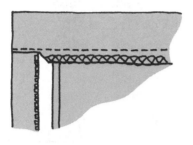

When constructing waistbands, sergers can aid in reducing bulk in the waist seam. Cut the waistband 1/4 inch narrower than usual. Serge the long edge that is usually turned under. Using a conventional machine, stitch the unserged edge of the band to the waistline, matching pattern symbols. Fold the band over as directed by the pattern instruction sheet. Do not fold under a seam allowance on the inside of the garment, except right above the zipper. With the right side of the garment up, use a conventional machine to stitch the long serged edge of the band to the garment.

APPLYING ELASTIC

FOR WOVENS, TURN SEAM ALLOWANCE UNDER

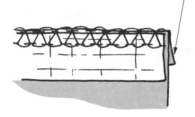

FOR KNITS, TRIM SEAM ALLOWANCE

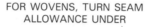

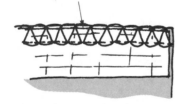

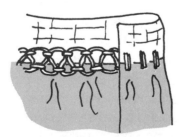

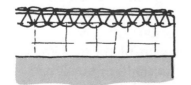

With a serger you will be able to apply elastic fast and easy. You can apply it so it will never bunch or twist. You will also be able to distribute the fullness where it is needed. Using a special elastic applicator foot can help. This foot stretches the elastic as it is being serged. The amount of stretch is adjustable.

The fastest and easiest way to apply elastic is to use flat construction. When using flat construction, the elastic is applied to the garment before the final side seam is sewn. This eliminates serging elastic in curved areas.

Here are two methods for applying elastic:

Flatlocked elastic. This method requires no casings and adds little bulk. Begin by adjusting the serger to flatlock. If using woven fabric, fold the seam allowance to the wrong side. Fold the seam allowance to the right side to reverse the stitch appearance on the outside of the garment. If using knit fabric, cut off the seam allowance.

Cut and mark the elastic according to the pattern instruction sheet. Place the elastic along the garment edge. Serge with the elastic side up, being careful not to cut the elastic. After serging, pull the elastic up until the stitches flatten.

Overlocked elastic. This method is a little bulkier, but can be used with soft elastic and lightweight fabrics. Use a 3- or 3/4-thread stitch. Leave a 1/4-inch seam allowance on the garment. Place the elastic on the fabric, right sides together. Serge the edges, being careful not to cut the

(Continued)

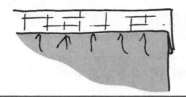

elastic. Stretch the elastic in front of the needle as you serge. After serging, pull the elastic up and the seam allowance toward the garment.

CONSTRUCTING ELASTIC CASINGS

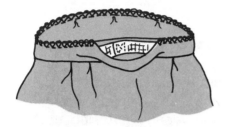

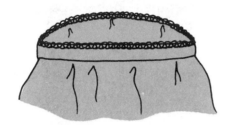

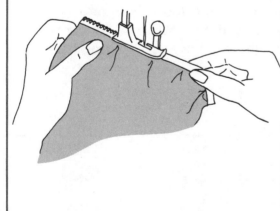

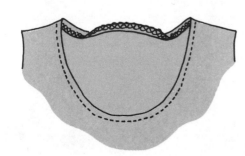

Elastic casings may be used to provide stretch at waistline and sleeve openings. They are also excellent for attaching 1/4-inch elastic to the legs of swim wear and aerobic wear. Here are two methods for constructing elastic casings:

Enclosed elastic bands. Prepare elastic according to the pattern instruction sheet or to fit the body. Try the elastic on to see if it fits comfortably. Cut out the band, making sure it is the appropriate length and 1/2 inch wider than the elastic.

Sew the band into a circle. Then press in half lengthwise. Using pins as markers, divide the band into quarters. Pin the band to the garment opening, matching quarter marks to seams or other pattern markings. Check pattern instruction sheet. Serge the band to the garment through all layers. Don't forget to remove pins before serging. Leave a 2-inch opening.

Insert the elastic into the opening and pull it through the casing. Adjust to the desired size. Lap the elastic ends and securely stitch together. Serge the opening closed.

Fold over elastic application. Divide and mark the top of the garment opening and elastic as directed on the pattern instruction sheet. Note that more elastic is usually allowed in the leg back. Adjust the serger to a medium to long stitch length and a medium to wide stitch width. Serge the elastic to the fabric edge on the wrong side of the fabric with the elastic side up. Hold the fabric and elastic behind the foot, stretching the elastic in front of the needle to fit the garment. Fold the fabric over the elastic to form a casing. Using a conventional machine adjusted to a long stitch, topstitch the casing in place 1/4 inch to 3/8 inch from the edge.

ATTACHING LACE

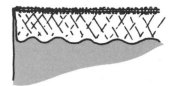

You will find the serger useful for attaching lace to garments. Here are four methods:

Narrow hemmed lace. Place the lace on the wrong side of the garment. Serge edges together using a narrow unrolled hem.

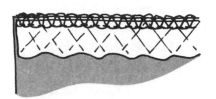

Flatlocked lace. Place the lace on the fabric with right sides together. If the fabric permits, try using transparent tape to hold the lace in place. Flatlock and then flatten the seam.

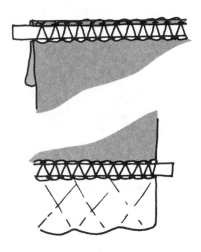

Lace with ribbon. Ribbon may be placed over the lace when lace is serged to the fabric. To do this, trim the seam allowance from the garment. Place lace on the fabric edge, wrong sides together. With the fabric right side up, place 1/8-inch ribbon next to the edge. Using a medium stitch width, serge over the ribbon. Be careful not to catch it in the stitching. Pull on the fabric and lace to flatten.

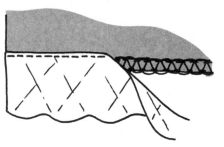

Overlapped lace. Serge the edge of the fabric. On the right side of the fabric, lap the lace 1/4 inch over the serged edge. Using a conventional machine, straight stitch or narrow zigzag the lace in place.

Unit 8   Evaluating the Project

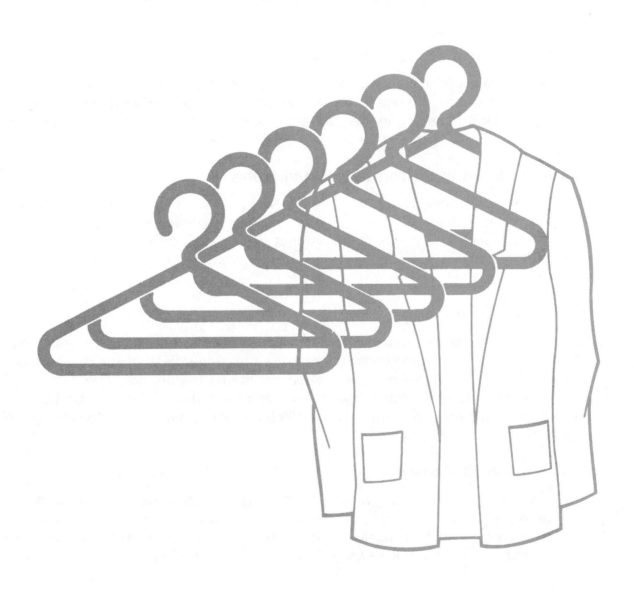

Unit 8
Evaluating the Project

The following forms are used to evaluate your learning from this class. They will help you see your strengths and weaknesses in sewing and serging skills. There are four forms.

Conventional Sewing Project Evaluation

This form may be used to evaluate your finished conventional sewing project. Some of the criteria in this form may have been evaluated as you constructed each portion. Other criteria deal with evaluating the garment as a whole. You, your teacher, or both of you may fill out this form.

Conventional Sewing Performance Evaluation

This form will help you evaluate your own learning. It will help you summarize the skills that you have mastered. It will give you an idea of which skills need practice. Finally, the form will show you some skills that you haven't tried yet. This will help you select future sewing projects that will improve your old skills and allow you to practice new ones.

Serged Project Evaluation

This form may be used to evaluate your finished serged project. When you use a serger, you will often use a conventional machine too. Regardless of the machine used, the same standards of quality apply when evaluating the project. The evaluation form "Conventional Sewing Project Evaluation" and the forms provided in Unit 6 may also be used to evaluate your serged project. Your teacher will tell you which forms to use and how to complete them.

Serger Operation Evaluation

This form will help you evaluate what you have learned about using a serger. It will help you summarize the skills you have mastered. It will give you an idea of additional skills that may be learned. For tasks performed on a conventional machine, you may want to use the "Conventional Sewing Performance Evaluation" form.

Name _____

Date _____ Period _____

Conventional Sewing Project Evaluation

Project description _____

For each section below, place a check in the column that indicates the proper evaluation.

	Poor	Fair	Good	Excellent	Comments
Overall appearance. Clean, neat, smooth, threads clipped.					
Harmony of pattern and fabric. Fabric texture and weight suited to design. Lining, trim, thread, zipper, and interfacing coordinated.					
Care coordination. All parts of the garment require the same care.					
Cut on-grain. All garment pieces are cut on-grain or on a grain that enhances garment shape.					
Marking. Marks do not show on right side of garment.					
Hand stitching. Appropriate stitch used, neatly done. Knots do not show.					
Machine stitching. Appropriate stitch length is used, stitching is straight. Topstitching is an even distance from the edge.					
Pressing. Shows evidence of being pressed as sewn. No press marks or wrinkles.					
Darts. Points tapered, smooth, and securely fastened at ends. Darts pressed down or toward center of garment.					
Seams. Appropriate stitch length used. Seams proper width, pressed flat and smooth. Seam ends meet. Plaids match. Stress seams (such as crotch) properly reinforced.					
Seam finishes. Proper finish for fabric, neatly done.					

(Continued)

Successful Sewing

Name _____

	Poor	Fair	Good	Excellent	Comments
Pockets (seam or patch). Securely stitched with reinforced upper corners. Smooth shape, any topstitching neatly done.					
Zipper. Appropriate method used. Stitching straight, no gap at top edge. Zipper is flat, smooth, well covered. Slides easily.					
Neck facing. Facing edge finished appropriately for fabric. Facing tacked at shoulders and zipper tape, smoothly shaped.					
Armhole facings. Facing edge finished appropriately for fabric. Facings tacked at seams, smoothly shaped.					
Collars and lapels. Free from bulk, smoothly shaped, neck seam clipped and trimmed. Interfacing used.					
Sleeves. Evenly gathered or eased, underarm seam reinforced.					
Cuffs. Sleeve evenly gathered to cuff, opening correctly done. Cuffs interfaced, even in width, neatly hemmed.					
Waistband. Any gathers or tucks joined evenly. Band uniform in width, free from bulk, interfaced, laps properly.					
Casings. Even in width, edge finished appropriately.					
Lining. Neatly attached to garment, fits garment. Ease allowed at hems if attached to garment.					
Hems. Uniform width, secure, flat, inconspicuous. Appropriate method used, fullness evenly distributed. Hand sewing neatly done.					
Buttonholes, buttons, and fasteners. Correctly placed, secure, appropriate for design. Buttons have shank if needed. Stitching neat, double thread used.					
Other (pleats, trims, etc.). Smooth, flat, free from bulk. Durable, neat, correctly done.					
Fit. Length appropriate, crotch length correct. Shoulders, waist, hips fit properly. Darts end at correct point.					

Name _____

Date _____ Period _____

Conventional Sewing Performance Evaluation

Rank yourself from 1 to 10 as to how well you feel you can perform the following tasks. When ranking, 1 represents little skill and 10 represents high performance.

	FABRICS
	Select appropriate fabric, pattern, notions, etc.
	Check care information.
	Make fabric grain perfect.
	Preshrink fabric.
	PATTERN
	Select pattern based on design principles and wardrobe plan.
	Take accurate body measurements.
	Select correct size and figure type.
	Make needed alterations.
	Read instruction sheet.
	Read pattern symbols.
	EQUIPMENT
	Thread the machine.
	Replace machine needle.
	Adjust stitch tension.
	Adjust stitch length.
	Straight stitch.
	Zigzag stitch.
	Serge stitch.
	Blind hem stitch.
	Stretch knit stitch.
	Use various decorative stitches.
	Follow seam guidelines.
	Backstitch.
	Machine embroider.
	Turn a square corner.
	Use small sewing equipment.
	Use pressing equipment.
	BASIC TECHNIQUES
	Lay out and pin pattern
	Cut out pattern.
	Mark with chalk, tailor's tacks, and tracing paper.
	Press.
	Staystitch.
	Construct plain seams.
	Clip seams.
	Trim and grade seams.
	Finish seams.

	BASIC TECHNIQUES (Continued)
	Construct flat-felled seams, French seams, slot seams, etc.
	Understitch.
	Clean finish.
	Gather and ease.
	Apply interfacing.
	Topstitch.
	Hand stitch.
	Construct darts.
	Construct tucks.
	Construct pleats.
	Construct patch pockets.
	Construct seam pockets.
	Construct ties.
	Insert an invisible zipper.
	Insert a centered and a lapped zipper.
	Construct a placket opening.
	Apply facing.
	Construct a yoke.
	Construct a collar.
	Construct set-in sleeves.
	Construct raglan sleeves.
	Construct sleeve openings.
	Construct cuffs.
	Construct rolled cuffs.
	Construct a waistband.
	Construct casings.
	Sew buttonholes and button loops.
	Apply stretch and nonstretch hem tape.
	Finish hems.
	Attach snaps, hooks, eyes, buttons.
	Sew belt loops.
	Sew knit ribbing.
	ADVANCED TECHNIQUES
	Sew appliques.
	Use specialty fabrics such as furs, lace, sheers, vinyl.
	Use border and directional prints, plaids, stripes.
	Use piping.
	Use stretch and napped fabrics.
	Construct linings and underlinings

Name _____

Date _____ Period _____

Serged Project Evaluation

Project Description _____

For each section below, place a check in the column that indicates the proper evaluation.

	Poor	Fair	Good	Excellent	Comments
Pattern and Fabric. Appropriate for a serged project. Serger used to fullest advantage in constructing the project.					
Thread. Type appropriate for task and decorative effect desired. Color matches or blends.					
Stitching. Serge stitch appropriate for fabric and purpose. Tension balanced. Stitches correct length and width. Serging free from puckers. No skipped or broken stitches.					
Decorative Stitching. Enhances appearance of project. Correctly and neatly done. Thread choice enhances stitch and project.					
Ending Stitching. Stitching secured at seam ends. Appropriate method used.					
Corners. Neatly turned. Appropriate method used. Correctly done.					
Edges and Seams. Stabilized when necessary. Appropriate method used. Correctly done.					
Ribbing. Attached correctly using appropriate method. Fullness evenly distributed.					
Elastic. Applied correctly using appropriate method. Fullness distributed correctly.					
Lace. Attached correctly using appropriate method. Ribbon, if used, not caught in stitching.					

Name _____

Date _____ Period _____

Serger Operation Evaluation

Rank yourself from 1 to 10 as to how well you feel you can perform the following tasks. When ranking, 1 represents little skill and 10 represents high performance.

	PATTERN/FABRIC
	Select appropriate pattern/fabric.
	Decide where to serge on project.
	Determine construction order.
	USING THE SERGER
	Replace machine needle(s)
	Change knives.
	Thread the serger.
	Remove thread from stitch finger.
	Use easy threading method.
	Resume stitching when threads break.
	Machine stitch.
	End stitching by cutting chain with knife.
	Secure chain at seam ends.
	Adjust the stitch tension.
	Adjust the stitch length.
	Adjust the stitch width.
	Adjust the differential feed regulator.
	Adjust the pressure regulator.
	Follow seam guidelines.
	Serge curves.
	Turn outside corners.
	Turn inside corners.
	Serge circles.
	Flatlock.
	Use rolled hem stitch.
	Care for serger.
	Solve machine problems.
	CONSTRUCTION TECHNIQUES
	Continuous stitch.
	Construct narrow double-stitched seam.
	Construct serged/topstitch seam.
	Construct decorative lapped seam.
	Construct flatlocked seam.

	CONSTRUCTION TECHNIQUES (Continued)
	Construct mock flat-felled seam.
	Construct French seam.
	Construct mock French seam.
	Construct gathers.
	Stabilize edges and seams.
	Construct finished-edge hem.
	Construct narrow turned-under hem.
	Construct eased hem.
	Construct blind hem.
	Construct flatlocked hem.
	Construct mock band hem.
	Construct narrow unrolled hem.
	Construct narrow rolled hem.
	Construct ribbon-finished hem.
	Construct lettuce-leaf hem.
	Use decorative stitching.
	Construct darts.
	Construct decorative tucks.
	Construct patch pockets.
	Construct seam pockets.
	Construct ties and straps.
	Construct belt loops.
	Construct center-gathered ruffles.
	Attach convertible collar.
	Attach Peter Pan collar.
	Attach ribbing.
	Construct sleeve openings.
	Attach cuffs.
	Construct waistbands.
	Apply elastic.
	Construct elastic casings.
	Attach lace.
	Serge sheer or slippery fabrics.
	Serge bulky fabrics.
	Serge stretchy fabrics.

notes

Unit 9   Additional Experiences

Unit 9
Additional Experiences

This unit is designed to help you broaden your sewing knowledge, skill, and creativity. After you master basic sewing techniques, you will find many new challenges waiting for you. Sewing never needs to be dull or boring. It can be as exciting and imaginative as you want to make it. Just let your imagination go and explore the endless variety of projects, fabrics, and techniques available.

In the following pages, you will find a few ideas to help you discover the world of creative sewing. However, you will not find many how-tos. It is your task to explore and discover all you can about these ideas. Your teacher may provide a number of current sewing references to help you. You might also visit your local fabric store and look for ideas and instructions there.

Your teacher may ask you to embellish your classroom project or a project that you do at home. Your teacher will provide you with guidelines and help you choose an appropriate idea to try. Don't be limited by the ideas included in the following pages. There are an endless variety of sewing projects you could do for additional experience. Feel free to explore other options.

Be sure to discuss with your teacher any techniques to be done as part of your in-class project. Also include these ideas on the project planning sheets provided in Unit 5. If your project is to be completed at home, your teacher will provide you with other planning and evaluation forms.

Lesson 47 Additional Experiences

Objectives

This lesson will help you to:
1. Research additional experiences that will expand your sewing knowledge, skill, and creativity.
2. Practice skills already learned by applying them to new, unusual, interesting, and challenging sewing projects.

Words to Know

applique
couching
embellishment
fraying

Gathering Information

Once you have learned basic sewing techniques, you will be ready to face new challenges. There is an endless variety of projects, fabrics, tools, and techniques to try. One of the hottest trends today is in the area of surface design. There are numerous ways to apply surface designs to garments and projects. This lesson will help you to explore a few possibilities.

EMBELLISHING SEWING PROJECTS

Adding surface design to garments and projects is called embellishment. There are a wide variety of techniques for applying surface designs. Decorative stitching, fraying, appliques, fabric paint, beads, and jewels are just a few of the embellishments that may be used. To get ideas, browse through fabric and craft stores, read books, and look at ready-to-wear fashions. You never know where you might find a great idea. You might even want to keep an idea notebook.

DECORATIVE STITCHING

ADJUST LENGTH/WIDTH

REPEAT ROWS

BUILT IN STITCHES

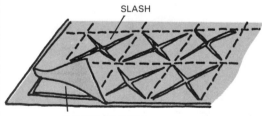

Machine stitching is a great way to add decorative detail to your project. Your machine may be able to add interest with a twin needle or machine embroidery. Even if your machine has limited stitch options, you may be able to do more than you think! Creative designs can be made by repeating rows of machine stitching. You can also adjust stitch length and width or use interesting thread color combinations.

Other creative ways to apply surface designs using your machine include couching. Couching is applying cord, narrow trim, or yarn to the surface of fabric by sewing over it. Plan your design and mark where you want to place the cording, trim, or yarn. Then stitch it in place using a zigzag stitch.

Don't forget your serger has great potential for embellishing garments and projects. Be creative! Make use of the overlock stitch, rolled edge, and flatlock stitch. Combine these techniques with decorative threads to design marvelous embellishments for your garments and accessories.

FRAYING

SLASH

MULTIPLE LAYERS

Fraying is a novelty effect created by sandwiching and stitching together several layers of tightly woven, natural fiber fabric. Some of the layers are then cut in spots to expose successive layers. The fabric is washed, dried, and brushed to make cut edges curl and fray.

A variation of this technique is to attach strips of cut fabric to a garment. Several layers of fabric may be used. Begin by marking placement lines on the garment; then stitch fabric strips in place. Wash, dry, and brush to create fraying.

APPLIQUES

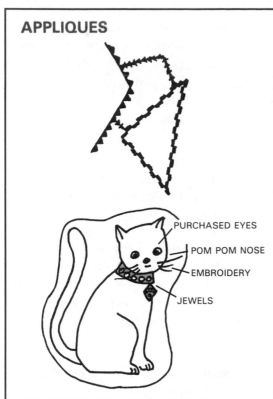

PURCHASED EYES
POM POM NOSE
EMBROIDERY
JEWELS

Appliques are fabric designs attached to the surface of a garment by fusing or hand or machine stitching. Appliques may be purchased ready-to-apply. You can also make your own appliques using various techniques, depending on the desired effect. Do a little research to find the most suitable method.

When making an applique, be sure to select fabrics compatible in weight and care requirements. Plan your design and sequence of steps before you begin stitching.

Appliques are often fused to the surface and then the raw edges are covered with decorative machine stitching. Stabilizers placed under the applique make stitching easier. Appliques may then be embellished by attaching buttons, ribbon, bows, sequins, fabric paint, cord, lace, rhinestones, or other trim. Permanent fabric glue may be used to attach decorative items.

FABRIC PAINTING

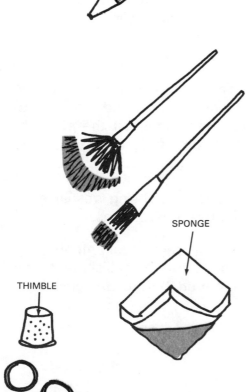

SPONGE

THIMBLE

New, easy-to-use fabric paints make embellishing garments fun and easy. These new paints are colorfast, nontoxic, and washable. They are available in pearl, glossy, gel, and glitter formulas for a variety of looks. They can be used to create colorful, permanent designs.

Paint can be applied to either woven or knit fabrics. Medium to heavy woven fabrics are easiest to paint. Begin by planning your design. You may want to transfer a design or pattern to the fabric before painting. Many commercial designs are available. Simply heat transfer them onto your fabric according to manufacturer's directions.

Before applying paint, prepare your fabric or garment by washing to remove sizing. Place a piece of cardboard or plastic between garment layers. This will prevent paint from bleeding onto another part of the garment. Use another piece of cardboard or plastic to protect the work surface.

Experiment! Use paint by squeezing from the bottle or apply with sponges, brushes, paint pads, kitchen tools, or sewing tools. Always practice painting techniques on fabric scraps before painting on your garment.

(Continued)

Fabric paint must be allowed to dry thoroughly before garments can be worn or laundered. Refer to manufacturer's directions for application tips, drying times, and laundering instructions.

BEADS, BUTTONS, AND TRIMS

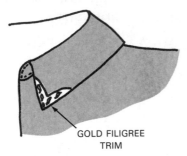

GOLD FILIGREE TRIM

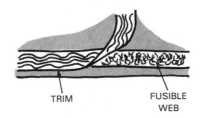

TRIM   FUSIBLE WEB

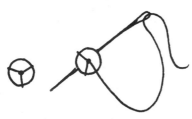

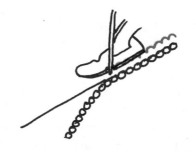

Surface decorations, such as beads, buttons, and trims, come in a wide variety of sizes, shapes, and colors. Use your imagination to combine them in creative ways.

Surface decorations may be purchased individually or as appliques. Some are designed to be ironed on; others to be sewn. Fusible web may be used to attach the sew-on variety. Test fuse before applying decorations to your project.

Beads and sequins may be attached to garments in several ways. To hand sew beads, use a beading needle and a double strand of waxed cotton-wrapped polyester thread. Some beads and sequins may be purchased by the yard and sewn to garments using a machine zigzag stitch. Careful stitch adjustment is necessary to avoid breaking the needle. Beads and sequins can also be made into appliques on backing fabric. These appliques can be permanently or temporarily attached to your garment.

Studs and rhinestones can be attached quickly and easily using a specialized tool. The tool neatly pushes the prongs on the studs and rhinestones through fabric and bends them securely in place.

Jewels can be attached using washable glue. Follow manufacturers directions.

Be sure to check care requirements for all embellishments. Some embellishments may have to be removed before dry cleaning or laundering.